BUSINESS ANALYSIS
Second Edition

BCS The Chartered Institute for IT
Our mission as BCS, The Chartered Institute for IT, is to enable the information society. We promote wider social and economic progress through the advancement of information technology science and practice. We bring together industry, academics, practitioners and government to share knowledge, promote new thinking, inform the design of new curricula, shape public policy and inform the public.

Our vision is to be a world-class organisation for IT. Our 70,000 strong membership includes practitioners, businesses, academics and students in the UK and internationally. We deliver a range of professional development tools for practitioners and employees. A leading IT qualification body, we offer a range of widely recognised qualifications.

Further Information
BCS The Chartered Institute for IT, First Floor, Block D, North Star House, North Star Avenue, Swindon, SN2 1FA, United Kingdom.
T +44 (0) 1793 417 424
F +44 (0) 1793 417 444
www.bcs.org/contact

BUSINESS ANALYSIS
Second Edition

EDITED BY
Debra Paul, Donald Yeates and James Cadle

bcs
The
Chartered
Institute
for IT

Published by British Informatics Society Limited (BISL), a wholly owned subsidiary of BCS The Chartered Institute for IT, First Floor, Block D, North Star House, North Star Avenue, Swindon, SN2 1FA, United Kingdom.
www.bcs.org

ISBN 978-1-906124-61-8

British Cataloguing in Publication Data.
A CIP catalogue record for this book is available at the British Library.

Typeset by Lapiz Digital Services, Chennai, India.
Printed at CPI Antony Rowe Ltd., Chippenham, UK.

CONTENTS

LIST OF FIGURES AND TABLES

CONTRIBUTORS

Malcolm Eva (contributor) has worked in the field of IS systems development as developer, systems analyst and business analyst for over 25 years. He has experience in university and college education, and also of training in the public and private sectors.

Craig Rollason (contributor) is a manager of business analysts at National Grid, with a specific focus on investment planning and project start-up. He has worked across the complete business analysis lifecycle in government, manufacturing and utilities. He is a Chartered Member of BCS.

Keith Hindle (contributor) has more than 30 years' experience of consulting and training in IS systems development and business analysis for organisations in the public and private sectors. He is a Chartered Member of BCS.

James Cadle (co-editor/contributor) is a Chartered Member of BCS and a specialist consultant in business analysis, systems analysis and project management with more than 30 years' experience in the UK and overseas. He is a Director of Assist Knowledge Development Ltd.

Debra Paul (co-editor/contributor) is Managing Director of Assist Knowledge Development Ltd. and has worked for more than 25 years in the IT industry delivering training and consultancy in her specialist fields of business analysis and business change. She is a Chartered Fellow of BCS.

Dot Tudor (contributor) is the Technical Director of TCC Limited. She specialises in project management, business analysis and agile approaches to business change. She is a Chartered Fellow of BCS.

Donald Yeates (co-editor/contributor) is a Chartered Fellow of BCS and a Visiting Executive Fellow at Henley Business School in the UK. He has worked in the IT industry for most of his career and is now an Executive Coach.

FOREWORD

Thoughts since the first edition

Since the first edition of this book was published, a lot has happened in the world of business analysis – much of it as a result of this book itself and the way it has acted as a standard text for the business analysis discipline.

Business analysis is now accepted as a mature discipline whose importance is seen alongside project management, solution development and service management. Before this publication there had been no definitive text for business analysis in the UK.

Business analysis has now held its first UK conference and has a stronger position at the heart of business change, an active membership group and an expanding examination and certification scheme via ISEB, which now has an exemption agreement with the IIBA.

In addition, the original text has spawned another publication *Business Analysis Techniques (72 Essential Tools for Success)*, which provides additional guidance and practical tips on a range of the business analysis techniques introduced in this volume.

It was difficult to see how the original text could have been bettered, but the authors should be commended in that they have achieved this with the second edition.

Paul Turner FBCS
March 2010

ABBREVIATIONS

BA	Business Analyst
BAM	Business Activity Model
BAMM	Business Analysis Maturity Model
BBS	Balanced Business Scorecard
BCS	British Computer Society
BPMN	Business Process Modelling Notation
CATWOE	customer, actor, transformation, *Weltanschauung* (world view), owner, environment
CBAP	Certified Business Analysis Professional
CEO	Chief Executive Officer
CI	configuration item
CMMI	Capability Maturity Model Integration
COTS	Commercial Off-the-Shelf (solution)
CSF	Critical Success Factor
DBMS	Database Management System
DCF	Discounted Cash Flow
DSDM	Dynamic Systems Development Method
ERP	Enterprise Resource Planning
FSA	Financial Services Authority
GMC	General Medical Council
HR	Human Resources
IET	Institution of Engineering and Technology
IIBA	International Institute of Business Analysts
IMIS	Institute for the Management of Information Systems
IRR	Internal Rate of Return

IS	Information Systems
ISEB	Information Systems Examinations Board
IT	Information Technology
itSMF	IT Service Management Forum
KPI	Key Performance Indicator
MoSCoW	must have, should have, could have, want to have but won't have this time
MOST (analysis)	mission, objectives, strategy and tactics (analysis)
NPV	Net Present Value
Ofcom	Office for Communications
Ofsted	Office for Standards in Education
PESTLE (analysis)	political, economic, sociocultural, technological, legal and environmental (analysis)
POST	Parliamentary Office of Science and Technology
RACI (chart)	responsible, accountable, consulted and informed (chart)
RASCI (chart)	responsible, accountable, supportive, consulted and informed (chart)
SBU	Strategic Business Unit
SDLC	Systems Development Lifecycle
SFIA	Skills Framework for the Information Age
SMART	specific, measurable, achievable, relevant and time-framed
SSADM	Structured Systems Analysis and Design Method
SSM	Soft Systems Methodology
STROBE	Structured Observation of the Business Environment
SWOT	strengths, weaknesses, opportunities and threats
UML	Unified Modelling Language
UP	Unified Process

GLOSSARY

Action Learning   This is a process through which participants study their own actions and experiences in order to learn from them.

Activity Sampling   This is an investigation technique carried out to determine the amount of time individuals spend on different aspects of their work. Activity sampling is a form of observation, and involves the collection of data that may be used for statistical analysis.

Agile   Agile methods are a family of processes for software development using incremental and iterative approaches.

Actor   This is a role that performs areas of work within a business system. Actors are modelled on swimlane diagrams and use case diagrams. Actors are usually user roles, and show the individual or group of individuals responsible for carrying out the work. An actor may also be an IT system, and time may also be an actor.

APM   The Association for Project Management, with 17,000 individual members and 500 corporate members, aims to develop and promote project management.

Apocryphal Tales   These are usually stories used to illustrate a point, although they are of doubtful authenticity. They may be an example of conventional wisdom or of a belief that is widely accepted.

Atern   DSDM Atern is the agile project management framework from the DSDM consortium.

Balanced Business Scorecard   A balanced business scorecard supports a strategic management system by capturing both financial and non-financial measures of performance. There are usually four quadrants: financial, customer, process, and learning and growth. The balanced business scorecard was developed by R. S. Kaplan and D. P. Norton.

Benefits Management   A process that is concerned with the delivery of the predicted business benefits defined in a business case. This process includes managing projects such that they are able to deliver the predicted benefits, and, after the project has been implemented, checking progress on the achievement of these benefits and taking any actions required in order to enable their delivery.

Boston Box   A technique used to analyse the market potential of the products and services provided by an organisation. It was defined by the Boston Consulting Group.

British Computer Society   *See* BCS – Chartered Institute for IT.

Business Activity Model (BAM)   A conceptual model that shows the set of business activities that would be expected to be in place, given the business perspective from which it has been developed. There are five typical types of business activity represented on a business activity model: planning, enabling, doing, monitoring and controlling activities. See *BUSINESS PERSPECTIVE*.

Business Actor   Business actors are people who have an interest in a project, either because they have commissioned it, they work within the business system being studied or they will be the users of a proposed new IT system. *See* STAKEHOLDER.

Business Analysis   This is an internal consultancy role. It has the responsibility for investigating business situations, identifying and evaluating options for improving business systems, defining requirements and ensuring the effective use of information systems in meeting the needs of the business.

Business Analysis Process Model   A framework for business analysis assignments that incorporates the strategic context and five sequential stages: Investigate Situation, Consider Perspectives, Analyse Needs, Evaluate Options and Define Requirements. The framework places standard modelling techniques in context to help analysts determine the most appropriate technique for individual business situations.

Business Architecture   A framework for a business system that describes its structure, processes, people, information and technology.

Business Case   A business case is a document that describes the findings from a business analysis study and presents a recommended course of action for senior management to consider. A business case would normally include an introduction, management summary, description of the current situation, options considered, analysis of costs and benefits, impact assessment, risk assessment and recommendations, plus appendices that provide detailed supporting information.

Business Environment   See *EXTERNAL BUSINESS ENVIRONMENT, INTERNAL BUSINESS ENVIRONMENT*.

Business Event   A business event triggers the business system to do something. Typically this is to initiate the business process that forms the business system response to the event. In effect, a business event tells us when a business activity should be triggered; it fires into life the process that carries out the activity. There are three types of business event: external, internal and time-based business events.

Business Option   A key step in developing a business case is to identify the options available to address the business problem or opportunity. A business option describes the scope and content of a proposed business solution and states what it is intended to achieve in business terms. See *TECHNICAL OPTION.*

Business Perspective   A view of the business system held by a stakeholder. The business perspective will be based upon the values and beliefs held by the stakeholder. These values and beliefs will be encapsulated in a defined world view. There may be several divergent business perspectives for any given business situation. See *CATWOE*

Business Process   A linked set of tasks performed by a business in response to a business event. The business process receives, manipulates and transfers information or physical items, in order to produce an output of value to a customer. See *BUSINESS PROCESS MODEL.*

Business Process Model   A diagram showing the tasks that need to be carried out in response to a business event, in order to achieve a specific goal. See *SWIMLANE DIAGRAM.*

Business Requirements Elicitation   The proactive investigation and collection of requirements for a solution required in order to resolve a business problem or enable a business opportunity. See *REQUIREMENTS ELICITATION*

Business Rule   Business rules define how business activities are to be performed. It is important that these rules are considered when modelling the processing to carry out the activity. There are two main types of business rule: constraints that restrict how an activity is performed and operational guidance rules, which describe the procedures for performing activities.

Business Sponsor   A senior person in an organisation who is accountable for delivering the benefits from a business change. The sponsor is also responsible for providing resources to the project team.

Business Strategy   A strategy describes the long-term direction set for an organisation in order to achieve the organisational objectives.

Business System   A set of business components working together in order to achieve a defined purpose. The components of a system include people, IT systems, processes and equipment. Each component may be a system in its own right. See *IT SYSTEM.*

Business User   An individual member of staff involved in a business change project from the customer side of the equation. A business user may adopt a number of business roles including business sponsor, domain expert and end user of a solution.

Capability Maturity Model Integration (CMMI)   A process improvement approach used to help integrate traditionally separate functions, set process improvement goals and priorities and provide guidance for quality processes.

Catwoe A technique from the Soft Systems Methodology that provides a framework for defining and analysing business perspectives. The mnemonic stands for: C – customer, A – actor, T – transformation, W – *Weltanschauung* (or world view), O – owner, E – environment. See *BUSINESS PERSPECTIVE, SOFT SYSTEMS METHODOLOGY.*

CBAP CBAP stands for Certified Business Analysis Professional from the International Institute of Business Analysis (IIBA). The IIBA publishes the Business Analysis Body of Knowledge (BABOK).

Change Control A process whereby changes to requirements are handled in a controlled fashion. The change control process defines the process steps to be carried out when dealing with a proposed change. These steps include documenting the change, analysing the impact of the change, evaluating the impact of the change in order to decide upon the course of action to take and deciding whether or not to apply the change. The analysis and decisions should be documented in order to provide an audit trail relating to the proposed change.

Class A class is a definition of the attributes and operations shared by a set of objects within a business system. Each object is an instance of a particular class. See *OBJECT.*

Class Model A technique from the Unified Modeling Language (UML). A class model describes the classes in a system and their associations with each other.

Cloud Computing A general term for the delivery of hosted services over the internet.

Competency (or Competence) A competency is a skill or quality that an individual needs in order to perform his or her job effectively.

Computer-Aided Software Engineering (CASE) An automated tool that provides facilities to support requirements engineering work. These facilities will include the production and storage of documentation, management of cross-references between documentation, restriction of access to documentation and management of document versions. Sometimes known as COMPUTER-AIDED REQUIREMENTS ENGINEERING.

Consensus Model The definitive, agreed BAM representing the activities needed by a business, and created from the individual stakeholder BAMs.

Cost–Benefit Analysis A technique that involves identifying the initial and ongoing costs and benefits associated with a business change initiative. These costs and benefits are then categorised as tangible or intangible, and a financial value is calculated for those that are tangible. The financial values are analysed over a forward period in order to assess the potential financial return to the organisation. This analysis may be carried out using standard investment appraisal techniques. See *PAYBACK PERIOD (OR BREAK-EVEN ANALYSIS) and DISCOUNTED CASH FLOW/NET PRESENT VALUE ANALYSIS.*

Critical Success Factors   The areas in which an organisation must succeed in order to achieve positive organisational performance.

Discounted Cash Flow   An investment appraisal technique that takes account of the time value of money. The annual net cash flow for each year following the implementation of the change is reduced (discounted) in line with the estimated reduction in the value of money. The discounted cash flows are then added to produce a net present value. See *NET PRESENT VALUE.*

Document Analysis   A technique whereby samples of documents are reviewed in order to uncover information about an organisation, process, system or data items.

DSDM Atern   DSDM Atern is an iterative project delivery framework that emphasises continuous user involvement and the importance of delivering the right solution at the right time.

Entity Relationship Diagram   A diagram produced using the entity relationship modelling technique. The diagram provides a representation of the data to be held in the IT system under investigation. See *ENTITY RELATIONSHIP MODELLING.*

Entity Relationship Modelling   A technique that is used to model the data required to support an IT system. The technique models the data required to describe the 'things' the system wishes to hold data about – these are known as the 'entities' – and the relationships between those entities.

Ethnographic Study   An ethnographic study is concerned with spending an extended period of time in an organisation in order to obtain a detailed understanding of the culture and behaviours of the business area under investigation.

Explicit Knowledge   The knowledge of procedures and data that is foremost in the business users' minds, and which they can easily articulate. See *TACIT KNOWLEDGE.*

External Business Environment   The business environment that is external to an organisation and is the source of forces that may impact the organisation. Types of forces may include the introduction of new laws, social trends or competitor actions. See *PESTLE ANALYSIS, FIVE FORCES ANALYSIS.*

Force Field Analysis   A technique to consider those forces inside and outside the organisation that will support adoption of a proposal and those that will oppose it. This technique was developed by Kurt Lewin and may be used in evaluating options for change and in change management.

Functional Requirement   A requirement that is concerned with a function that the system should provide, i.e. what the system needs to do.

Gap Analysis   The comparison of two views of a business system, the current or 'as is' view and the desired or 'to be' view. The aim of gap analysis is to determine where the current situation has problems or 'gaps' that need to be resolved. This leads to the identification of actions to improve the situation. The business activity modelling technique may be used to provide an ideal view, which can then be compared with a view of the current situation. An alternative approach is to use the business process modelling technique, using 'as is' and 'to be' process models.

Holistic Approach   The consideration of all aspects of a business system: the people, process and organisational areas, in addition to the information and technology used to support the business system.

IMIS   The Institute for the Management of Information Systems.

Impact Analysis   The consideration of the impact a proposed change will have on a business system and on the people working within it.

Information Systems Examinations Board   The vocational qualification division of BCS, offering examinations in over 200 countries.

Institution of Engineering and Technology   One of the world's leading professional bodies for engineering and technology, with over 150,000 members in over 120 countries.

Intangible Benefit   A benefit to be realised by a business change project for which a credible, usually monetary, value cannot be predicted. See *TANGIBLE BENEFIT.*

Intangible Cost   A cost incurred by a business change project for which a credible, usually monetary, value cannot be predicted. See *TANGIBLE COST.*

Internal Business Environment   The internal capability of the organisation that affects its ability to respond to external environment forces. Techniques such as MOST analysis or the resource audit may be used to analyse the capability of the internal business environment. See *MOST ANALYSIS* and *RESOURCE AUDIT.*

Internal Rate Of Return   A calculation that assesses the return on investment from a project, defined as a percentage rate. This percentage is the discount rate at which the net present value is equal to zero, and it can be used to compare projects to see which are the better investment opportunities. Alternatively, this rate may be used to compare all projects with the return that could be earned if the amount invested was left in the bank.

Interview   An investigation technique to elicit information from business users. An agenda is prepared prior to the interview and distributed to participants. The interview is carried out in an organised manner, and a report of it is produced once it has been concluded.

ISEB   See *INFORMATION SYSTEMS EXAMINATION BOARD.*

IT System   A set of automated components hosted on a computer that work together in order to provide services to the system users. See *BUSINESS SYSTEM.*

itSMF   An internationally recognised forum for IT service management professionals.

Key Performance Indicators   These are defined performance targets or measures that assess the performance of an organisation. Key performance indicators are often identified in order to assess the organisation's performance in the areas defined by the critical success factors. See *CRITICAL SUCCESS FACTORS.*

McKinsey 7-S   A technique developed by the McKinsey consultancy organisation. The 7-S model is used to consider key areas for the implementation of business change.

MoSCoW   An approach to prioritising requirements. MoSCoW stands for:

- Must have: a key requirement, without which the system has no value.

- Should have: an important requirement that must be delivered, but, where time is short, could be delayed for a future delivery. This should be a short-term delay.

- Could have: a requirement that would be beneficial to include if it does not cost too much or take too long to deliver, but that is not central to the project objectives.

- Want to have (but Won't have this time): a requirement that will be needed in the future, but that is not required for this delivery.

Most Analysis   An analysis of an organisation's mission, objectives, strategy and tactics to identify any inherent strengths or weaknesses, for example from a lack of strategic direction or unclear objectives. See *INTERNAL BUSINESS ENVIRONMENT.*

Net Present Value   The amount an investment is worth once all of the net annual cash flows in the years following the current one are adjusted to today's value of money. The net present value is calculated using the discounted cash flow approach to investment appraisal. See *DISCOUNTED CASH FLOW.*

Non-Functional Requirement   A requirement that defines a constraint or performance measure with which the system or the functional requirements must comply.

Object   An object is something within a business system for which a set of attributes and functions can be specified. An object is an instance of a class. See *CLASS.*

Payback Calculation   An investment appraisal technique where a cash-flow forecast for a project is produced using the current values of the incoming and outgoing cash flows, with no attempt to adjust them for the declining value of money over time. See *DISCOUNTED CASH FLOW*.

Pestle   A technique used to analyse the external business environment of an organisation. The technique involves the analysis of the political, economic, sociocultural, technological, legal and environmental forces that may impact upon an organisation. See *BUSINESS ENVIRONMENT*.

Porter's Five Forces   A technique used to analyse the industry or business domain within which an organisation operates.

Project Initiation Document (PID)   A document that defines the business context for a project and clarifies the objectives, scope, deliverables, timescale, budget, authority and available resources.

Process   *See* BUSINESS PROCESS.

Process Model   *See* BUSINESS PROCESS MODEL.

Protocol Analysis   A technique used to elicit, analyse and validate requirements. Protocol analysis involves requesting the users to perform a task and to describe each step as they perform it.

Prototyping   A technique used to elicit, analyse and validate requirements. Prototyping involves building simulations of a system in order to review them with the users. This technique helps the business users to visualise the solution and hence increases understanding about the system requirements.

Questionnaires   A technique used to obtain quantitative information during an investigation of a business situation. Questionnaires are useful to obtain a limited amount of information from a large group of people.

Raci or Rasci   Linear responsibility matrix charts that identify stakeholder roles and responsibilities during an organisational change process.

Requirement   A feature that the business users need the new system to provide.

Requirements Catalogue   An organised set of requirements where each individual requirement is documented using a standard template. See *REQUIREMENT*.

Requirements Elicitation   Requirements elicitation is an approach to understanding requirements that requires the analyst to be proactive in drawing out the requirements from the business users and helping them to visualise the possibilities and articulate their requirements.

Requirements Management   Requirements management aims to ensure that each requirement is tracked from inception to implementation (or withdrawal) through all of the changes that have been applied to it.

Resource Audit   A technique to analyse the capability of an organisation. The resource audit considers five areas of organisational resource: tangible resources – physical, financial and human – and intangible resources – know-how and reputation.

Rich Picture   A pictorial technique offering a free-format approach that allows analysts to document whatever is of interest or significance in the business situation. This technique originated from the soft systems methodology. See SOFT SYSTEMS METHODOLOGY.

Risk   A problem situation that may arise with regard to a project or a business situation. Potential risks are identified for each option in a business case. The probability of the risk occurring and the likely impact of the risk are assessed, and suitable countermeasures are identified. See *BUSINESS CASE*.

Risk Management   The identification, assessment, monitoring and control of significant risks during the development, design and implementation of IT systems.

Root Definition   A perspective of a business situation based upon an individual world view that gives rise to a valid business system.

Scenarios   A technique used to elicit, analyse and validate requirements. A scenario will trace the course of a transaction from an initial business trigger through each of the steps needed to achieve a successful outcome.

SFIA and SFIA plus   The Skills Framework for the Information Age (SFIA) and the extended version provided by BCS (SFIAplus). Standard frameworks for the definition of skills and competencies in the information systems industry.

Six Sigma   A business management approach developed by Motorola in the early 1980s that aims to improve business processes by identifying and removing the causes of errors.

Shadowing   A technique used to find out what a particular job entails. Shadowing involves following users as they carry out their jobs for a period such as one or two days.

Six Thinking Hats   A thinking tool developed by Edward de Bono for individuals and for groups, to improve the thinking process.

Smart   A mnemonic used to ensure that objectives are clearly defined, in that they are specific, measurable, achievable, relevant and time-framed.

Soft Systems Methodology   A methodology that provides an approach to analysing business situations, devised by Peter Checkland and his team at Lancaster University.

Special-Purpose Records   A technique that involves the business users in keeping a record about a specific issue or task. Typically the record is based on a simple structure, for example a five-bar gate record.

Stakeholder   An individual, group of individuals or organisation with an interest in a change. Categories of stakeholder include customers, employees, managers, partners, regulators, owners, suppliers and contractors.

Stakeholder Analysis   The analysis of the levels of power and interest of stakeholders in order to assess the weight that should be attached to their issues. This technique provides a means of categorising stakeholders in order to identify the most appropriate stakeholder management approach.

Stakeholder Management   The definition of the most appropriate means to be adopted in order to engage with different categories of stakeholder. The approach to stakeholders will vary depending on their level of interest in the project and the amount of power or influence they wield to further or obstruct it.

Strategic Analysis   The application of techniques in order to analyse the pressures within an organisation's external business environment and the level of internal organisational capability to respond to these pressures.

Strategy   The direction and scope of an organisation over the longer term. The strategy is defined in order to achieve competitive advantage for the organisation through its configuration of resources within a changing business environment. The strategy also needs to fulfil the stakeholders' expectations.

Strobe   A technique that represents a formal checklist approach to observation, where the analyst is investigating specific issues rather than observing generally. STROBE stands for STRuctured Observation of the Business Environment and is used to appraise a working environment.

Swimlane   A row on a business process diagram or model that indicates who is responsible for a given process or task. Typical swimlanes represent departments, teams, individuals or IT systems.

Swimlane Diagram   A technique used to model business processes. A swim-lane diagram models the business system response to a business event. The model shows the triggering event, the business actors, the tasks they carry out, the flow between the tasks and the business outcome. See *BUSINESS PROCESS MODEL*.

SWOT Analysis   A technique used to summarise the external pressures facing an organisation and the internal capability the organisation has available to respond to those pressures. The mnemonic stands for strengths, weaknesses, opportunities and threats. SWOT analysis is used during strategy analysis.

Tacit Knowledge   Those aspects of business work that a user omits to articulate or explain. This may be due to a failure to recognise that the information is required or to the assumption that the information is already known to the analyst. See *EXPLICIT KNOWLEDGE*.

Tangible Benefit   A benefit to be realised by a business change project for which a credible, usually monetary, value can be predicted. See *INTANGIBLE BENEFIT*.

Tangible Cost   A cost incurred by a business change project for which a credible, usually monetary, value can be predicted. See *INTANGIBLE COST*.

Task   On a business process model or swimlane diagram, a piece of work carried out by a single actor at a specific moment in time.

Task Modelling   The technique for developing a model that describes the human activities and task sequences required by a business system. The task model elaborates the tasks identified by mapping business processes on to specific individuals or workgroups.

Technical Option   A technical option describes how the business solution may be implemented using information technology.

Unified Modeling Language   The Unified Modeling Language (UML) is a suite of diagrammatic techniques that are used to model business and IT systems.

Use Case   A use case is something that an actor wants the IT system to do; it is a 'case of use' of the system by a specific actor and describes the interaction between an actor and the system.

Use Case Description   A use case description defines the interaction between an actor and a use case.

Use Case Model   A technique from the UML. A use case model consists of a diagram showing the actors, the boundary of the system, the use cases and the associations between them, plus a set of use case descriptions.

Value Chain   A concept developed by Michael Porter to identify the primary and support activities deployed within organisations to deliver value to customers.

Value Proposition   A clear statement of the value that a product or service delivers, or is perceived to deliver, to an organisation's customers.

Workshop   An investigation technique whereby a meeting is held with business actors from a range of business areas in order to elicit, analyse or validate information. An agenda is prepared prior to the workshop and distributed to participants. The workshop is run by a facilitator; actions and decisions are recorded by a scribe.

PREFACE

Business Analysis has taken great strides forward since the first edition of this book was published in 2006. This new edition reflects this progress and incorporates much new material.

The main audience for this book is still practising Business Analysts at all levels. It offers them a wide-ranging source of practical guidance on how to approach business analysis and how to use key techniques. It will therefore appeal to people wanting to improve their understanding of business analysis. The book also supports everyone wanting to achieve industry qualifications in business analysis especially those studying for ISEB qualifications in Business Analysis.

In addition, the book will be useful for business analysis and information systems students at university, and for managers in other Information Systems disciplines who need to understand business analysis.

The book includes material drawn from research discussions and conversations with practitioners in business analysis in the UK, Australia, the USA and Canada. Some important additions since the first edition include:

- The introduction of new analysis techniques now more widely used such as Ishikawa diagrams and spaghetti maps.
- An expanded explanation of requirements engineering – now taking up four chapters.
- More on the process and techniques of investigating business needs.
- A more detailed treatment of benefits realisation including the use of benefits realisation maps.

Throughout the business world public, private and not for profit organisations face immense challenges. Business Analysts must respond by developing practical, creative and financially sound solutions. We are reminded about the financial implications of the solutions proposed by business analysts by the question posed by a manager from a large car manufacturer, whose response to a business case proposal was to ask 'how many more cars do we need to sell to pay for this?' Business managers and senior business analysts will be comforted to know that producing the business case is still an important part of this book.

On a personal level we'd like to welcome James Cadle to the editorial team and thank him for his efforts in producing this edition. Also thanks must go to Alan Paul – husband of Debbie – for reviewing much of the book and improving it. Thanks also to Charlotte Parke for interpreting Debbie's jottings and creating an excellent rich picture.

BCS publications team members Matthew Flynn, Karen Greening and Sarah Woodall made it all come together in the end and their detailed examination of what had been written has, we hope, saved us from embarrassing ourselves too much. Also, we thank the BCS legal team for their work in protecting copyright.

Debra Paul, *Sonning Common, England*
Donald Yeates, *Fetcham, England*

1 WHAT IS BUSINESS ANALYSIS?

Debra Paul

INTRODUCTION

This is a book about business analysis, a relatively new discipline that promises to offer great benefit to organisations by ensuring that business needs are aligned with implemented business change solutions. Many of those solutions will involve new or enhanced information systems, but others may have a broader scope incorporating changes to areas such as business processes and job roles. The reason for producing this book is to provide guidance about business analysis that reflects the breadth of the role and the range of techniques used. While most organisations use the term 'business analysis' and employ business analysts, there continues to be a lack of clarity about what this really means and this often creates more questions than answers. What do business analysts do? What skills do they require? How do they add value to organisations? Also, in the absence of a standard definition of business analysis and a standard business analysis process model, problems have arisen:

- Organisations have introduced business analysis so as to make sure that business needs are paramount when new information technology (IT) systems are introduced. However, recognising the importance of this in principle is easier than considering how it might be achieved.

- Some business analysts were experienced IT systems analysts and have been less comfortable considering the business requirements and the range of potential solutions that would meet those requirements.

- Many business analysts come from a business background and have a limited understanding of IT and how computer systems are developed. While knowledge of the business is invaluable for business analysts, problems can occur where IT forms part of the solution and the analyst has insufficient understanding of IT. This can cause communication difficulties with the developers, and may result in failure to ensure that there is an integrated view of the business and the computer system.

- Some business analysts, as they have gained in experience and knowledge, have felt that they could offer beneficial advice to their organisations – but a lack of understanding of their role has caused organisations to reject or ignore this advice.

This chapter examines the business analysis discipline and considers how we might define the business analyst role. In Chapter 4 we describe a process model for business analysis, where we provide an overview of two aspects:

how business analysis is undertaken and the key techniques to be used at each stage. Much of this book provides guidance on how the various stages in this process model may be carried out. Business analysis work is well defined where there are standard techniques that have been used in projects for many years. In fact, many of these techniques have been in use for far longer than the business analyst role has been in existence. In this book we describe numerous techniques that we feel should be within any business analyst's toolkit, and place them within the overall process model. Our aim is to help business analysts carry out their work, to improve the quality of business analysis within organisations and, as a result, to help organisations to adopt business improvements that will ensure their success.

THE ORIGINS OF BUSINESS ANALYSIS

Developments in IT have enabled organisations to create information systems that have improved business operations and management decision-making. In the past this has been the focus of IT departments. However, as business operations have changed, the emphasis has moved on to the development of new services and products. The question we need to ask now is 'What can IT do to exploit business opportunities and enhance the portfolio of products and services?'

Technology has enabled new business models to be implemented through more flexible communication mechanisms that enable organisations to reach out to the customer, connect their systems with those of their suppliers and support global operation. The use of IT has also created opportunities for organisations to focus on their core processes and competencies without the distraction of the peripheral areas of business. These days, the absence of good information systems would prevent an organisation from developing significant competitive advantage. Yet for many years there has been a growing dissatisfaction in businesses with the support provided by IT. This has been accompanied by recognition by senior management that IT investment often fails to deliver the required business benefit. In short, the technology enables the development of information systems, but these often fail to meet the requirements of the business and deliver the service that will bring competitive advantage to the organisation. This situation applies to all sectors, including the public sector. In July 2003 the Parliamentary Office of Science and Technology (POST) (2003) report on Government IT projects listed six UK government departments and agencies where there had been recent high-profile IT difficulties. The chairman of the Public Accounts Committee commented on 'one of the worst IT projects I have ever seen'. The perception that, all too frequently, information systems do not deliver the predicted benefits continues to be well founded.

THE DEVELOPMENT OF BUSINESS ANALYSIS

The impact of outsourcing

In a drive to reduce costs, and sometimes in recognition of a lack of IT expertise at senior management level, many organisations have outsourced their IT services rather than employ their own internal IT staff. They have transferred much of their IT work to specialist service providers. This approach has been based upon the belief that specialist providers, often working in countries where costs are lower than in the UK, will be able to deliver higher quality at lower cost. So, in organisations that have outsourced their IT functions, the IT systems are designed and constructed using staff employed by an external supplier. This undoubtedly has advantages both for the organisation purchasing the services and for the specialist supplier. The latter gains an additional customer and the opportunity to increase turnover and make profit from the contractual arrangement; the customer organisation is no longer concerned with all staffing, infrastructure and support issues and instead pays a specialist provider for delivery of the required service. In theory this approach has much to recommend it, but, as is usually the case, the flaws begin to emerge once the arrangement has been implemented, particularly in the areas of supplier management and communication of requirements. The issues relating to supplier management are not the subject of this book, and would require a book in their own right. However, we are concerned with the issue of communication between the business and the outsourced development team. The communication and clarification of requirements is key to ensuring the success of any IT system development, but an outsourcing arrangement often complicates the communication process, particularly where there is geographical distance between the developers and the business. We need to ask ourselves 'How well do the business and technical groups understand each other?' and 'Is the communication sufficiently frequent and open?' Communication failures will usually result in the delivered IT systems failing to provide the required level of support for the business.

Investigation of the outsourcing business model has identified that, in order to make such arrangements work, new roles are required within the organisation. A study by Feeny and Willcocks (1998) listed a number of key skills required within organisations that have outsourced IT. This report specifically identified business systems thinking, a core element of the business analyst role, as a key skill that needs to be retained within organisations operating an outsourcing arrangement. The outsourcing business model has undoubtedly been a catalyst for the development of the business analysis function as more and more organisations recognise the importance of business representation during the development and implementation of IT systems.

Competitive advantage of using IT

A parallel development that has helped to increase the profile of business analysis and define the business analyst role has been the growing recognition that three factors need to be present in order for IT systems to deliver competitive advantage. First, the needs of the business must drive the development of the IT systems; second, the implementation of an IT system must be accompanied by the necessary business changes; and third, the requirements for IT systems must be defined with rigour and accuracy. The traditional systems analyst role operated primarily in the last area, but today's business challenges require all three areas to be addressed.

Successful business change

During the last few years organisations have broadened their view from IT projects to business change programmes. Within these programmes, there has been recognition of the need for roles and skill sets that will enable the successful delivery of business change initiatives. The roles of the programme manager and change manager have been well defined, with a clear statement of their scope and focus within the business change lifecycle. Figure 1.1 shows a typical lifecycle.

Figure 1.1 Business change lifecycle

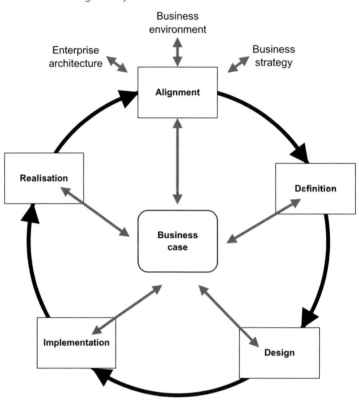

The early part of the business change lifecycle is concerned with the analysis of the organisation and its business needs and requirements, in order to determine new ways of working that will improve the organisation's efficiency and effective-ness. Later business change activities are concerned with change design and development, business acceptance testing and, after implementation, benefits review and realisation. Clearly, extensive analysis is required here and the nature of this work falls within the remit of business analysis. However, in many organisations a coherent approach to business change, which includes business analysts in the business change lifecycle, is still awaited.

The importance of the business analyst
The delivery of predicted business benefits, promised from the implementation of IT, has proved to be extremely difficult, with the outsourcing of IT services serving to add complication to already complex situations. The potential exists for organisations to implement information systems that yield competitive advantage, and yet this often appears to be just out of reach. Organisations also want help in finding potential solutions to business issues and opportunities, sometimes where IT may not prove to be the answer, but it has become apparent that this requires a new set of skills to support business managers in achieving it. These factors have led directly to the development of the business analyst role. Having identified the

business analyst role, we now need to recognise the potential this can offer, particularly in a global economic environment where budgets are limited and waste of financial resources is unacceptable. The importance of delivering the business benefits predicted for business change initiatives has becoming increasingly necessary to the survival of organisations.

The use of consultants

Many organisations use external consultants to provide expert advice throughout the business change lifecycle. The reasons are clear: they can be employed to deal with a specific issue on an 'as-needed' basis, and they bring a broader business perspective and thus can provide a dispassionate, objective view of the company. On the other hand, the use of external consultants is often criticised, particularly in public-sector organisations, because of the lack of accountability and the absence of any transfer of skills from the external consultants to internal staff. Cost is also a key issue. Consultancy firms often charge daily fee rates that are considerably higher than the employment cost for an internal analyst and, whilst the firms may provide consultants who have a broad range of expertise, this is not always guaranteed. The experiences gained from using external consultants have also played a part in the development of the internal business analysis role. Many business analysts have argued that they can provide the same services as external consultants and can, in effect, operate as internal consultants. Reasons for using internal business analysts as consultants, apart from lower costs, include speed (internal consultants do not have to spend time learning about the organisation) and the retention of knowledge within the organisation. These factors have been recognised as particularly important for projects where the objectives concern the achievement of business benefit through the use of IT, and where IT is a prime enabler of business change. As a result, although external consultants are used for many business purposes, the majority of business analysts are employed by their organisations. These analysts may lack an external viewpoint but they are knowledgeable about the business domain and, crucially, will have to live with the impact of the actions they recommend. Consequently, there have been increasing numbers of business analysts working as internal consultants over the last decade.

THE SCOPE OF BUSINESS ANALYSIS WORK

A major issue for business analysts, based on feedback from a wide range of organisations, is the definition of the business analyst role. Discussions with several hundred business analysts across a range of business forums have highlighted that business analysis job descriptions are unclear and do not always describe their responsibilities accurately. A quick survey of the job advertisements for business analysts also reflects a range of possibilities. For example, in some cases the job description of a business analyst seems, on close inspection, to be similar to that of an analyst/programmer, e.g. 'Candidates must have experience of SQL.' In other organisations the business analysts are required to work with senior stakeholders and need to have detailed business domain knowledge. Even though the role of the business analyst emerged almost 20 years ago, a formal definition of the role is still debated hotly whenever there is a group of business analysts.

The range of analysis activities

One way in which we can consider the business analyst role is to examine the possible range of analysis activities. Figure 1.2 shows three areas that we might consider to be within the province of the business analyst. Consultants, both internal and external, who specialise in strategic analysis often have to get involved in business process redesign to make a reality of their strategies, and good systems analysts have always needed to understand the overall business context of the systems they are developing. However, it is useful to examine them separately in order to consider their relevance to the business analyst role.

Figure 1.2 Potential range of the business analyst role

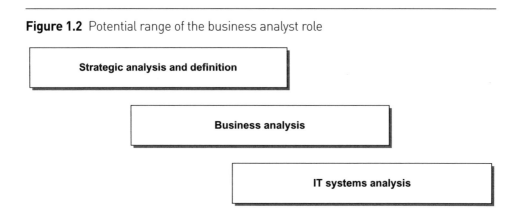

Strategic analysis and definition

Strategic analysis and definition is typically the work of senior management, often supported by strategy consultants. Some business analysts, albeit a minority, may be required to undertake strategic analysis and identify business transformation actions, but most will probably have a role to play in supporting this activity. In the main, we believe that strategic analysis is mostly outside the remit of business analysis. We would, however, expect business analysts to have access to information about their organisation's business strategy and be able to understand it, as their work will need to support the achievement of this strategy. Given that business analysts often have to recommend process and IT system solutions, it could be argued that they define the tactics that will deliver the business objectives and strategy. Hence, it is vital that they are able to work within the strategic business context. It may also be the case that some business analyst roles will require strategic-level thinking. The use of IT to enable business improvements and the opportunities presented by technology will need to be considered during any strategy analysis. The business analysts are the specialist team within organisations that should be able to advise on the use of technology to drive business change. Given these issues, we feel that although strategic analysis work is not core to business analysis, business analysts will need a good understanding of strategy development processes. Chapter 3 explores a range of strategic analysis techniques and provides an overview of the strategic planning process.

IT systems analysis

At the other end of our model, there is the IT discipline called systems analysis. The systems analyst role has been in existence for over 40 years and can be defined clearly. Systems analysts are responsible for analysing and specifying the IT system requirements in sufficient detail to provide a basis for the evaluation of software packages or the development of a bespoke IT system. Typically, systems analysis work involves the use of techniques such as data modelling and process or function modelling. This work is very specific to describing the computer system requirements, and so the products of systems analysis define exactly what data the computer system will record, what processing will be applied to that data and how the user interface will operate.

Some organisations consider this work to be of such a technical nature that they perceive it to be completely outside the province of the business analyst. They have decided that modelling process and data requirements for the IT system is not part of the role of the business analyst, and have separated the business analysis and IT teams into different departments. The expectation here is that the IT department will carry out the detailed IT systems modelling and specification. The job role 'systems analyst' tends to be used rarely these days, and the detailed specification of the requirements is often undertaken by systems designers or developers.

However, in some organisations the term 'IT business analyst' has been adopted to identify a business analyst working in the area traditionally known as systems analysis. The essential difference here is that a business analyst is responsible for considering a range of business options to address a particular problem or opportunity; on the other hand an IT business analyst, or systems analyst, works within a defined scope and considers options for the IT solution.

In some organisations there is little divide between the business analysts and the IT team. In these cases the business analysts work closely with the IT developers and include the specification of IT system requirements as a key part of their role. In order to do this, the business analysts need a more detailed understanding of IT systems and how they operate, and need to be apply to use the approaches and modelling techniques that fell historically within the remit of the system analyst job role.

Business analysis

If the two analysis disciplines described above define the limits of analysis work, the gap in the middle is straddled by business analysis. Hence Figure 1.2 highlights the possible extent of business analysis work. Business analysts will usually be required to investigate a business system where improvements are required, but the range and focus of those improvements can vary considerably.

It may be that the analysts are asked to resolve a localised business issue. They would need to recommend actions that would overcome a problem or achieve business benefits. However, it is more likely that the study is broader than this and requires investigation into several issues, or perhaps ideas, regarding increased efficiency or effectiveness. This work would necessitate extensive and detailed analysis. The analysts would need to make recommendations for business changes and these would need to be supported by a rigorous business case.

Another possibility is that the business analyst is asked to focus specifically on enhancing or replacing an existing IT system in line with business requirements.

In this case the analyst would deliver a requirements document defining what the business requires the IT system to provide.

Whichever situation applies, the study usually begins with the analyst gaining an understanding of the business situation in hand. A problem may have been defined in very specific terms, and a possible solution identified, but in practice it is rare that this turns out to be the entire problem and it is even rarer that any proposed solution addresses all of the issues. More commonly, there may be a more general set of problems that require a broad focus to the study. For any changes to succeed, the business analyst needs to consider all aspects, for example the processes, IT systems and resources that will be needed in order to improve the situation successfully. In such cases, techniques such as stakeholder analysis, business process modelling and requirements engineering may all be required in order to identify the actions necessary to improve the business system. These three topics are the subjects of later chapters in this book.

Realising business benefits

Analysing business situations and identifying areas for business improvement is only one part of the process. The analyst may also be required to develop a business case in order to justify the required level of investment and ensure any risks are considered. One of the key elements of the business case will be the identification and, where relevant, the quantification of the business benefits. Organisations are placing increased emphasis upon ensuring that there is a rigorous business case to justify the expenditure on business improvement projects. However, defining the business case is only part of the picture; the delivery or 'realisation' of these business benefits once the solution has been delivered is also gaining increasing focus. This is largely because there has been a long history of failure to assess whether or not the business benefits have been realised. The business analyst will not be the only person involved in this work, but supporting the organisation in assessing whether predicted business benefits have been delivered is a key element of the role.

Taking a holistic approach

There appears to be universal agreement that business analysis requires the application of an holistic approach. Although the business analyst performs a key role in supporting management to exploit IT in order to obtain business benefit, this has to be within the context of the entire business system. Hence, all aspects of the operational business system need to be analysed if all of the opportunities for business improvement are to be uncovered. Figure 1.3 represents the four views that it is useful to consider when identifying areas for improving a business system.

This model shows us that business analysts need to consider these four aspects when analysing a business system. For each area, we might consider the following:

- **The processes:** are they well defined and communicated? Is there good IT support, or are several 'workarounds' in existence? Does the process require documents to be passed around the organisation unnecessarily?

- **The people:** do they have the required skills for the job? How motivated are they? Do they understand the business objectives that they need to support?

- **The organisational context:** is there a supportive management approach? Are jobs and responsibilities well defined? Is there effective cross-functional working?
- **The technology:** do the systems support the business as required? Do they provide the information needed to run the organisation?

Figure 1.3 The four views of a business system

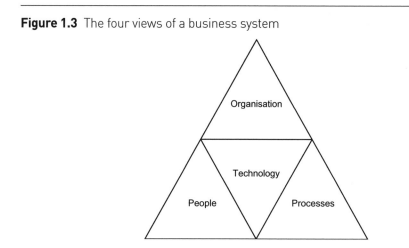

We need to examine and understand these four areas if the business system is to be effective. It is often the case that the focus of a business analysis or business change study is on the processes and the IT support. However, even if we have the most efficient processes with high standards of IT support, the system will have problems if the staff members do not have the right skills to carry out their work or the organisation structure is unclear.

It is vital that the business analyst is aware of the broader aspects relating to business situations such as the culture of the organisation and its impact on the people and the working practices. The adoption of an holistic approach will help ensure that these aspects are included in the analysis of the situation.

Business analysis places an emphasis on improving the operation of the entire business system. This means that, although technology is viewed as a factor that could enable improvements to the business operations, there are other possibilities. The focus on business improvement rather than on the use of automation per se results in recommendations that typically, but not necessarily, include the use of IT. There may be situations where a short-term non-IT solution is both helpful and cost-effective. For example, a problem may be overcome by developing internal standards or training members of staff. These solutions may be superseded later by longer-term, possibly more costly, solutions but the focus on the business has ensured that the immediate needs have been met. Once urgent issues have been handled, the longer-term solutions can be considered more thoroughly. It is important that our focus as business analysts is on identifying opportunities for improvement with regard to the needs of the particular situation. If we do this, we can recommend changes that will help deliver real business improvements.

Supporting business change

It is often observed that even when the business analysts have defined excellent solutions that have been well designed and developed, business improvement initiatives can fail during implementation. The business analyst may be required to support the implementation of the business changes, and Figure 1.3 offers an effective structure for identifying the range of areas to be considered. One aspect may be the business acceptance testing – a vital element if business changes are to be implemented smoothly. The business analyst's involvement in business acceptance testing can include work such as developing test scenarios and working with users as they apply the scenarios to their new processes and systems. The implementation of business change may require extensive support from business analysts, including tasks such as:

- writing procedure manuals and user guides;
- training business staff in the use of new processes and IT systems;
- defining job roles and writing job role descriptions;
- providing ongoing support as the business staff begin to adopt the new, unfamiliar approaches.

Chapter 14 explores further the implementation of business change and the key elements to be considered.

THE ROLE AND RESPONSIBILITIES OF A BUSINESS ANALYST

So where does this leave us in defining the role and responsibilities of a business analyst? Although there are different role definitions, depending upon the organisation, there does seem to be an area of common ground where most business analysts work. The responsibilities appear to be:

- To investigate business systems, taking an holistic view of the situation. This may include examining elements of the organisation structures and staff development issues as well as current processes and IT systems.
- To evaluate actions to improve the operation of a business system. Again, this may require an examination of organisational structure and staff development needs, to ensure that they are in line with any proposed process redesign and IT system development.
- To document the business requirements for the IT system support using appropriate documentation standards.

In line with this, we believe the core business analyst role should be defined as:

An internal consultancy role that has the responsibility for investigating business situations, identifying and evaluating options for improving business systems, defining requirements and ensuring the effective use of information systems in meeting the needs of the business.

However, this definition is expanded by considering the guiding principles that underpin business analysis. These principles explain why business analysis is so important for organisations in today's business world and impose responsibilities that business analysts must recognise and accept.

The guiding principles for business analysis are:

- **Root causes, not symptoms:** to distinguish between the symptoms of business problems and their root causes, and to investigate and address the root causes.

- **Business improvement, not IT change:** to recognise that IT systems should enable business opportunity, to analyse opportunities for business improvement and to enable business agility.

- **Options, not solutions:** to challenge predetermined solutions, and identify and evaluate options for meeting business needs.

- **Feasible, contributing requirements, not all requests:** to be aware of financial and timescale constraints, to identify requirements that are not feasible and do not contribute to business objectives, and to evaluate stated requirements against business needs and constraints.

- **The entire business change lifecycle, not just requirements definition:** to analyse business situations and support the effective development, testing, deployment and post- implementation review of solutions.

- **Negotiation, not avoidance:** to recognise conflicting stakeholder views and requirements, and negotiate conflicts between stakeholders.

- **Business agility, not business perfection:** to enable organisations to be responsive to external pressures and to recognise the importance of timely, relevant solutions.

Further to the definition and guiding principles, in some organisations there are business analysis roles that apply to the strategic analysis or systems analysis activities described above. This is typically where business analysts are in a more senior role or choose to specialise. These aspects are:

- **Strategy implementation:** here, the business analysts work closely with senior management to help define the most effective business system to implement elements of the business strategy.

- **Business case production:** more senior business analysts usually do this, typically with assistance from finance specialists.

- **Benefits realisation:** the business analysts carry out post-implementation reviews, examine the benefits defined in the business case and evaluate whether or not the benefits have been achieved. Actions to achieve the business benefits are also identified and sometimes carried out by the business analysts.

- **Specification of IT requirements,** typically using standard modelling techniques such as data modelling or use case modelling.

THE BUSINESS ANALYSIS MATURITY MODEL

As the business analysis function has developed within organisations, a progression has emerged reflecting this development process. The business analysis maturity model (BAMM) shown in Figure 1.4 was developed by Assist Knowledge Development Ltd., in conjunction with Matchett Ltd., to represent the development and maturity of business analysis.

Figure 1.4 The business analysis maturity model

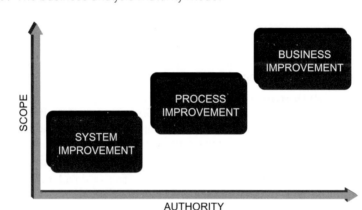

This model reflects discussions with hundreds of business analysts (BAs) working for numerous organisations across the UK and in Australia. These BAs have come from different backgrounds – some from IT, and many from business areas – and have brought different skills and knowledge to their business analysis teams. The model uses two axes: the scope of the work allocated to the BA and the BA's authority level. The scope may be very specific, where an initial study has identified the required course of action and the analyst now needs to explore and define the solution in greater detail. Alternatively, the scope may only have been defined at an overview level, with the BA having to carry out detailed investigation to uncover the issues before the options can be explored. The authority of the BA can also vary considerably, ranging from a very limited level to the ability to influence and guide at senior management level.

The business analysis maturity model shows three levels of maturity found when business analysis is developing. The first of these is where the business analysis work is concerned with defining the requirements for an IT system improvement. At this level, the scope is likely to be well defined and the level of authority to be limited to the project on which the business analyst works. The next level is where the business analysis work has moved beyond a specific area or project, so that the analysts work cross functionally on the business processes that give rise to the requirements. The third level is where the scope and authority of the analysts are at their greatest. Here, the business analysis work is concerned with improving the business and working with senior management to do this.

These levels of maturity apply to three perspectives on business analysis: the individual analysts, the business analysis teams within an organisation, and the business analysis profession as a whole. At each level, the application of techniques and skills, the use of standards and the evaluation of the work through measures can vary considerably. One of the points often raised about the BAMM is its link to the capability maturity model integration (CMMI) represented in Figure 1.5. The CMMI was developed by the Software Engineering Institute (SEI) at Carnegie Mellon University and is an approach used for process improvement in organisations. If we consider the BAMM in the light of the CMMI, we can see that the five levels of the CMMI apply at each level of it.

Figure 1.5 The capability maturity model integration

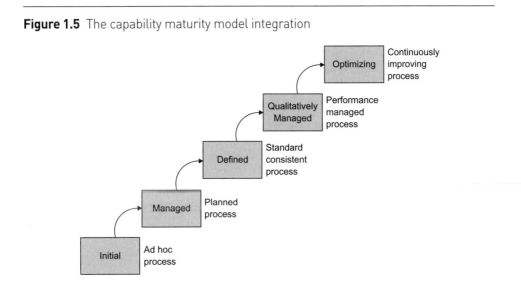

An organisation working to develop its business analysis function may begin by aiming the BAs at requirements definition work. In doing this, the BAs may initially have to develop their own process and standards. Therefore they would be at the System Improvement level of the BAMM and the Initial level of the CMMI. By contrast, an organisation that has employed business analysts for some time may have analysts that can work at all three levels of the BAMM. The analysts working at the Business Improvement level may have a defined process, standards and measures that are managed for each assignment. These BAs are working at the Managed level of the CMMI.

The business analysis profession could also be examined in the light of the BAMM and the CMMI. A panel discussion at the 2009 Business Analysis Conference, organised by the International Institute of Business Analysis, considered whether or not Business Analysis should be deemed to be a profession.

The discussion looked at various aspects of what makes a profession. The factors identified were:

- **Qualifications:** that determine the standard of skills and abilities of the individual professional and that are recognised by employing organisations.
- **Standards:** techniques and documentation standards that are applied in order to carry out the work of the profession.
- **Continuing professional development:** a requirement for the continuing development of skills and knowledge in order to retain the professional status.
- **Code of conduct:** a definition of the personal behaviours and standards required from a member of the profession.
- **Professional body:** a body with responsibility for defining technical standards and the code of conduct, promoting the profession and carrying out disciplinary action where necessary. This might require the removal of members where they do not reach the standard required by the code of conduct.

The conference considered the issue of professionalism, and the consensus was that, while business analysis had certainly increased in professionalism, there was still some way to go before it could be called a profession. While the Information Systems Examinations Board (ISEB) Diploma in Business Analysis has become a widely accepted qualification, it is still possible to practise as a business analyst without qualifications, although this is increasingly rare. There are some recognised business analysis standards and techniques, and some benchmarks, such as this book, have appeared in the last few years. Continuing professional development is not a requirement for the majority of business analysts. Many business analysts are members of BCS – the Chartered Institute for IT – and this professional body has a defined code of conduct for its members and provides standards and promotion for the profession. Gradually the picture is becoming clear, and a business analysis profession is developing.

THE FUTURE OF BUSINESS ANALYSIS

Business analysis has developed into a specialist discipline that can really offer value to organisations. The place of business analysis within the business change lifecycle is critical if organisations are to benefit from those changes. Business analysis offers an opportunity for organisations to ensure that technology is deployed effectively to support their work, and also to identify relevant options for business change that take account of budgetary and timescale pressures. Business analysts can also offer objective views that can challenge the received wisdom and identify where real business benefits can accrue. Over the last few years, business analysts have continued to develop their skills such that the breadth of work they can engage in has become extensive. As internal consultants, experienced business analysts are not just able to bridge IT and 'the business'; they can also improve areas where success has traditionally been a struggle, such as the achievement of predicted business benefits. Further, where outsourcing initiatives operate across departmental boundaries and sometimes have impacts upon the entire organisation, the work carried out by business analysts is vital if the new partly in-house, partly outsourced processes and technology are going to deliver effectively. The challenge for the analysts is to ensure that they develop the extensive toolkit of skills, both behavioural and technical, that will enable them to engage with the problems and issues facing their organisations, and assist in their resolution. The challenge for organisations is to support the analysts in their personal development, ensure they have the authority to carry out business analysis to the extent required by the situations they face, and listen to their advice. This book has been developed primarily for the business analysis community but also to help professionals face the challenges of today's business environment; we hope all business managers, staff and analysts will find it useful.

REFERENCES

Feeny, D. and Willcocks, L. (1998) Core IS Capabilities for exploiting information technology. *Sloan Management Review*, **39**, 9–21.

Parliamentary Office of Science and Technology (POST) (2003) Report on Government IT projects.

FURTHER READING

Cadle, J., Paul, D. and Turner, P. (2010) *Business Analysis Techniques*. BCS, Swindon.

Harmon, P. (2007) *Business Process Change*, 2nd edn. Morgan Kaufmann, Boston, MA.

Johnson, G., Scholes, K. and Whittington, R. (2008) *Exploring Corporate Strategy*, 8th edn. FT Prentice Hall, Harlow.

Porter, M.E. (1980) *Competitive Strategy: Techniques for Analysing Industries and Competitors*, Free Press, New York.

Senge, P.M. (2006) *The Fifth Discipline: The Art and Practice of the Learning Organization*, revised edn. Broadway Business, New York.

Skidmore, S. and Eva, M. (2004) *Introducing Systems Development*. Palgrave Macmillan, Basingstoke.

Yeates, D. and Wakefield, T. (2004) *Systems Analysis and Design*. FT Prentice Hall, Harlow.

USEFUL WEBSITES

International Institute of Business Analysis *IIBA BA Body of Knowledge* at www.theiiba.org

2 THE COMPETENCIES OF A BUSINESS ANALYST

Craig Rollason

INTRODUCTION

Good business analysts can make the difference between a poor and a great investment in business and IT improvements. They can also help to resolve issues without jumping to premature conclusions. But what exactly is a good business analyst? This chapter aims to address this question by identifying and describing the competencies that business analysts need in order to be effective in the modern business environment. Competence has been described by the Working Group on Vocational Qualifications (1986) as 'the ability to do a particular activity to a prescribed standard'. For the purposes of this chapter, we define a competency as something a business analyst needs in order to perform his or her job effectively. The set of business analysis competencies can be divided into three broad groups, as illustrated in Figure 2.1.

Behavioural skills and personal qualities concern the way you think and how you interact with the people around you. They are not specific to business analysis, but are general skills that are important for developing and progressing in any business environment. Behavioural skills are arguably more important than technical or business skills, since they are a prerequisite for working with other people. It is often said that it is easier to give a person with good behavioural skills the techniques they need for their job than to graft behavioural skills on to a good technician. One of the main reasons for this is that good behavioural skills take many years to develop. We shall have more to say on developing competencies later in this chapter.

Business analysts also require business knowledge, which helps them to develop a good understanding of the organisation and the business domain or sector within which it operates. This knowledge is vital if a business analyst is to offer advice and insights that will help improve the organisation's performance. Business knowledge can be developed through reading relevant literature or studying for business qualifications and can be given context by working in a variety of business and project environments.

The techniques of business analysis are those specific to the role that differentiate it from other business or IT roles. They are the technical skills required particularly of the business analyst role. Each of the competencies shown in Figure 2.1 is discussed in the sections that follow; those marked with asterisks are covered in more detail in specific chapters of this book.

Figure 2.1 The competencies of a business analyst

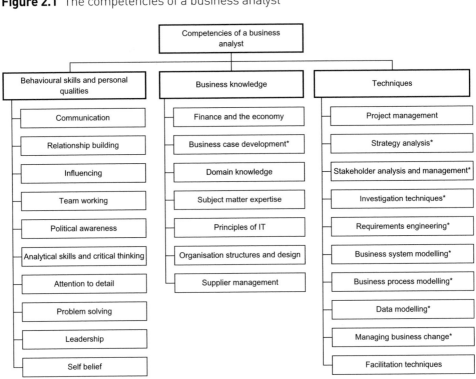

BEHAVIOURAL SKILLS AND PERSONAL QUALITIES

These are the interpersonal skills and characteristics that are useful for a business analyst.

Communication

Communication is perhaps the most important skill a human possesses. It encompasses a wide range of skills such as building rapport, listening, influencing and building empathy. Much analysis work involves collecting and analysing data and then presenting back information that brings new perspectives on the project, so as to propose a course of action. Poor communication skills are often cited as problematic for IT staff and this is explained by the fact that communication at the system level is between computer and human. This type of communication is based on logic. Generally, computers are predictable and do as they are told. When dealing with people, a logical approach does not always apply and many IT professionals become frustrated with business colleagues when there is a failure to do 'the obvious thing'.

Business analysts need to communicate with business colleagues in a language and style they are comfortable with and avoid what they perceive as 'techno-babble'.

Spending time with the intended audience will help you to understand what the communication norms are and what will be effective.

It is important, too, that business analysts can adjust their communication to align with the people they are talking to. The managing director, for example, will most likely have a different view and different interests, and use different language, from shop-floor workers.

Relationship building

This is an extension of communication skill and concerns the ability to get on well with people, at a working if not a social level. Some people seem to possess this ability naturally but others have to work at it – either way, it is essential for a business analyst. As a business analyst, you need to get people to impart information and share opinions with you, and also to discuss ideas for change. All of these things will be very much easier if the people concerned like and trust you. Those who possess this skill naturally seem to take a real interest in other people, making them feel respected and important. This approach is often vital for successful relationship building.

Influencing

Business analysts often conclude their analysis by recommending a course of action. If that conclusion is at odds with preconceived ideas about what is required or calls for radical or unexpected action, then the ability to influence is essential. Successful influencing requires a concerted effort. Emailing the decision-makers with a set of PowerPoint slides is not enough. You need to understand the people who will influence the decision. Some are obvious, such as the project sponsor, project management, governance committees, project boards and other steering groups. Some are hidden, such as networks of colleagues, with personal agendas and hidden information. Identifying each of these stakeholders and understanding the amount of power they exert over the decision-making processes will allow you to target and influence the decision-makers most effectively. Once decision-makers have been identified, you can then define a course of action to take the decision forward. This may involve briefing other colleagues, such as more senior staff or representatives on decision-making groups, or influencing business colleagues directly.

The influencing itself needs careful consideration and prior planning. Business analysts have to develop an understanding of where the other party stands on their proposal, the likely resistance and the influencing style needed to approach the person or group. For example, some managers might defer all decisions to another group, require all information at a very detailed level or ask only for a high-level summary. Some are interested in all the technicalities, others in just the 'vision' or the 'big picture'. Tailoring the approach is vital for a successful outcome.

The analysis itself may be questioned, and business analysts are often themselves influenced to take or suggest another course of action. This may involve another round of influencing, facilitating a round-table discussion or seeking support from senior colleagues on the best course of action. This is especially true when the business analyst is caught in the middle of opposing views. It also suggests that another personal quality that business analysts need from time to time is the ability to withstand pressure.

Team working

Business analysts often work in teams. The nature of business analysis work is that it requires information to be collected from many sources, such as business colleagues, IT suppliers and internal suppliers as well as project team members or management. Hence, a team approach is often used.

An understanding of your role within the team and of what needs to be done and an appreciation of the working style of others are, therefore, important to ensure that the project objectives are achieved.

Political awareness

This is a bit like an elephant – hard to describe, but you know it when you see it. One way of defining such awareness is to use the word 'nous', which one dictionary describes as 'common sense; gumption', but that doesn't quite convey what we mean. The term 'streetwise' also captures part of what we are getting at. Essentially, what we are talking about is an ability to work out what is and is not politically acceptable in an organisation and to use the right organisational levers to get things done. This means knowing the sources of power within the organisation, understanding what they like and don't like and tailoring our approach accordingly. Having political awareness, by the way, emphatically does not mean accepting the status quo; it does mean using resourcefulness and being astute to get results, even in the face of opposition.

Analytical skills and critical thinking

Since the role we are talking about here is that of business analyst, it is clear that analytical skills form a major part of the job, but what does this mean in practice? It means not settling for the obvious, not accepting things at face value and not jumping to premature conclusions. It means digging deeper and deeper until the true situation is uncovered and the real problem has been defined. It involves sifting through masses of often conflicting data and determining which is relevant and which is not and presenting the results of the analysis in a form suitable for the relevant stakeholders. And it involves challenging received wisdom at every turn: Why do you do this? What value does it add? Where is it done? How is it done? Who is or should be responsible? When should it happen? Some analysts seem to believe that the job simply consists of amassing of more and more data in the hope that the answer will somehow magically reveal itself, but it will not do so without the active and critical intervention of the analyst. Over time the analyst will be able to assess the level of analysis required for a specific situation. One maxim often used advises doing 20 per cent of the analysis required to get an answer that is 80 per cent of the right answer, and then being 100 per cent convincing in your influencing. This doesn't mean taking shortcuts on the analysis; it does mean recognising the key factors rather than trying to analyse everything.

Attention to detail

Although it is sometimes true that the answer to a business problem is obvious, in most cases this is not so and the real solution is only revealed after painstaking research. In addition, many business cases (see Chapter 13) fail because there is insufficient detailed evidence for the proposed change. When a project is handed over to the IT specialists, they often find that many important issues of detail have not been addressed. So it appears that having an eye for detail is also an important attribute of a good business analyst.

Problem solving

There are many techniques associated with problem solving, and numerous books and training courses address the topic. Chapter 4 describes an approach to creative problem solving. However, here we are talking about the problem-solving mindset. A business analyst has to approach an issue with the attitude that problems can be solved. A variation on this is that even if the optimal solution cannot be implemented, for financial, technical or political reasons, the business analyst must be pragmatic and be prepared to find other solutions that will yield at least some business benefit.

Leadership

Leadership is a competency that is often associated with line-management job roles. However, the fundamental characteristics of leadership – developing a vision, taking ownership of that vision and ensuring the actions to achieve that vision are implemented – can be applied to all types of work. Thus, leadership is also applicable to business analysis and in this context may be defined as creating a vision of the options available to address a business issue, advising stakeholders in order to obtain agreement about the vision and then driving the business change process towards the achievement of that vision.

No two projects are the same. Each project has different objectives, constraints and stakeholders, and hence the required approach, skills and resources will differ. It is important to assess each situation on its own merits, decide what is needed and then design the analysis process. The word 'analysis' is used here in the broad context of analysing business systems, not just IT systems. Business analysts need to consider all aspects of the environment within which they work, including the people, culture and processes as well as commercial and technical aspects. Getting the vision and actions right will require holistic thinking and rigorous analysis, and will position the project for success with key business stakeholders.

Self belief

This last quality is one that is often overlooked, but is extremely important. It does not relate to having an enormous ego and wanting to carry all before you. It does mean that you have sufficient confidence in yourself, in the quality of your analysis and in the correctness of your solution to be able to withstand pressure and sustain your arguments. Self belief is a key competence for working effectively with stakeholders across the broad range of situations likely to be encountered by business analysts.

BUSINESS KNOWLEDGE

This section considers the range of business knowledge and understanding that is essential as a background and foundation for the business analyst's work.

Finance and the economy

The universal language of business is finance. Even in the public and not-for-profit sectors of the economy, finance plays a key role in deciding what funds are available and what can and cannot be done. A business analyst needs to have a good working knowledge of the economy and of the basics of business finance. This includes a general understanding of financial reports such as the balance sheet and profit-and-loss account, of financial analysis tools such as ratio analysis, and of the principles of costing.

Business case development

Much of the business analyst's work will be to assess the costs and benefits of delivering a project to the organisation. Thus, when communicating analysis findings, you will need to ensure that you have a view on the financial impact that the project will have. IT in its own right is only an enabling tool for business benefits to be achieved, and a business analysis project may involve other specialists such as management accountants to understand and model the business activities and determine how IT can deliver financial benefit. To develop the business case, a basic understanding of finance is required along with the financial workings of the business area being considered. Business analysts involved in business case preparation will need to understand basic investment appraisal techniques and work closely with the finance department. These techniques are explained in Chapter 13. Over recent years many business analysts have developed a greater understanding of the benefits and costs of technical solutions. This is a positive development, since it enables analysts to discount costly options quickly, and appreciate the true value and impact of their work on their organisations.

Domain knowledge

This is a good general understanding of the business domain, or sector, in which your organisation operates, be it private, public or not-for-profit. Apart from the general domain, there is more specific domain knowledge, for instance of the supermarket or local government sectors. The reasons why this knowledge is required are threefold:

- It enables you to talk sensibly with the business people involved in the project, in a language that they can understand. (The personal qualities of communication and relationship-building also help here.)

- It will help you to understand what would and would not be acceptable or useful in this business domain. Issues of profit, for instance, are unlikely to be of interest when working in a social-security department.

- It may enable you to take ideas, particularly those relating to best practice or 'best value' (a UK government term), from part of a sector and apply them elsewhere.

Subject matter expertise

This takes the domain knowledge to a lower level of detail. A good understanding of the business area in which you work is important in order to establish credibility with your customer. The level of expertise required will again depend on the type of work being done; for example, if the project is concerned with strategic matters, this will require an understanding of industry structures, organisation design, business models and business drivers for strategic change. At a more operational level, a discussion on the replacement of existing systems will require an understanding of how the existing systems are configured to meeting current business needs. Business analysts may be specialists in particular business domains, with a strong and detailed understanding of the subject area, who can pinpoint very quickly areas for improvement, and identify what needs to change or to be analysed by using existing knowledge and contacts. Alternatively, they could be generalists with outline knowledge about individual business areas who rely on others to bring the relevant detailed knowledge. There is no right or wrong answer to being a specialist or a generalist. Both are valuable, depending on the organisational context. The key point is to assess how well your competencies meet the needs of the current situation and to recognise your strengths and weaknesses. You can then take any necessary actions such as developing specialist knowledge, requesting input from specialists or asking for a new perspective from a generalist who can take a broader view.

Principles of IT

Many business analysts do not come from an IT background and say – rightly – that their job is not to be expert in IT-related issues; that, after all, is why there are systems analysts, software engineers and so on. However, as so many business analysis projects result in the use of IT in some way, a general understanding of the field seems necessary so that business analysts can communicate meaningfully with the IT professionals.

The extent to which you will need technical knowledge will depend on the nature of the analysis work being undertaken. Although strong technical knowledge is often useful, this may be better obtained from those with specialist skills, for example systems analysts, developers or external suppliers. The key requirement is that the business analyst can understand the technical terms used by IT specialists and help the business users to appreciate any impacts on the organisation. However, since business analysts often investigate IT solutions, they should also possess an understanding of IT fundamentals, including areas such as:

- how computers work, including operating systems, application software, hardware and networks;

- systems-development lifecycles, for example the 'V' model or the unified process;

- systems-development approaches, for example the dynamic systems development method (DSDM), agile development and the unified modelling language (UML);

- the relative pros and cons of developing systems and of buying them 'off the shelf';

- trends and new opportunities that IT brings. such as ecommerce, grid computing and mobile technologies, and how these impact systems development.

Organisation structures and design

As well as involving processes and IT, many business analysis projects involve restructuring organisations to a greater or a lesser degree, for example to remove handoffs, to centralise a process or to improve the customer service. Because of this, it is important for a business analyst to have a good understanding of the various organisation structures that may be encountered – functional, project, matrix and so on – and of their relative strengths and weaknesses.

Supplier management

Many organisations use external suppliers to deliver their IT systems, either on an ad-hoc basis or perhaps through a more comprehensive outsourcing arrangement. In recent years, outsourcing arrangements have been extended to cover whole business processes or even an entire business function. For example, many organisations have outsourced payroll activities for several years, but some have now extended this to cover much of the human resources (HR) work, from recruitment to HR record keeping. The selection and contracting of suppliers tends to fall within the domain of the supplier management function. However, for some outsourcing contracts the business analyst may carry out or be involved in this work, and so needs a broad understanding of procurement and supplier management processes. As a minimum, business analysts should be aware of the different contractual arrangements that are available, for example:

- **Time and materials:** where the contracted party is paid on the basis of the time worked.

- **Fixed price delivery:** where the contracted party is paid the price that they originally agreed for the delivery of piece of work according to the precise specification.

- **Risk and reward:** where the contracted party has agreed to bear some or all of the risk of the project, for example by investing resources such as staff time, materials or office space, but where the potential rewards are greater than under other contractual arrangements.

Business analysts should also understand the supplier management process, and should be able to engage with suppliers to ensure that they deliver their services effectively.

TECHNIQUES

Finally, we consider the techniques that the business analyst will need to apply during assignments.

Project management

The Association for Project Management's *Body of Knowledge* (APM, 2006) has seven sections that describe the work of a project manager. The Project Management Institute's equivalent publication (PMI 2008) lists the project management context and processes, scope management, integration management, time management, cost management, quality management, human resource management, communications management, risk management and procurement management. It is unlikely that a business analyst will be called upon to display skills in all of these areas, but where the project team is small the analyst may be required to undertake the project manager role. Larger projects often employ a specialist project manager. However, there are some project skills that an analyst should have. For example, understanding project initiation is vital since it allows the analyst to understand, or even define, the terms of reference for the project. It is also important that analysts understand project management planning approaches – as they will have to work within a plan – and are aware of particularly relevant aspects such as dependencies between tasks, quality assurance and risk management.

Strategy analysis
This covers a range of techniques that can be used to understand the business direction and the strengths and weaknesses of an organisation, or part of an organisation. Strategy analysis is explored in more detail in Chapter 3.

Stakeholder analysis and management
This includes understanding who are the stakeholders in a business analysis project and working out how their interests are best managed. Stakeholder analysis and management is the subject of Chapter 6.

Investigation techniques
Clearly, to get to the root of a business issue the analyst will have to undertake detailed analysis of the area. Investigation techniques are reviewed in Chapter 5.

Requirements engineering
This is the set of practices and processes that lead to the development of a set of well-formed business requirements, from which the business and IT solutions can be developed. The topic is examined in Chapters 9, 10 and 11.

Business system modelling
Business system modelling is an approach to visualising business systems through the creation of conceptual models. The techniques concerned are described in Chapter 7.

Business process modelling
Whereas a business system model looks at the entire business system in overview, more detailed process models are used to map and analyse how the business processes actually work and to help identify opportunities for process improvement. Business process modelling is the subject of Chapter 8.

Data modelling
Analysing the data held and used within a business system affords valuable insights into how the system operates. For example, what are the data items that are held about our customers? What are the relationships between customers, products and suppliers? The entity relationship modelling and class modelling techniques are discussed in Chapter 11.

Managing business change
This covers the techniques needed to implement changes within an organisation and to make them 'stick'. Managing business change is the subject of Chapter 14.

Facilitation techniques
The interpersonal skills required for effective facilitation – usually exhibited within the context of a workshop – are those described under the heading 'Behavioural skills and personal qualities' on page 19. However, there are other qualities that provide the basis for skilled facilitation. It is necessary to apply the process for effective facilitation, in particular in the preparation for a workshop. The analyst also needs the knowledge of a range of techniques and the ability to apply them. These techniques include such approaches as brainstorming, mind-mapping, the use of Post-it notes, Edward de Bono's 'six thinking hats' (de Bono 1990) and so on. There is not the space to covers these topics in depth here, but an introduction to some is provided in Chapter 5. In addition, the 'Further reading' section at the end of this chapter identifies some useful publications. Effective facilitation usually results from a combination of the right qualities in the facilitator and the choice of the right techniques to match the task and the cultural context of the organisation in which it is being used.

THE RIGHT COMPETENCIES FOR THE RIGHT SITUATION

A key task for the management of business analysts is to ensure that there is a good fit between the competencies needed for the analysis to be carried out. Putting a junior analyst is a situation where higher-level skills are required can be demotivating, and the reverse is also true. Figure 2.2 offers a simple model for thinking about the situation and the competencies and skill levels required.

Figure 2.2 Skill analysis matrix

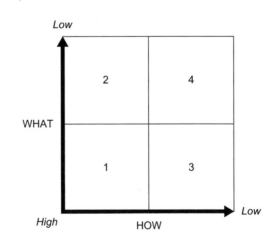

In quadrant 1, the analysis to be done is well understood, as is the process for doing it. This would be the starting point for a new analyst. As an example, analysing the costs and benefits of an end-user-requested bug fix to a system might fall into this category. This might equate to level 3 or 4 in the SFIAplus framework (which is described later in this chapter).

In quadrant 2, the analysis that needs to be done is not clearly understood, although how it is to be done is understood. This would be work for a more experienced analyst. For example, a new collaborative technology that has a predefined way of being deployed might be introduced into the organisation. However, the organisation might be unsure which are the high-value areas in which this technology should be deployed, leading to the need for some feasibility analysis. This may equate to level 4 or 5 in the SFIAplus framework.

In quadrant 3, the analysis that needs to be done is understood, although it is not clear how it is to be done. As with quadrant 2, this would be work for a more experienced analyst. For example, the organisation may want to move from a variety of packaged systems solutions to a single enterprise resource planning (ERP) system. However, the way to achieve this may not be clear if the organisation has never attempted such a thing before. This may equate to level 4 or 5 in the SFIAplus framework.

In quadrant 4, neither the analysis to be done nor how it is to be done are understood. This type of work is for the experienced analyst, and borders on a need for consulting skills. The analyst needs to facilitate the organisation in its thinking about what it is trying to achieve. In this example the brief can be as vague as 'We need to reduce costs', 'We need to improve sales' or 'We need to innovate more'. This may equate to level 6 in the SFIAplus framework.

HOW CAN I DEVELOP MY COMPETENCIES?

Earlier sections of this chapter have identified a wide range of competencies that a business analyst will eventually want to master, but to someone new to the role the list may appear rather daunting. Also, of course, the question 'Do I have to have all of these competencies in order to be a useful analyst?' is raised. The answer to this is clearly 'no', and business analysts usually start out in the role with well-developed competencies in some areas and less ability in others.

The first step in developing as a business analyst is to understand the competencies required of a business analyst in your organisation. This should include an assessment of both the current and the future competencies required. Your HR department or line management may be able to provide an outline definition of the competencies required and many organisations have internal skills frameworks that define the competency requirements for different roles and grades. Alternatively, you could use an existing framework such as the Skills Framework for the Information Age (SFIA) which has been developed by e-skills UK and the SFIA Foundation. This framework is described more fully in the next section.

Essentially, there are three ways in which business analysts can develop their competencies: training, self-study and work experience.

Training

This is particularly useful for the concrete techniques and, to some extent, for the behavioural skills and personal qualities. Classroom-based training allows skills to be learned and practised in a relatively safe environment, with a tutor on hand to offer support, guidance and encouragement. It also allows course delegates to share knowledge and experience, which helps to enrich the learning experience. Computer-based training can also be useful, in particular where the need is to gain knowledge. Some training courses lead to industry qualifications, such as those offered by the ISEB. Industry qualifications are discussed further in the next section.

Self-study

Self-study is an excellent way for analysts to grow their business knowledge. As well as textbooks, reading publications such as the *Financial Times*, the *Economist*, the *Harvard Business Review* and other technical and professional journals will broaden and deepen the analyst's understanding of the business world. The internet also provides a wealth of resources, including specialist websites, articles and blogs.

Work experience

This provides an opportunity to use and improve techniques and to deepen business knowledge. It is also the best arena in which business analysts can develop their behavioural skills and personal qualities. The performance of most analysts improves over time as their experience grows, but this can be heightened and accelerated if your organisation operates a proper coaching or mentoring programme. Even if it does not, there is a lot to be said for working, or having discussions, with more experienced business analysts whose work you respect. However, it is important to adapt their approach to your personality and competencies; what works for one person does not necessarily work for another.

INDUSTRY SKILLS FRAMEWORKS

SFIA – pronounced 'sofia' – and SFIAplus, the British Computer Society's (BCS's) model, are the two major frameworks for the definition of skills in the information systems industry. These frameworks include six categories of skill, including 'strategy and architecture', 'business change', and 'solution development and implementation'. There are 86 skills defined, covering an extensive range of areas. Several levels are defined for each skill, and these definitions can be used to build job role descriptions. The levels are numbered 1 to 7: level 1 is follow, 2 is assist, 3 is apply, 4 is enable, 5 is ensure and advise, and 6 is initiate and influence. The information in the frameworks can be used to build descriptions of the skills levels required by the business analyst roles within an organisation.

SFIA

SFIA is owned and maintained by the SFIA Foundation, a not-for-profit organisation whose members are:

- BCS, the Chartered Institute for IT;
- e-skills UK;
- the Institution of Engineering and Technology (IET);
- the Institute for the Management of Information Systems (IMIS);
- the IT Service Management Forum (itSMF).

SFIA is used worldwide in all sectors of industry and government as the preferred framework for defining the skills required of IT professionals. The licence to use the framework is free of charge, though the SFIA Foundation requires a royalty from those using it to support a commercial offering. The Foundation accredits consultants and partners, and provides training in the use of the framework.

The business analysis skill
The business analysis skill in SFIA is part of the 'business change' skill category of the SFIA framework. The SFIA description of the business analysis skill is:

> The methodical investigation, analysis, review and documentation of all or part of a business in terms of business functions and processes, the information used and the data on which the information is based. The definition of requirements for improving any aspect of the processes and systems and the quantification of potential business benefits. The creation of viable specifications and acceptance criteria in preparation for the construction of information and communication systems.

Business analysis skill levels are defined at levels 3, 4, 5 and 6. SFIA provides a more detailed definition of the skill requirements for each level of a given skill. For example, business analysis level 5 is described as follows:

- Takes responsibility for investigative work to determine business requirements and specify effective business processes, through improvements in information systems, information management, practices, procedures, and organisation change.
- Applies and monitors the use of required modelling and analysis tools, methods and standards, giving special consideration to business perspectives.
- Conducts investigations at a high level for strategy studies, business requirements specifications and feasibility studies.
- Prepares business cases which define potential benefits, options for achieving these benefits through development of new or changed processes, and associated business risks.
- Identifies stakeholders and their business needs.

Table 2.1 shows the SFIA and SFIAplus description of Business Analysis skill levels 3–6. Other skills in the SFIA framework that are likely to be used to describe the skill requirements for business analysts include:

- business process improvement;
- stakeholder relationship management;
- requirements definition and management.

Table 2.1 SFIA and SFIAplus description of Business Analysis skill levels 3–6

Level 3   Investigates operational needs and problems, and opportunities, contributing to the recommendation of improvements in automated and non-automated components of new or changed processes and organisation. Assists in defining acceptance tests for these recommendations.

Level 4   Investigates operational requirements, problems, and opportunities, seeking effective business solutions through improvements in automated and non-automated components of new or changed processes. Assists in the analysis of stakeholder objectives, and the underlying issues arising from investigations into business requirements and problems, and identifies options for consideration. Identifies potential benefits, and available options for consideration. Works with clients/users in defining acceptance tests.

Level 5   Takes responsibility for investigative work to determine business requirements and specify effective business processes, through improvements in information systems, information management, practices, procedures, and organisation change. Applies and monitors the use of required modelling and analysis tools, methods and standards, giving special consideration to business perspectives. Conducts investigations at a high level for strategy studies, business requirements specifications and feasibility studies. Prepares business cases which define potential benefits, options for achieving these benefits through development of new or changed processes, and associated business risks. Identifies stakeholders and their business needs.

Level 6   Takes full responsibility for business analysis within a significant segment of an organisation where the advice given and decisions made will have a measurable impact on the profitability or effectiveness of the organisation. Establishes the contribution that technology can make to business objectives, defining strategies, validating and justifying business needs, conducting feasibility studies, producing high-level and detailed business models, preparing business cases, overseeing development and implementation of solutions, taking into account the implications of change on the organisation and all stakeholders. Guides senior management towards accepting change brought about through process and organisational change.

SFIAplus

SFIAplus provides the same description for the business analysis skill set as
SFIA, but it also provides additional details on the following:

- a list of related skill sets (given in full at the end of this section);
- technical overview, including typical tools and techniques;
- overview of training, development and qualifications;
- careers and jobs;
- professional bodies;
- standards and codes of practice;
- communities and events;
- publications and resources.

SFIAplus also provides additional information for each level for a particular skill
(levels 3–6 in the case of business analysis). This information covers the following
headings:

- background;
- work activities;
- knowledge/skills;.
- training activities;
- professional development activities;
- qualifications.

While SFIAplus provides more detail than SFIA, it is important to realise that
the two frameworks should be implemented in different ways. SFIAplus should
be treated as a standard and is not designed to be customised, whereas SFIA is
intended to be used as a basis for tailoring to an organisation's needs. As a result,
care should be taken when choosing which of the two is most appropriate for a
specific organisation.

SFIAplus enables organisations to classify and benchmark their IT skills and to
train and develop their teams to meet the defined skill requirements. As a business
analyst, this provides a basis for you to gauge where you are against the skills and
corresponding level of competence defined in the framework. You could obtain an
objective assessment of your competencies from your line manager and peers. This
can be used to look ahead to assess how you, and your employing organisation,
want your skill set and career to develop. The final step is to identify a set of actions
that will help you with your development. You could try some or all of the following:

- Seek out assignments that give you opportunities to develop.
- Identify a role model who demonstrates your desired competencies. Ask them
  what is required, or ask them to mentor your development or arrange to work
  for them.

- Use training providers to target specifically those areas that need development.
- Consider a secondment to an organisation that excels in the required competencies.
- Do your own research into specific competencies. There are many more detailed books covering the competencies identified in this chapter.
- Ask for regular feedback from your boss or peers.
- Join an industry specialist group such as one of the BCS specialist groups that focus specifically on the competencies, such as project management.
- Develop as you go and gain from experience. Record what you've learned so that you don't forget it.

The full list of skills related to the Business Analysis skill provided by SFIAplus comprises:

- benefits management;
- business modelling;
- business process improvement;
- change implementation, planning and management;
- data analysis;
- usability requirements analysis;
- organisation design and implementation;
- requirements definition and management;
- stakeholder relationship management;
- system design.

INDUSTRY QUALIFICATIONS

There are two examination bodies offering professional qualifications in business analysis in the UK. These are the ISEB, which is a division of BCS, and the International Institute of Business Analysts (IIBA).

ISEB/BCS
ISEB offers a range of qualifications for business analysts covering the subjects of business analysis, change management and consultancy. There are three levels of qualification:

- the foundation certificate in:
  - business analysis (described below);
  - IT-enabled business change.

- the practitioner certificate in:

  o benefits management and business acceptance;

  o business analysis essentials;

  o modelling business processes;

  o organisational context;

  o requirements engineering.

- higher qualifications:

  o the diploma in business analysis (described below);

  o the certificate in information systems (IS) consultancy practice.

ISEB foundation in business analysis
The foundation in business analysis covers the broad range of business analysis principles and techniques, and is based upon the information contained within this book.

ISEB business analysis diploma
Candidates will be awarded the relevant diploma once they have passed written examinations in the compulsory and specialist modules, and have passed an oral examination specialising in the particular diploma subject area.

IIBA CBAP
The IIBA has created the Certified Business Analysis Professional (CBAP), a designation awarded to candidates who have successfully demonstrated their expertise in this field. This is done by detailing hands-on work experience in business analysis through the CBAP application process, and passing the IIBA CBAP examination. The CBAP may also be used towards the ISEB diploma in business analysis.

SUMMARY

Competence development is the most important aspect of career development for any professional. This chapter has sought to categorise and describe the most common competencies for being a successful business analyst. Every organisation will have a different interpretation of what a business analyst does, and we have seen the importance of matching the competencies to the role an individual is expected to perform. If you wish to develop and improve your performance you need to understand your levels of competence in the various skill areas and then take the necessary steps to improve.

Historically, business analyst jobs and qualifications have focused on the construction of systems that meet business requirements. This has meant that the focus is on collecting requirements in an organised and logical fashion, which are then used to select or build systems that meet those needs. The need for people who can do this is now a lot wider, and there is much more emphasis on the importance of this task, often as a result of the sourcing options available to organisations. Where external suppliers are used, defining IT requirements is even more important, particularly where they are located in another country – offshore sourcing, as this is known. Critically, the stakes are being raised higher for IT projects. IT departments that cannot show or communicate how they add value are becoming an endangered species. Business analysts can only survive and evolve if they offer a much broader set of competencies that allows them to demonstrate how they can identify, analyse and develop options for adding value to their organisations.

It is in the area of behavioural skills and personal qualities that perhaps the biggest challenges for business analysts lie. Staff involved in IT projects have been characterised in the past as showing far more aptitude for communicating with machines than with human beings. In addition, anyone working in business change is only too aware of the apprehension and even resentment that change projects engender. So, business analysts face a major challenge. They need to use all of their behavioural skills to invalidate the stereotypes and overcome the opposition, so that they can work with their business colleagues to deliver the business improvements their organisations demand.

REFERENCES

Association for Project Management (2006) *Body of Knowledge*. APM Publishing, www.apm.org.uk/bodyofknowledge.asp

de Bono, E. (1990) *Six Thinking Hats*. Penguin, London.

Project Management Institute (PMI) (2008) *A Guide to the Project Management Book of Knowledge*, 4th edn.

FURTHER READING

Cadle, J., Paul, D. and Turner, P. (2010) *Business Analysis Techniques*. BCS, Swindon.

Laborde, G.Z. (1987) *Influencing with Integrity*. Anglo American Book Company, Bancyfelin, Wales.

Stanton, N. (2009) *Mastering Communication*, 5th edn. Palgrave Macmillan.

Townsend, J. and Donovan, P. (1999) *The Facilitator's Pocketbook*. Management Pocketbooks, Alresford.

Whiddett, S. and Hollyforde, S. (2003) *A Practical Guide to Competencies*, 2nd edn. Chartered Institute of Personnel and Development, London.

Zuker, E. (1991) *The Seven Secrets of Influence.* McGraw-Hill.

USEFUL WEBSITES

www.sfia.org.uk

www.bcs.org

www.management-standards.org

www.theiiba.org

3 STRATEGY ANALYSIS

Donald Yeates

INTRODUCTION

This chapter is about four aspects of strategy analysis:

- understanding what strategy is and why it is important – the assumption being that strategy is important;
- exploring some ideas about how strategy is developed;
- implementing strategy;
- working out what all of this means for business analysts.

There is no intention here to try and turn you into a strategic planner, but the aim is to enable you to understand the process of strategy development, be comfortable with the tools that managers use and be able to use them yourself as you explore how new or different information systems could push forward the activities of the organisation that employs you.

THE CONTEXT FOR STRATEGY

Why do organisations bother about strategy? What advantage do they hope to get? Let's look at what's happening in the world. Most of us would probably support the idea that business is becoming increasingly unpredictable and changes are more turbulent. The information revolution and the digital economy have caused much of this dramatic change, and barriers between previously separate businesses are falling like dominoes. For example, who will be the big financial players in the future? It could be the global banks, or retail outlets like Tesco and Sainsbury's, or strong brands like Amazon and Virgin. If you're working in the finance sector, how do you know where to move next?

There are some big changes that organisations face and that strategy development tries to moderate. First there are the changes to the ways we are employed. There is much more use of part-time and contract employees, who may have little long-term loyalty to their employer and who have their own individual career and work/life balance plans. The growth of knowledge-based industries and the continuous change experienced by organisations means that individual employees, consultants or contractors – permanent, full-time or part-time – have become valuable assets. This is becoming more than ever the case as organisations everywhere, in both the public and the private sectors, flatten their organisation structures, decentralise decision-making and give more freedom to individuals to do business, deal with customers and resolve problems. There are no longer jobs for life, and attitudes to work have changed. We all now want greater job satisfaction, higher rewards, more personal recognition and flexible working environments.

Society has also changed. There is greater freedom of expression and of thought. Freedom of information legislation means that individuals have access to evidence and decisions taken by government that were previously hidden. There is less respect for authority and office unless it has been earned. Our attitudes to change, direction, reorganisation and other people knowing better than we do have shifted, and the development and implementation of new strategies need to take this into account.

Organisations are responding to these changes by doing everything they can to increase their flexibility and responsiveness, which means that they seek to reduce employment costs. Without trade unions to apply a brake, we see central government and European institutions taking this role instead.

The world is full of contradictions, for example:

- **Global versus local:** globalisation creates the largest markets ever known, and until we have intergalactic businesses this will remain the case. But it also means that the players in a global market can be small. Having a global reach doesn't mean being the biggest. The scarcity of the product, its brand reputation and its distribution channels make the difference. The paparazzi know this: one paparazzo, a camera, the right moment – and the internet sells the product across the world in less than a day.

- **Centralised versus decentralised organisation structures:** finance may be a central process, but prices and discounts are set locally.

- **Hard and soft management:** developing strategy is seen as a 'hard' discipline like finance and technology, but the creativity and change skills that make strategy work are the 'soft' skills.

Finally, there are two questions. How can anyone create, formulate or build a strategy if the future is inherently unknowable and unpredictable? And how can it be implemented in a coherent way in decentralised structures with delegated authorities and an ever-changing environment? This makes it appear very difficult for a business analyst to understand the nature and permanence – or impermanence – of the business strategies against which information systems (IS) strategies are to be built. However, as we shall see through an examination of the nature of strategy and the use of some well-tried tools, effective steps can be taken to deal with this difficulty.

WHAT IS STRATEGY?

The concept of strategy begins in a military context and the word 'strategy' is derived from the Greek word *strategia*, meaning 'generalship'. The term has a 'getting ready for battle' sense to it, and it concerns the deployment of troops, weapons, aircraft and ships before engagement with the enemy begins. Once the enemy is engaged, then battlefield tactics determine the success of the strategy. The transfer of these ideas to business is easy to make, and we expect to deal with:

- **The goal or mission of the business:** in strategy terms this is often referred to as the 'direction'.
- **The timeframe:** strategy is about the long term. The problem here is that it differs widely across industries, with petrochemicals and pharmaceuticals at the really long end and domestic financial services products at the short end.
- **The organisation of resources:** such as finance, skills, assets and technical competence, so that the organisation can compete.
- **The environment:** within which the organisation will operate, and its markets.

A popular definition is given by Johnson, Scholes and Whittington (2008):

Strategy is the direction and scope of an organisation over the long term, which achieves advantage for the organisation through its configuration of resources within a changing environment and to fulfil stakeholder expectations.

However, writers and gurus have offered their own definitions for at least the last 30 years, including George Steiner (1979), who did not so much define it as paint a picture of it by saying that strategy:

- is what top management does;
- is about direction;
- sets in motion the important actions necessary to achieve these directions;
- is what the organisation should be doing.

Finally, another definition from Johnson, Scholes and Whittington (2008) is more helpful to us when considering strategy analysis. They wrote that strategic decisions are concerned with:

- the direction of an organisation's activities;
- matching these activities to the environment;
- the capability of the organisation to support the chosen direction;
- the values and expectations of stakeholders;
- the implementation and management of change.

Strategies exist at different levels in an organisation, ranging from corporate strategies at the top level affecting the complete organisation, down to the operational strategies for product or services offerings. Typical levels of strategy could be:

- **Corporate strategy** concerned with the overall purpose and scope of the business. Strategies at this level are influenced by investors, governments and global competition, and by the context set out earlier in this chapter. This is the basis of all other strategies and strategic decisions.

- **Business unit strategy:** below the corporate level are the strategic business units (SBUs). Each of these organisational units has a distinct external market, different from those of other SBUs. SBU strategies address choice of products, pricing, customer satisfaction and competitive advantage.

- **Operational strategy:** focusing on the delivery of the corporate and SBU strategies through the effective organisation and development of resources, processes and people.

STRATEGY DEVELOPMENT

This section begins with some fundamental questions: How do we start to develop a strategy? Where does strategy development come from? How do we know what kinds of strategy to develop? We can identify several starting points:

- **Strategy associated with an individual,** often the founder of a business. UK examples include Stelios Haji-Ioannou of easyJet, Ken Morrison of Morrisons supermarkets, Richard Branson and Alan Sugar. In already established businesses, we might suggest Allan Leighton of Asda and the Royal Mail and Stuart Rose of Marks & Spencer, both introduced into these businesses to turn them around and to change their strategy. So strategy sometimes starts and is strongly associated with an individual leader. This can work all the way down an organisation, where new leaders bring new ideas – strategies – to operating units, divisions and departments.

- **Decentralised and empowered organisations** where all managers are encouraged to use the techniques of strategy analysis and be 'intrapreneurial' – internally entrepreneurial – and actively create and champion new initiatives.

- However, strong individual strategy champions aren't always necessary in order to create new strategies. Groups of managers may meet regularly and review trends in the market and their own business progress; they plan new actions and try them out. Strategy evolves in an incremental way.

- **Strategies resulting from a formal planning process.** Some organisations find this to be essential, especially those for which strategy is truly long term.

We could, therefore, see the origins of strategy development as in Figure 3.1.

The sizes of the triangles shown in Figure 3.1 are not necessarily the same and, indeed, change over time. Formal planning or intrapreneurial strategies may follow entrepreneurially driven strategy as an organisation grows; a crisis may

Figure 3.1 Strategy creation

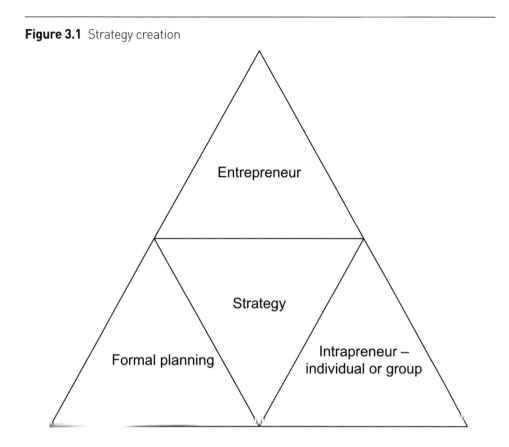

call for new entrepreneurial strategies, perhaps associated with a new chief executive, and the cycle then begins again.

The three different ways in which strategies come about are described by Johnson, Scholes and Whittington (2008) as seeing strategy development through three different lenses. These lenses are the design lens, the experience lens and the ideas lens.

The design lens of formal planning sees strategy resulting from 'the deliberate positioning of the organisation' through a detailed and comprehensive analysis and a subsequent directive strategy that is formulated by top management and pushed down through the organisation. A key factor here is that the structure of the organisation and all of the central systems can be aligned to report on the performance of the strategy. It is unlikely that any organisation could withstand frequent major revisions of strategy of this kind. It is also unlikely that strategy by design always gets it right: certainly not in every detail. It is likely that adaptations and incremental changes will be made to the strategy.

This brings us to the experience-lens (intrapreneur) view of strategy develop-ment, where the collective experience of the organisation and its organisational culture operate on the existing strategy to give it a new form. In other words, the strategy is modified to fit a continually evolving environment, and each modification may form the basis for the next, and so on. Although this seems a sensible approach, these small slow steps, taken as they are rooted in a collective experience and a past strategy, are unlikely to be innovative and may produce responses that are just 'more of the same' and inadequate as answers to bigger-than-normal external changes.

Entrepreneurial strategies come through the ideas lens and are the result of an innovative climate or the introduction of new thinkers, very often new chief executive officers (CEOs). These ideas can also come from environmental scanning – looking at what's happening outside the organisation and identifying new opportunities or stronger competitor pressure, new customer demands or imminent technological change.

We also have to recognise another force in the making of strategy: politics. So far the development of strategy has been considered as a rational, logical and organised process. It often is developed like this, and in this chapter we'll consider many of the tools that are used to inform the strategy process. However strategy is developed, it can't always be done by flashes of inspiration with no hard work! There are views now that show organisations as political systems, which manipulate the formation of strategy through the exercise of power. Different interest groups form around different strategic ideas or issues, and compete for resources and the support of stakeholders to achieve the dominance of their ideas. On this basis, strategic direction is not achieved through a universally accepted rational analysis, but through the promotion of specific ideas of the most powerful groups. This power comes from five main sources:

- **Dependency:** other departments are dependent on those that have control over the organisation's resources. The power of the HR department increases, for example, if all new staff requisitions have to be authorised by it.

- **Financial resources:** where are the funds to invest in the development of new ideas, product or services. Who has these funds? What financial frameworks constrain or give freedom to different groups?

- **Position:** where do the actors live in the organisation structure, and how does their work affect the organisation's performance?

- **Uniqueness:** no other part of the organisation can do what the powerful group does.

- **Uncertainty:** power resides with people, and groups can cope with the unpredictable effects of the environment and protect others from its impact.

It is interesting, therefore, when considering strategic direction and the implementation of strategy to assess the extent to which politics influences the outcome.

Finally, there is the 'garbage can' model for strategy formulation. This is the process that is furthest away from cool, calm and scientific deliberation. It is said to be most appropriate where there is collective and great uncertainty about what to do, where the technology or technological change is unclear or unknown and where strategy-makers' preferences and ideas are unclear and their choices about what to do are inconsistent. The garbage can therefore stores many different processes and solutions that are thrown into it independently of each other. Indeed, the problems, solutions and decision-makers are not necessarily connected, and it seems to be a chance alignment of components that generates the required action when the garbage can is inspected. So when there is a need to do something – a choice opportunity, as it is called – we look in the garbage can and find a collection of solutions and ideas that that we can use now, but that were not intended for us, or to be used in this way, when they were thrown into the bin.

So we know that there are many different drivers for strategy development, and even though strategy appears to be formulated in different ways they will all incorporate some external analysis – 'What's happening out there?' – some internal analysis – 'Where do we fit in to what's happening out there?' – and some consideration of how new strategies could be implemented.

We do all of this in order to provide a written statement of our strategy. This written statement is needed for many reasons:

- It provides a focus for the organisation and enables all parts of it to understand the reasons behind top-level decisions and how each part can contribute to its achievements.

- It provides a framework for a practical allocation of investment and other resources.

- It provides a guide to innovation, where new products, services, systems etc. are needed.

- It enables appropriate performance measures to be put in place that measure the key indicators of our success in achieving the strategy.

- It tells the outside world, and especially our outside stakeholders, about us and enforces the expectations that they develop about us.

EXTERNAL ENVIRONMENT ANALYSIS

Most organisations face a complex and changing external environment of increasing unpredictability. Let us take as an example a retail electrical and electronics store that faces some or all of the following external changes:

- **The state of the national and local economies:** product demand is influenced by local employment and incomes and the cost of credit.

- **Product cost:** price competition is high and there's a continuing shift to move manufacturing to lower-cost economies, with the possible impact on supply and after-sales support.

- **Changes in consumer lifestyles and tastes:** the high cost of housing leads to a greater incidence of smaller houses and a growth in the supply of flats, calling for small TVs and kitchen equipment. DVDs (digital versatile disks) replace videocassette technology.

- **Changes in technology:** there's a greater demand for smaller devices, flatter screens and multi-purpose devices.
- **New marketing approaches:** consumers are buying over the internet or from catalogue retailers.

With a little thought it would have been possible to identify these kinds of environmental trends, but many of the more dramatic changes have come from surprising places. When the deregulation of the UK financial services sector stimulated supermarket banks and insurance companies, existing banks sought to obtain critical mass by takeover, while mutual societies such as building societies became public companies, rewarded their members and were themselves predators or victims in takeovers. This dash for growth and the subsequent poor risk analysis, coupled with less than robust scenario analysis, brought them of course to the financial crisis of 2008 and to completely different kinds of ownership, never before seen in the lifetimes of the managers in these businesses. Equally dramatic and unexpected are the activities of environmental or animal rights campaigners or a sudden change in technology that changes generally accepted business models.

There is a framework to help organisations assess their broad environment: the PESTLE (sometimes called PESTEL or just PEST) analysis. This is an examination of the political, economic, sociocultural, technological, legal and environmental issues in the external business environment.

Political influences include:

- trade regulations and tariffs;
- social welfare policies.

Economic influences include:

- business cycles;
- interest rates;
- money supply;
- inflation;
- unemployment;
- disposable income;
- availability and cost of energy;
- the internationalisation of business.

Taken together these economic factors determine how easy – or not – it is to be profitable, because they affect demand.

Sociocultural influences include demand and taste issues, and how tastes and preferences change over time. Specific influences include:

- demographics (for example, an ageing population in Europe);
- social mobility – will people move in order to work, or stay where they are even if unemployed and relying on state support? (To some extent this is now a political issue, with an enlarged Europe enabling a freer movement of labour across the community);
- lifestyle changes (for example, the desire to retire earlier, and general changes in people's views about work/life balance);
- concern for the environment, including waste disposal, recycling and energy consumption.

Technological issues include:

- government spending on research, the quality of academic research and the 'brain drain';
- the focus on technology, and support for invention and innovation;
- the pace of technological change and the creation of technology-enabled industries.

Legal issues include:

- legislation about trade practices and competition;
- environmental-protection legislation, such as new laws on recycling and waste-disposal industries;
- employment law, such as that regarding employment protection and discrimination.

Environmental issues include:

- global warming and climate change;
- animal welfare;
- waste, such as unnecessary packaging.

It is important that we do not view PESTLE analysis as a set of checklists, since these are not of themselves useful in making a strategic assessment. The key tasks are to identify those few factors that will really affect the organisation, and to develop a real understanding of how they might evolve in the future. How can this be done? In some cases a few issues may be so important that they provide a natural focus. It may also be helpful to get some outside expert opinion.

Having examined the external environment, we should now consider the competition our organisation faces. Few businesses have no competition, and most seek to develop and keep a competitive advantage over their rivals. They aim to be different or better in ways that appeal to their customers. An analysis tool that helps to evaluate an industry's profitability and hence its attractiveness is Michael Porter's five forces model (Porter 1980). This is shown in Figure 3.2. In the centre is the competitive battleground, where rivals compete and competitive strategies are developed. Organisations seek to understand the nature of their competitive environment. Additionally, they will be in a stronger position if they understand the interplay of the five forces and can develop defences against the threats they pose.

Figure 3.2 Porter's five forces model

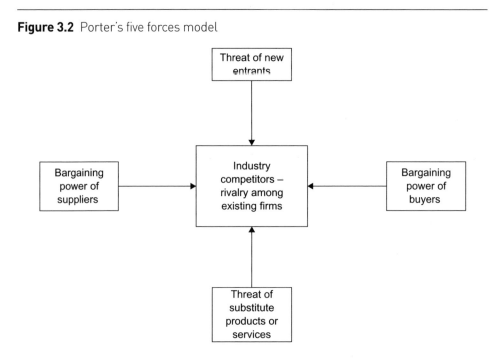

New entrants may want to move into the market if it looks attractive, and if the barriers to entry are low. Globalisation and deregulation both give new entrants this opportunity, but there are barriers to entry that organisations build. These include:

- **Economies of scale:** if substantial investment is necessary before a new entrant can compete, then this may be a deterrent.

- **Product differentiation:** if existing products and services are seen to have strong identities that are supported by high expenditure or branding, then new entrants may be deterred from entry.

- **Substantial capital investment** by a new entrant.

- **Access to distribution channels:** existing distribution channels may be committed to existing suppliers, thus requiring new entrants to find new and different distribution channels.

- **Technologies** and the use of patented processes.

Supplier power limits the opportunity for cost reductions when:

- there is a concentration of suppliers, and supplying businesses are bigger than the many customers they supply;
- the costs of switching from one supplier to another are high because of supply contracts, interlinking systems with suppliers, supply logistics or the inability of other suppliers to deliver;
- the supplier brand is powerful, e.g. the power of 'Intel Inside';
- customers are fragmented.

Customer power – or the 'bargaining power of buyers', as Porter called it – is high when:

- there is a small concentration of buyers and many small organisations in the supplying industry, as for example in the supply of food to supermarkets;
- alternative sources of supply are available and easy to find;
- the cost of the product or service is high, encouraging the buyer to search out alternatives;
- switching costs are low.

The threat from substitute products – for example, budget air travel instead of cross-channel ferries – is high when:

- product substitution from new technologies is more convenient – DVDs for videos, for example;
- the need for the product is replaced by a different need;
- we decide to 'do without it'.

Another example that affects us all is the impact of high-speed trains on airlines – particularly between London, Paris and Brussels.

All of these forces impact on the competitive battleground in some way. On the battleground itself there is competitive rivalry. This is high when:

- there are many competing firms;
- buyers can easily switch from one firm to another;
- the market is growing only slowly or not growing at all;
- the industry has high fixed costs, and responding to price pressure is difficult;
- products are not well differentiated, and so there is little brand loyalty;
- the costs of leaving the industry are high.

Porter's framework is simple to use and understand, and it helps to identify the key competitive forces affecting a business. It is widely used in the development of strategies. There are, however, some weaknesses, of which the most often mentioned is that government is not treated as the sixth force. Porter's response is that the role of government is played through each of the five forces – legislation affects entry and rivalry for example – and so it has not been ignored. There are also views that it is difficult to apply the model to not-for-profit organisations and that since the 1980s the increasing development of international businesses has led to a more complex set of competitive and collaborative relationships. Nonetheless, the framework is widely accepted as a useful analytical tool.

Having worked hard on our PESTLE and Porter analyses, we will have much useful data about the attractiveness of the business we have and the external conditions it may face. How can the data be used? Generally, even with good data, the world springs surprises on organisations from time to time. There is a high level of uncertainty, and some different approaches are need in order to understand potential future impacts. Scenarios may be used to do this. They look at the medium- and long-term future, and by evaluating possible different futures prepare the organisation to deal with them, and managers to deal with future shocks.

Scenarios begin by identifying the potential high-impact and high-uncertainty factors in the environment. It is tempting to choose just two scenarios – good and bad – when doing this, but really four or more are needed, and they should be plausible and detailed. Next, what futures could these factors construct, and what combination of these factors could build a plausible scenario? In doing this we are concerned with predetermined events such as demographic changes, key uncertainties – often political and economic, including regulation and world trade – and driving forces such as technology and education. This information comes from the PESTLE analysis.

INTERNAL ENVIRONMENT ANALYSIS

The external environment creates opportunities and threats and can give an 'outside-in' stimulus to the development of strategy. Successful strategies depend on something else as well: the capability of the organisation to perform. Can an organisation continue to change its capability so that it constantly fits the environment in which it operates? Can it always be innovative in the way it exploits this capability? We shall look at two techniques in this section to address these issues – the Resource Audit and portfolio analysis using the Boston Matrix. All of this begins, however, with an understanding of the current business positioning, and for this we will use the MOST analysis technique. MOST analysis examines the current mission, objectives, strategy and tactics, and considers whether these are clearly defined and supported within the organisation. We can define the MOST terms as follows:

- **Mission:** a statement declaring what business the organisation is in, and what it is intending to achieve;

- **Objectives:** the goals against which the organisation's achievements can be measured;
- **Strategy:** the approach that is going to be taken by the organisation in order to achieve the objectives and mission;
- **Tactics:** the detailed means by which the strategy will be implemented.

A clear mission driving the organisation forward, a set of measurable objectives and a coherent strategy will enhance the capability of the organisation and be a source of strength. On the other hand, where there is a lack of direction, unclear objectives and an ill-defined strategy the internal capability is less effective and we have a source of weakness.

Reflecting on core competences starts the strategy process from inside the organisation, and so is an 'inside-out' approach based on the belief that competitiveness comes from an ability to create new and unexpected products and services from a set of core competences. The resource audit can help us to identify core competences or may highlight where there is a lack of competence that could undermine any competitive moves. There are five key areas to examine. First, there are three sets of tangible resource:

- the **physical** resources that the organisation owns or has access to, including features such as buildings, plant and equipment and land;
- the **financial** resources that determine the organisation's financial stability, capacity to invest in new resources and ability to weather fluctuations in the market;
- the **human** resources and their expertise, adaptability, commitment, etc.

Second, there are the intangible resources such as the **know-how** of the organisation, which may include actual patents or trademarks, but may also be derived from the use of technology that is specific to the business, for example manufacturing technology. Another intangible resource is the **reputation** of the organisation, for example the brand recognition and the belief that is held about the quality of the brand, and the goodwill – or antipathy – that this produces. An analysis of the organisation's resources will identify where these provide a source of competence – strengths – or where there is a lack of capability – weaknesses.

Some organisations have a single or limited range of products, and can focus their efforts on delivering these products in such a way that they delight their customers. However, many businesses have a diversified range of products and services; they might all be computer software but different products are produced for different markets and for different users. Each will have developed its own strategic direction, perhaps using the tools described in this chapter, and decisions have to be taken now about the resources to be put into each product or service. Portfolio analysis was developed to address this problem. The underlying idea is that the portfolio of businesses is managed to achieve balance with a mixture of high-growth, profit-maximising, investment-needing and declining businesses making up a balanced overall organisation.

The original portfolio matrix – the Boston Box – was developed by the Boston Consulting Group. This analysis concentrates on immediate financial gain and does not connect with any long-term strategic direction or core competences. A company's strategic business units (SBUs) – parts of an organisation for which there is a distinct and separate external market – are identified, and the relationship between each SBU's current or future revenue potential is modelled against the appropriate management of it. Put simply, as in Figure 3.3, the cows are milked, the dogs are buried, the stars get the gold and the wild cats are carefully examined until they behave themselves or join the dogs and die.

Figure 3.3 The Boston box

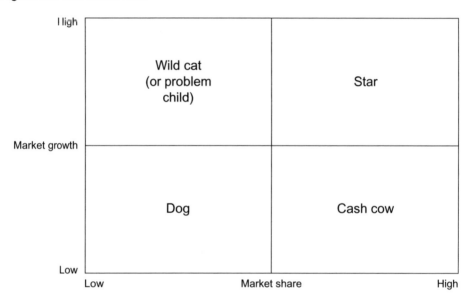

A successful product or SBU starts as a wild cat and goes clockwise round the model until it dies or is revitalised as a new product, service or SBU. The wild cats or problem children are unprofitable but are investments for the future. The stars strengthen their position in a growth industry until they become the big profit earners. They are mature products or services, often market leaders, and provide the funding for the other segments of the matrix. The dogs are businesses that have low market share in markets with low growth. The cash cows are mature products in well-established markets where they are the market leaders; they are the most profitable products in the portfolio.

SWOT ANALYSIS

SWOT (strengths, weaknesses, opportunities, threats) analysis is often used to pull together the results of an analysis of the external and internal environments.

Too often one sees it used as the first analytical tool before enough preparatory analysis has been done. When this approach is adopted the results are usually weak, inconclusive and insufficiently robust to be of much use. If we use the techniques we described earlier they help identify the major factors both internal and external to the organisation that the business strategy needs to take account of. Hence, the SWOT analysis is where we summarise the key strengths, weaknesses, opportunities and threats in order to carry out an overall audit of the strategic position of a business and its environment. A SWOT analysis is often represented as a two-by-two matrix, as shown in Figure 3.4.

Figure 3.4 Format of a SWOT matrix

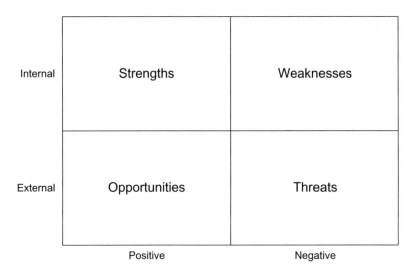

The language of a SWOT analysis is important. It needs to be brief, with strengths and weaknesses related to critical success factors. Strengths and weaknesses should also be measured against the competition. All statements should be specific, realistic and supported by evidence. Some examples – not for the same organisation – could be:

- **Strengths:** strong product branding – market research shows a high awareness of our brands compared with the competition. We secure 'best space' in all branches of the top five supermarkets.

- **Weaknesses:** we have poor cash flow. Against industry benchmarks we are in the bottom quartile. We exceed our overdraft limits on 19 days every quarter.

- **Opportunities:** demographic change in Europe will provide a greater market for our products.

- **Threats:** low market growth will see increased concentration of business through acquisition. The poorest-performing businesses will fail.

It is important to get the balance between the external and the internal analysis right. Completely changing the nature of the organisation because of what the external analysis says leads to radical change; basing everything on an internal analysis may lead to little or no change. Either case could be right, of course, but both analyses are likely to contribute towards the creation of a new strategic direction.

IMPLEMENTING STRATEGY

Implementing new strategies implies risk because it involves change. In Chapter 14 we discuss how business change should be managed to maximise the benefits and minimise the risks of implementing change. In this section we consider three particular aspects of implementing strategy: the context for the strategy, the role of the leader and two tools that we can use – the balanced business scorecard (BBS) and the McKinsey 7-S Model. We will deal with some of the contextual issues first. There are five of these:

- **Time:** how quickly does the new strategy need to be implemented? What pace of change is needed?

- **Scope:** how big is the change? Is the new strategic direction transformational or incremental?

- **Capability:** is the organisation used to change? Are the experiences of change positive or negative? Are the change implementers skilled?

- **Readiness:** is the whole organisation, or the part of it to be affected, ready to make the change?

- **Strategic leadership:** is there a strategic leader?

In this context, the strategic leader will have the key role. The strategic leaders we read about are usually the top managers, but strategic leadership does not have to be delivered from the top – there are many successful strategic changes that have been driven from other parts of organisations. The key characteristics seem to be that the leader does the following:

- Challenges the status quo all the time, and sets new and demanding targets, never being prepared to tolerate unsatisfactory behaviour or performance.

- Establishes and communicates a clear vision of the direction to be taken, why it has to be taken and how the journey will be achieved. This means establishing the new mission, setting out objectives, identifying the strategies for achieving them and defining the specific tactics to deliver them. The leader will also clearly communicate the values that underpin the new ways of doing business.

- 'Models the way'. Such leaders demonstrate through their behaviour how everyone else should behave and act in order to deliver the strategy.

- Empowers people to deliver their parts of the strategic change within the vision, values and mission that have been set out – the leader cannot be everywhere.

- Celebrates success with those who achieve it.

Two tools that help in the implementation of strategy are the McKinsey 7-S model, shown in Figure 3.5, and the balanced business scorecard, shown in Figure 3.6.

Figure 3.5 The McKinsey 7-S model

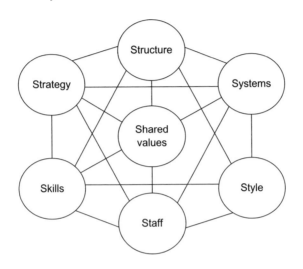

The McKinsey 7-S model supposes that all organisations are made up of seven components. Three are often described as 'hard' components – strategy, structure and systems – and four as 'soft' – shared values, style, staff and skills.

These are the seven levers that can be used in the implementation of strategic change. All seven need attention if the implementation is to be successful, because if there is a change in one, others will be affected. Changing the strategy means that all of the other components have to change as well:

- The structure, which is the basis for building the organisation, will change to reflect new needs for specialisation and coordination resulting from the new strategic direction.

- Formal and informal systems that supported the old system must change.

- The style or culture of the organisation will be affected by a new strategic direction. Values, beliefs and norms that developed over time may be swept away.

- The way in which staff are recruited, developed and rewarded may change. New strategies may mean relocating people or making them redundant.

- Skills or competences acquired in the past may be of less use now. The new strategy may call for new skills.

- Shared values are the guiding concepts of the organisation, the fundamental ideas that are its basis. Moving from being an 'engineering first' company to a 'customer service first' company, for example, would change the shared values.

The Balanced Business Scorecard can be thought of as the strategic balance sheet for an organisation, since it captures both the financial and the non-financial components of a strategy. It therefore shows how the implementation process is working and the effectiveness with which the levers for change are being used. The BBS supplements financial measures with three other perspectives on organisational performance: customers, learning and growth, and internal business processes. Vision and strategy connect with each of these, as shown in Figure 3.6.

Figure 3.6 The balanced business scorecard

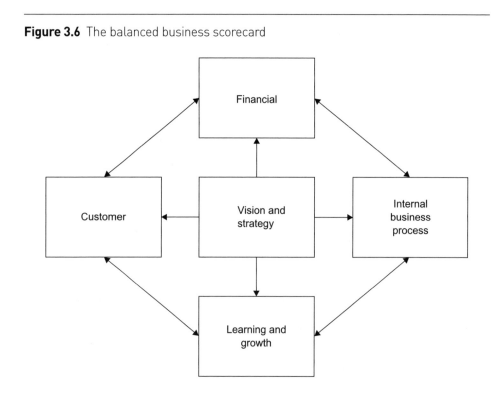

Although the emphasis of the BBS is to measure all aspects of performance, people perhaps pay more attention to the non-financial measures, since these have not previously been measured – but financial measures retain their importance. The customer perspective assesses those critical success factors that provide a customer focus. It forces a detailed examination to be made of statements such as 'superior customer service', so that everyone can agree what it means, and measures can be established to show the progress being made. But it might be that little progress is possible without new skills and different attitudes – a link to the learning and growth perspective, which in turn could generate a need for new internal processes to give the newly skilled people the tools to use. Each perspective then answers questions like these:

- **Financial:** to succeed financially and have the resources to deliver our strategy, how must we be seen by our stakeholders?
- **Customer:** to achieve our vision, what do we want customers to say about us?
- **Learning and growth:** how will we sustain our ability to change and improve so that we constantly keep ahead of the competition?
- **Internal business processes:** what are the business processes that we must excel at in order to deliver customer value?

Having a strategy is not enough by itself, but the task of implementing it is difficult. Apart from the issues associated with change, the environment gives a shifting context within which to work. But without an effective implementation the work in developing the strategy will be of doubtful value.

SUMMARY

In this chapter we have looked at the reasons why organisations develop strategies and how they might do this. We have explored the complexity of this process and offered ideas about how strategies are developed, taking account of entrepreneurial approaches and formal planning. The chapter also described the external factors influencing strategy – the outside-in approach – and an internal analysis approach – the inside-out approach. Finally we looked at the implementation of strategy and IS strategy considerations.

REFERENCES

Johnson, G., Scholes, K. and Whittington, R. (2008) *Exploring Corporate Strategy,* 8th edn. FT Prentice Hall, Harlow.

Porter, M. (1980) *Competitive Strategy: Techniques for Analysing Industries and Competitors,* Free Press, New York.

Steiner, G. (1979) *Strategic Planning.* Free Press, New York.

FURTHER READING

Bannock, G., Davis, E., Trott, P. and Uncles, M. (2003) *Dictionary of Business.* Economist Books, London.

Grant, R.M. (2010) *Contemporary Strategy Analysis,* 7th edn. John Wiley & Sons Ltd, Chichester.

Kaplan, R.S. and Norton, D.P. (1996) Using the balance scorecard as a strategic management system. *Harvard Business Review,* January/February.

Mintzberg, H., Lampel, J., Quinn, J. and Ghoshal, S. (2003) *The Strategy Process: Concepts Contexts Cases.* Pearson Education Limited, Harlow.

Porter, M. (1998) *Competitive Advantage: Creating and Sustaining Superior Performance.* Free Press, New York.

Thompson, J. with Martin, F. (2005) *Strategic Management: Awareness and Change*, 5th edn. Cengage Learning EMEA, London.

Whipp, R. (2002) The politics of strategy making. In Warner, M. (ed), *The International Encyclopaedia of Business and Management.* Thomson Learning, London.

4   THE BUSINESS ANALYSIS PROCESS MODEL

Debra Paul

INTRODUCTION

There are many tools and techniques available for the business analyst to use but, because of the nature of business analysis work, an overview framework is useful to place these in context and help you determine the most appropriate technique for each individual situation. In this chapter we set out a business analysis process model as a framework within which both standard modelling techniques and organisational templates can be used. This approach also incorporates the principles of requirements engineering to highlight best practice when defining system requirements.

AN APPROACH TO PROBLEM-SOLVING

One of the requirements of business managers is that business analysts examine the entire business area and take a thoughtful or even creative approach to developing ideas for solutions. Creative problem-solving is vital in the current business world as, increasingly, organisations need to develop innovative ideas in order to respond to changes in the business environment, including actions from competitors. However, many people find this difficult; often because they feel under pressure to produce ideas very quickly. In this context, Isaksen and Treffinger's (1985) creative problem-solving model, shown in Figure 4.1, provides a useful framework for understanding problems and developing creative solutions, particularly as the model emphasises the need to investigate and analyse rather than leap to quick, possibly premature, solutions.

This model proposes an approach that may be applied usefully to business analysis. In this section we describe the implications and suggestions that the model has for you as a business analyst. The first stage, **mess finding**, is where we often begin when undertaking a problem investigation. In business analysis this stage is concerned with finding out about the complexity of the problem situation. Many problems are poorly defined, and each problem situation is likely to be complex and to contain various issues and concerns. In other words there is likely to be a 'mess', and different situations will have different components to that mess. Identifying this as the starting point in this model helps to emphasise that you need to gain some understanding about the complete situation before diving into options and solutions. The rich picture approach, described in Chapter 7, is particularly useful to help document and analyse the 'mess' in problematic business situations. Mind maps, also described in that chapter, are similarly helpful.

Figure 4.1 A problem-solving model

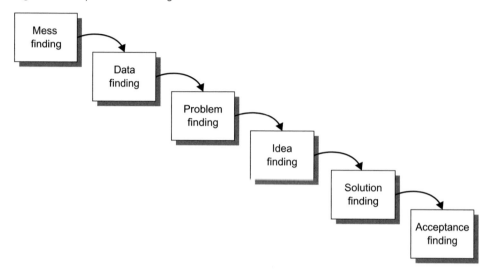

Data finding, the second stage of the model, is concerned with analysing the opinions, concerns, knowledge and ideas uncovered in the previous stage, in order to identify where this information can be quantified and supporting data obtained. It is often useful to examine the rich picture or mind map to clarify your thinking about the situation. It is particularly important to consider which information is factual and which is based on opinion. This can help lead us to the aspects that we can, and should, verify; it also emphasises the need to divorce opinion from fact. Chapter 5 explains some techniques that will help you to obtain quantitative data, such as questionnaires and activity sampling.

Problem finding then uses the work of the previous two stages to help uncover the heart of the problem. We now know the complexity of the situation facing us and have been able to quantify some elements, whilst appreciating that other elements are personal views or opinions. We may have been presented with a statement of the problem at the outset, but at this point, having carried out the previous two stages, it is important to revisit this in order to really understand where the problems lie. Finding the right problem to solve is often a necessary part of business analysis, as analysts are often pointed at symptoms and they have to dig deeper in order to find out where the real problems lie.

These first three stages are concerned with understanding the problem, and they provide a structure for doing so. The next two stages focus on developing solutions.

First there is **idea finding,** during which business analysts try to generate a wide range of ideas. Analysts often use brainstorming approaches to uncover ideas, but this can be difficult since it requires a group to generate ideas 'cold'. Sometimes this works, but often different approaches need to be used along with brainstorming in order to stimulate ideas, so during this stage it may be useful to employ some creative thinking techniques. Two examples of techniques that can provide stimuli for creative ideas are assumption reversal, where assumptions about a situation are listed and reversed, and random words or pictures, where unrelated words or pictures are used to generate different ideas about a situation. More information about these techniques can be found in the creative thinking texts mentioned in the 'Further reading' section of this chapter.

Once some ideas have been identified, they can be evaluated. We can then focus on the ideas that could provide solutions to the problem(s). This is the **solution finding** stage, and it is significant that this stage appears so late in the model. Business analysts are often expected to deliver solutions quickly, and yet here we can see that it is important to resist the pressure to do so at too early a stage; there are other aspects that need to be considered first. Also, Isaksen and Treffinger (1985) stress the importance of identifying criteria to help evaluate solutions, and this would not be possible without the earlier work. It is therefore important to work through the earlier stages, since they will help you to develop better, more appropriate solutions that will be more beneficial to the business situation.

The final stage in the model is **acceptance finding,** which is concerned with managing the implementation of the solution, an aspect that is critical to the success of any change project but often fraught with difficulty. Chapter 12 considers how a robust business case may be made in order to obtain approval from the business for the recommendations. Chapter 13 examines the area of managing the implementation of change and hence the acceptance by the organisation of the new working practices.

TIIE PROCESS MODEL

One of the aspects that make business analysis work so interesting is the range and nature of business analysis projects. The business systems under consideration can be very varied, and for a particular project business analysts may need to apply several techniques and analyse a number of different views. Sometimes the project may be to investigate a problematic part of the organisation and produce outline recommendations for ways forward. Other projects may require the business analyst to analyse and document specific system requirements. So the challenge faced in developing a process model is to offer something that is sufficiently flexible while providing a framework that will help people to carry out their work. Our process model, shown in Figure 4.2, is intended to provide this help.

The process model sets out the key stages for a business analysis project, with each stage representing the areas that need to be considered. However, it should be noted that although some projects may require a detailed exploration of all of the stages, other projects may focus on a subset of the model, possibly just one stage. One of the most important aspects of a business analysis project is to decide what the focus is and which areas need to be investigated. For example, on some projects the focus may be to explore possible improvements to how part of the organisation works. In this case we might begin by examining all of the current working practices, including the staffing and job roles, and the work might focus on analysing and evaluating the options for the future business system. Another project may

Figure 4.2 The business analysis process model

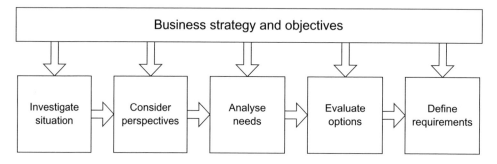

focus on the IT system needs. In this case, although understanding the situation and all of the stakeholder perspectives would be important, the potential for the use of IT to improve the business system would dominate the analysis. The rest of this chapter describes the stages of this process model.

INVESTIGATING THE SITUATION

This stage is concerned with uncovering issues and problems. The terms of reference for the project, or possibly a more detailed project initiation document, are needed in order to set out the context within which the business analysis work will take place. A key area for the analyst is to clarify the objective of the study and tailor the approach accordingly – often a task that requires a good deal of skill. During the initial period of business analysis work the analyst may be presented with a statement of 'the problem'; it is important to investigate further in order to determine exactly where the problems lie, and not to confuse symptoms of problems with the real issues. It is also vital that the analyst does not make false assumptions or accept all of the information provided without question. As shown at the top of the model, business analysis also requires an appreciation of the business context, particularly the overall business objectives and strategy for the organisation or business unit. It is important that these should be available during the investigation stage so that the analysts can understand the business context for the work they have been asked to carry out. Once the analyst has begun to understand the situation, some form of description will be required: first so that there is a record of the results of the investigation so far, and second to help other members of the team understand the situation.

Investigation techniques
There are many investigative approaches that business analysts can use, and these are explored in detail in Chapter 5. It is important that we consider the range of possible investigative approaches and choose those that are most appropriate to the work in hand.

The level of detail required during this stage may vary considerably depending on the focus of the business analysis work. If the analyst is trying to gain an overall appreciation of the business area, for example to identify the key stakeholders and acquire an understanding of their views and opinions in order to appreciate the nature of the work and the range of people and skills, then often the techniques used will be those that provide an overall perspective and generalised view: interviewing, observation and workshops would be particularly useful. However, if the work is concerned with eliciting more detailed information such as data requirements or the flow of a business process, then the most appropriate fact-finding techniques are those that focus on the detail, such as scenario analysis or prototyping. Much of the information gained here may be subjective and may require more detailed analysis; in this case, techniques such as record-searching or questionnaires may be very useful in order to quantify some of the information put forward.

Documenting business situations

There are a number of useful techniques for documenting the initial investigation of a business system. Typically a high-level overview of the situation will be required during the initial investigation, particularly where the issues are complex and originate from different causes. As we mentioned earlier, a "rich picture" can be very useful in capturing the essence of a situation, and an alternative, but similar, approach is the mind map, which also allows for a degree of structuring of the information. These techniques are described in further detail in Chapter 5.

Stage summary
Procedure

(i)   Study background material: project initiation document, terms of reference.

(ii) Carry out initial investigation with key stakeholders.

(iii) Document the results of the investigation using meeting reports plus a diagram such as a rich picture or a mind map.

Inputs

- Terms of reference or project initiation document
- Business objectives and strategy

Outputs

- View of the existing business situation, including meeting reports and diagrams such as rich pictures, mind maps and fishbone diagrams
- List of issues/problems
- Business needs log

Techniques

- Investigation techniques such as interviewing, observation and workshops
- Quantitative investigation techniques such as questionnaires, sampling and document analysis

- Rich pictures – from Soft Systems Methodology, developed by Checkland (1981)

- Mind-maps (Buzan and Buzan 2000)

- Spaghetti maps (see Chapter 5)

- Fishbone diagrams, also known as Ishikawa diagrams (Ishikawa 1990)

CONSIDERING PERSPECTIVES

This stage is concerned with analysing stakeholders and their perspectives on the situation. Many stakeholders hold very strong views about why problems exist, what needs to be done to improve the situation and where the focus of the business system should lie. Where some of the issues arise from differences in stakeholder view, it is vital that they be explored and, where possible, taken into account when making recommendations for the way forward.

Stakeholder identification and analysis

Every business situation will affect a range of individuals and organisations. Among this group there will be people or groups with varying levels of interest and power. Some stakeholders may be directly affected by any recommendations and may hold strong views on how the systems and working practices should be changed. Others may be affected only indirectly, and, whilst having opinions, may be less concerned about the nature of the new system. The range of possible stakeholders and mechanisms for stakeholder analysis and management are discussed in detail in Chapter 6.

Stakeholder perspectives

Stakeholders often have different views on what is important about a business system and the improvements that are needed. These views are often contradictory and can lead to hidden agendas, conflicts and inconsistent priorities. As business analysts, it is important that we are aware of the potential for such conflicts and are alert to situations where these might arise. We can often detect where they might originate by considering the underlying sets of values and beliefs held by the different stakeholders. For example, we might reflect on what an individual stakeholder considers to be the main focus of the business system and, critically, why this is the case. Understanding these values and beliefs allows the analyst to approach issues and problems from an informed position and, hence, to have an improved chance of resolving the situation. Chapter 6 considers the importance of analysing stakeholders and their perspectives, and explains how this may be done by considering the world view of each stakeholder. This may be expanded using the CATWOE (customer, actor, transformation, *Weltanschauung*, owner, environment) approach, originally developed by Checkland (1981), which is discussed in Chapter 7.

Business activity modelling

The stakeholder perspectives can be analysed further by considering the business activities that would be required to fulfil a particular perspective. This approach, developed from Checkland's (1981) work and extended by Wilson (1992), allows analysts to build a conceptual model of a business system envisaged by a particular stakeholder. For example, where a manager believes a training organisation should focus on quality, there would be an emphasis on activities such as:

- the development of highly skilled staff;
- the introduction of customer-focused processes;
- monitoring of customer satisfaction levels.

An alternative view could be that the focus should be on 'no frills' training. In this system the emphasis would be on the following activities:

- keeping costs low;
- monitoring the number of attendees at events.

This approach allows business analysts to consider where the priorities lie and what the focus of the new, improved business system should be. One stakeholder's view may take precedence over the others, or several models may be synthesised to provide an agreed business activity model. The business activity modelling technique is explained further in Chapter 7.

Stage summary
Objectives
The objective of this stage is to take stock of the range of stakeholder perspectives about the business system under investigation. These perspectives may then be analysed to uncover stakeholder values and beliefs, and developed into business activity models. However, where there is a narrow remit for the business analysis work (for example, if we are concerned primarily with improving a particular process), whilst it will be important to identify and manage the stakeholders, consideration of the entire business system may be beyond the scope of our work.

Procedure

(i) Identify key stakeholders whose perspectives are important to the business analysis project.

(ii) Investigate the values, beliefs and priorities of the key stakeholders.

(iii) Develop and analyse the stakeholder perspectives.

(iv) Build conceptual models of activities to fulfil the stakeholder perspectives.

(v) Explore and resolve conflicts between stakeholder perspectives.

(vi) Synthesise conceptual models into one view of the desired business system.

Inputs

- Terms of reference or project initiation document
- Business objectives and strategy

- Identified stakeholders (from the documentation of the existing business system)

Outputs

- Stakeholder perspectives
- Business activity models based upon individual stakeholder perspectives
- Agreed single business activity model

Techniques

- Investigation and negotiation techniques
- Stakeholder identification and analysis
- Analysis of stakeholder perspectives
- Business activity modelling

ANALYSING NEEDS

The focus of this stage is to identify where improvements can be made to the business system. The approach used is known as 'gap analysis' whereby a current or 'as is' view is compared with a desired, future or 'to be' system. This method contrasts with the traditional, more systematic approach to business or systems improvement, where new features are added on to an existing set of procedures or an IT system. With gap analysis the emphasis is on understanding where we want to be and, by looking at where we are now, identifying what needs to change to take us there.

Analysing activities

If we have developed a business activity model from a stakeholder perspective, this can be used to carry out a detailed analysis of the desired business system by examining each activity in turn. This analysis will allow us to identify where there are issues that need to be addressed in any solution that we recommend. As the model provides a conceptual picture of the desired business activities, it allows the business analyst to see where the current business system is lacking. When examining the model, the range and extent of the gaps found will vary from activity to activity. Some activities may be in place and operating satisfactorily, but others may be inadequate in the current business system and some may not exist at all. There may be good support for the activity from the organisation's information systems, or support may be poor and in need of improvement. Identifying the gaps at this level will help us to determine the potential for change to the business system and the degree to which this is required. The business activity model may identify a range of areas to be considered in the light of the current business situation. However, it is possible that some aspects may be beyond the scope of the business analysis work.

Analysing business processes

Another approach to gap analysis focuses on the business processes carried out within the business system. Whereas the activities modelled on the business activity model show a conceptual view of *what* activities are to be included within the desired business system, business process models allow us to consider *how* the work is carried out. A business process begins with a trigger, which is sometimes called a business event, and concludes when the goal of the process has been achieved. This view of the business situation cuts across departments and job roles in order to show a more results-oriented view that is focused on meeting customer needs. The approach we take to this work is to model the current business process and then to consider possible changes to the process before designing the required process. Hence, we develop a current or 'as is' model that provides a basis for developing the required or 'to be' model. When redesigning a process we can look for small changes that affect one or two process steps, or we might decide to design a completely new process. The business process modelling technique is explored in further detail in Chapter 8.

Stage summary

Objectives

The objectives here are to explore the differences between the current and desired situations and to identify the opportunities for business change by analysing these differences or 'gaps'.

Procedure

(i)   Examine the activities on the business activity model.

(ii) Consider how well each activity is carried out in the current business system and how well it is supported by the organisation's information systems.

(iii) Identify the key business events to be handled within the business system and develop 'as is' business process models for the key business events.

(iv) Develop 'to be' business process models for the key business events.

(v)   Analyse the gaps between the existing and the desired situation. Use these as a basis for identifying potential business system improvements.

Inputs

- Agreed business activity model
- View of the existing business system
- Business objectives and strategy

Outputs

- Analysis of activities, including identified weaknesses
- 'As is' and 'to be' business process models
- List of potential improvements to the business system

Techniques

- Gap analysis
- Activity analysis
- Business process modelling

EVALUATING OPTIONS

This stage is concerned with examining the potential improvements identified so far, developing some business options and evaluating them for acceptability and feasibility. The analysis of the gaps between the existing and desired systems will have produced some ideas for improvements, and the work now is to develop these ideas into business options. These may include options for changes in a number of areas; for example, they may change the business processes, the job roles, the management structure or the IT systems. At this point, the changes are likely to be defined in outline only but in sufficient detail so that a business case may be developed to support the recommendations and provide a basis for decision-making. Once the work to define the changed areas begins in earnest, there may be a need for further consideration of options. For example, where changes are required to the supporting IT systems, this may be agreed in principle at this stage but it is likely that the detailed options for the new IT system will need to be evaluated, and the business case revisited, at a later date.

Identifying potential options
The first step is to identify possible options by considering where improvements might be made and which ones would result in the greatest potential benefits. Once a number of options have been identified, these can be reduced to a shortlist of those that are to be developed further. Business objectives and strategy are considered as part of the development and evaluation of options, since they must be supported by any changes.

Assessing feasibility
All of the options that are to be considered in detail need to be evaluated for business, technical and financial feasibility. Chapter 13 explores these aspects of evaluation in further detail. In addition, aspects such as the impact of options on the organisation and the risks that may be associated with an option also need to be considered, since they will affect the acceptability of the options. Impacts and risks may give rise to additional costs that need to be fed into the cost/benefit analysis for the option. Consideration of the business objectives and strategy should also form part of this work, since any new business system will need to be aligned with the strategy and support delivery of the business objectives.

Stage summary
Objectives
The objective of this stage is to collect together the range of potential changes into packages of improvement actions. These packages form the basis for developing a set of options that are then developed and documented in further detail. They are then presented to business managers for consideration.

Procedure

(i) Identify a range of business options.

(ii) Explore the acceptability of options and reduce them to a shortlist.

(iii) Develop and document each option in detail. In particular, consider the business, technical and financial feasibility of each option.

(iv) Develop a business case, including presenting options and recommendations to business managers.

Inputs

- Project initiation document / terms of reference
- Business objectives and strategy
- List of potential improvements to the business system

Outputs

- Shortlist of business options
- Business case, including options, feasibility assessment and recommendations

Techniques

- Business options identification
- Cost/benefit analysis, including quantification of costs and benefits and investment appraisal techniques
- Impact analysis
- Risk analysis

DEFINING REQUIREMENTS

This stage is concerned with gathering and documenting the detailed requirements for changes to the business system. These changes may be to any (or all) of the four aspects of a business system described in Chapter 1: the business processes, the supporting IT systems, the people carrying out the work or the organisation structure. Where the changes are to the business processes, the modelling techniques described in Chapter 8 should be used to define how the new processes should look. If the recommendations include the implementation of redesigned processes, this is likely to require changes to the structure of the organisation and the job roles, plus development of staff skills. It is sometimes the case that the improvements to the business system can be made just through changes such as improved job definitions or additional training for staff. However, more extensive change is usually required, for example to the business processes, and it is likely that this will require enhancements to existing IT systems or even the introduction of a new IT system. Business analysts have a responsibility to define the requirements comprehensively and accurately, since their documentation will form the basis for the development of the system. If the requirements are not documented clearly, then this is likely to cause problems not only during the development of the system but also once it has been implemented. It is vital, therefore, that the requirements can be related directly to a business need and hence will support the business objectives.

Requirements engineering

The requirements engineering approach has been developed as a response to the lack of rigour often found in requirements documentation. Requirements engineering proposes a framework to help analysts improve their requirements work by highlighting the need for proactive analysis, organisation, documentation and management of stated requirements. The requirements engineering approach is described in Chapters 9 and 10.

Modelling IT systems

There are many modelling techniques available to business analysts. These techniques originated mainly from systems analysis and design approaches such as UML. Each modelling technique provides insight into a particular aspect of the IT system. For example, techniques such as object class modelling and entity relationship modelling provide a clear and unambiguous means of documenting the system data. Business analysts find such techniques extremely useful when exploring requirements, since they help to build rigour into the requirements analysis activity. Building and comparing models of a system will help generate additional questions, and uncover omissions, errors and inconsistencies. Chapter 11 provides an overview of some of the more popular modelling techniques used by business analysts. There are many books devoted to explaining systems modelling techniques in detail, some of which are included in the list of further reading for Chapter 11. Approaches for delivering the requirements are discussed in Chapter 12.

Stage summary

Objectives

The objective of this stage is to produce a well-formed requirements document setting out the business requirements for the new business system. This document must include clear textual descriptions of the requirements and sufficient information to trace each requirement from its origin through to its resolution. Modelling techniques may be used to represent the process and data requirements diagrammatically and hence improve the rigour of the requirements definition.

Procedure

(i) Gather the requirements:

    (a) Elicit and analyse the business requirements for the new business system.

    (b) Document and manage the requirements.

    (c) Validate the documented requirements.

(ii) Document the requirements for the new business system, including as appropriate:

- business process models;
- catalogue of business requirements;
- models of the IT processing and data;
- glossary of terms.

Inputs

- Selected option for revised business system
- Business objectives and strategy
- Terms of reference/project initiation document

Outputs

- 'To be' process models
- Job definitions
- Revised organisational structure
- Validated requirements document, including:

    o requirements catalogue;
    o models of business process and system requirements;
    o glossary of terms.

Techniques

- Business process modelling
- Job design
- Investigation techniques
- Requirements elicitation, analysis and validation
- Requirements documentation and management
- IT systems modelling techniques

DELIVERING CHANGES

Once the business analysts have considered and analysed the situation, developed options for improvement and defined the requirements to be delivered, it is important to consider how the requirements are to be delivered, the changes implemented and the business benefits realised. In the main this work is not the responsibility of the business analyst, but we have to carry out certain tasks and provide support to the project team. Figure 4.3 shows an extended version of the

Figure 4.3 Extended business analysis process model

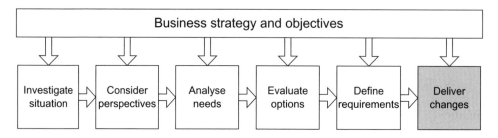

business analysis process model, including a stage where the business analyst works to support the delivery of business change.

Delivering the requirements
The requirements will need to be converted into the business change solution. This solution may include process, people, organisational and IT system change. The lifecycle and the approach to be adopted to develop and deliver the changes will need to be determined. This decision will have an impact upon the roles of the project team, the deliverables to be produced and the techniques to be used. Chapter 12 discusses these issues. The extent of the business analyst role will depend upon the lifecycle and the approach adopted for the project.

Implementing the business changes
The implementation of the business changes will need to consider aspects such as the culture of the organisation, the emotional impact of change and the realisation of the business benefits. These issues are discussed in Chapter 14. Again, the business analyst will not be responsible for this work, but will support the implementation of the changes and the review of the benefits.

Stage summary
Procedure

(i) Decide the lifecycle and approach to be adopted.

(ii) Develop the business change solution.

(iii) Plan the implementation:

    (a) Consider the environment for the change.

    (b) Consider the culture of the organisation.

    (c) Define the learning approach and develop the required learning materials.

(iv) Review the predicted benefits.

(v) Identify any actions required to realise the benefits.

Inputs

- Business change process and organisation design
- IT software solution
- Business case

Outputs

- Business change plan
- Communication plan
- Training approach and materials
- Revised job roles and descriptions
- Post-implementation review document
- Benefits realisation plan

Techniques

- Power/impact stakeholder analysis
- Cultural web analysis
- McKinsey 7-S analysis
- Concerns-based adoption model

SUMMARY

Business analysis projects are usually concerned with improving the working practices within business systems. This may involve changes to a range of aspects that form the business system, including staff capability, business processes or the supporting information systems. Increasingly, business analysts are also required to support the development of solutions, delivery of business changes and realisation of business benefits. The business analysis process model is intended to help business analysts in deciding how to structure their assignments. The model also includes references to some of the techniques in popular use and identifies when they may be particularly useful.

REFERENCES

Buzan, T. and Buzan, B. (2000) *The Mind Map Book*. BBC Books, London.

Checkland, P. (1981) *Systems Thinking, Systems Practice*. John Wiley & Sons, Chichester.

Isaksen, S. and Treffinger, D. (1985) *Creative Problem Solving: The Basic Course.* Nicholas Brealey Publishing, London.

Wilson, B. (1992) *Systems, Concepts, Methodologies and Applications.* John Wiley & Sons, Chichester.

FURTHER READING

de Bono, E. (1990) *Six Thinking Hats.* Penguin Books, London.

Ishikawa, K. (1990) *Introduction to Quality Control.* Productivity Press, New York.

5   INVESTIGATION TECHNIQUES

Debra Paul and Malcolm Eva

INTRODUCTION

When business analysts first enter an area of study, they need a range of tools and techniques to help them understand the breadth and depth of issues. While they will be making use of background research, workshops, one-to-one interviews and quantitative methods for the verification of data, they must also use diagnostic tools for understanding a problem area and different approaches to documenting their findings according to the focus. This chapter will look at the different focuses of investigation and means of documenting the findings and at various techniques for conducting the study.

The assumption behind the chapter is that the analyst will be responsible for performing a broad study that begins with general understanding of a situation and then produces a diagnosis of the underlying causes followed by the requirements for a solution. The terms of reference for most analysis studies will be significantly narrower than that, nevertheless, all the techniques described in this chapter will be useful at one time or another. We advocate a toolbox approach to analysis rather than a strict checklist method, and the more tools that are available, the more flexible and responsive the analyst can be.

PRIOR RESEARCH

If analysts are working with an unfamiliar client organisation (or division or department) they should spend time gathering background information prior to beginning the work. There are various sources available, but the internet has made access to such background information much simpler than it was before.

Study the company website
This is the quickest and simplest way to get a view of what the organisation does, what its values are, how it brands itself and how it wants to be perceived. Depending upon the nature of the organisation and the sector to which it belongs, there should be access to reports on its performance and its products or services as well as opportunities to interact by placing an order or making a query, giving feedback or generally exploring.

At this stage we'll be looking particularly at the organisation's branding, its apparent values and priorities, and how easy it is to navigate and interact with the site. If the site shows feedback or reviews from customers it is worth looking at these, particularly if any are less than wholeheartedly positive. However, such material is likely to be selected to show the company in its best light. It may be worth exploring other websites, for example hotel or restaurant review sites, for customer reactions.

One useful inference from the design of the website is how the company views its place strategically, in terms of the balance between the cost of its products and their perceived quality. The design of the site will often give an indication of the level of quality it aims at: primary colours, flashing icons and liberal use of exclamation marks and words like 'bargain' all suggest a more populist approach and a low price market for its offerings, while a quieter background, carefully composed photographs and moderated colours all imply a concern with a perception of quality. Interpreting a website this way can provide early insights into the business imperatives for the organisation.

We can also evaluate the ease of navigating around the site, and the ease of placing an order or making an enquiry. These things will give an idea of the level of user friendliness of the site and the expected standards of technology presentation and achievement. This in turn can give clues about the technological maturity of the company – is the technology subordinate to the business intention, or are the developers showing off their skills at the expense of the company's message?

Study company reports

If we are approaching a commercial company in the role of an external consultant, it is useful to look at company reports to confirm the health of the company. The statutory documents, for example the profit and loss account and the balance sheet for UK-based companies, are publicly available from Companies House. These documents can provide information about the levels of debt, liquidity and gearing and the trends in growth or stagnation over the previous years, and give insights into where there may be problems. The shareholders' reports will also set out the future direction of the company as agreed by the directors, and state the targets and achievements at which they are aiming over the next year.

Studying these reports at the outset of a project can also save unnecessary effort later, as a recent experience showed. Following an invitation to carry out consultancy work for a new client, an examination of this company's entry at Companies House uncovered the fact that it was about to be suspended for non-submission of accounts over the previous two years. A failure to carry out this research could have ended with unpaid invoices.

Study procedure manuals and documentation

Many business analysis projects will have a scope that is more local than those suggested above, and more focused on specific sets of processes. The prior research for such projects will include studying current system documentation and perhaps existing analysis documents for the current system, and also procedure manuals. These give us an idea of the expected 'as is' process, but – another note of caution – over time such documentation will naturally become unrepresentative of the actual course of the process. It will tell you not so much the 'as is' description as the 'what we thought it ought to have been'.

Studying the documentation is never a substitute for proper investigation and analysis. Rather it is a preparation, a way of obtaining a prior understanding of the domain in question that gives the analyst a gateway into various lines of investigation.

Study the organisation chart of the target area of the company
The 'family tree' gives the structure and, to an extent, the culture of the organisation. Understanding the job roles and reporting lines is a valuable preparation for the more detailed investigation to follow.

INVESTIGATION TECHNIQUES

After the prior research has been done and the analyst feels prepared to begin the more interactive part of the investigation, it is time to prepare the study proper.

There will be a variety of techniques available, depending upon the size of the domain in question, its location, the numbers of stakeholders to be consulted, and the nature of the information to be ascertained.

The Techniques can be categorised broadly as **qualitative** – understanding what is needed – and **quantitative** – concerned with volumes and frequencies. Qualitative techniques can be further broken down into one-to-one sessions and collaborative sessions. The most common of the qualitative one-to-one approaches to investigation are interviewing, or one-to-one meetings with stakeholders, and observation sessions. Collaborative approaches include workshops or focus groups.

Interviews
The interview is a key tool in the business analyst's toolkit. A well-run interview can be vital in achieving a number of objectives. These include:

- making an initial contact with key stakeholders and establishing a basis for the business analysis work;
- building and developing rapport with different business users and managers;
- acquiring a range of information about the business situation, including any personal issues and problems.

Interviews tend to take place on a one-to-one basis, which is one reason why they can be invaluable in identifying personal concerns. They focus on the views of an individual and provide an environment where interviewees have an opportunity to discuss their concerns and feel that they are given individual attention. If two analysts carry out some interviews it is more difficult to build up the level of trust required in order to share these concerns. Interviewing can be quite time consuming, so the interviewer has a responsibility to ensure that the interviewee's time is not wasted, the required information is acquired and a good degree of understanding is achieved.

The following three areas are considered during fact-finding or requirements interviews:

- current functions that need to be fulfilled in any new business system;
- problems with the current operations that need to be addressed;
- new features required from the new business system.

The last point can be the hardest part of an interview, as we are asking business users to think beyond their experience. They may offer vaguely worded suggestions, and the skill of the interviewer is needed in order to draw out more detailed information.

Advantages and disadvantages of interviewing

One of the major benefits of conducting an interview is that it gives an opportunity to build a relationship with the business stakeholders. Whether we are helping the business to improve operations or to replace legacy IT systems, it is critical that we understand the perspectives of the people involved with the business system. This means that we need to appreciate what they do, their concerns and what they want from any new processes or systems. For their part, the stakeholders need to have confidence in the analysts, to know that we are aware of their concerns, are professional, and are not leaping to a solution that overlooks the user's own needs and worries. Spending time to form good relationships early on in the project will increase the opportunities to understand the context and details of the business users' concerns and needs.

The second major benefit is that the interview can yield important information. The focus of the information will vary depending upon the needs of the project, but it will usually include details about the current operations, including difficulties in carrying out the work, and will help with the identification of requirements for the new business system.

Additional advantages of interviews include:

- the opportunity to understand different viewpoints and attitudes across the stakeholder community;
- the opportunity to investigate new areas that arise;
- a chance to collect examples of documents, forms and reports that the clients use;
- appreciation of political factors that may occur;
- study of the environment in which the business staff carry out their work.

While interviewing is an effective technique, there are some disadvantages. Interviews take time and can be an expensive approach, particularly if the business users are dispersed around the country. They take up the interviewees' time, which it is often difficult for them to spare from a busy schedule, and this may mean that people try to hurry the interview or resent the time that it takes. It is also important to realise that the information provided during an interview may be opinion from just one interviewee's perspective, and may need to be confirmed by quantitative data before any firm conclusions are drawn. Where several interviewees have different views, the analyst will also have to coordinate these views and identify gaps and conflicts. This may create a need for follow-up discussions and further investigative work.

Preparation for interviewing

The interviewing process is greatly improved when the interviewer has prepared thoroughly, as this saves a lot of time by avoiding unnecessary explanations and demonstrates interest and professionalism.

The classic structure of Who?, Why?, What?, When? and Where? provides an excellent framework for preparing for interviews.

Who?

This involves identifying which stakeholders we will interview and considering the order in which they will be interviewed. We usually begin with the more senior stakeholders, as this helps us to understand the context for the problem before moving to the details, so it is useful to interview someone who can provide an overview. A senior person is also able to identify the key people to see and make any necessary introductions.

The level of authority of the interviewee will dictate the nature of the questioning. The STOP model (Figure 5.1) illustrates a simple hierarchy.

- The 'S' represents the strategic level of management. Our concerns at this level are to confirm the terms of reference, to understand any management information requirements and to agree the approach to the investigation.

- The 'T' represents the tactical level, or middle management. Here we are concerned with understanding issues of performance, targets and management control. This often entails reporting requirements. The interviewee will be able to tell us what processes and functions are carried out in the department and who the key people are, but we should not expect detailed description of how the processes are executed. The tactical level, aware of higher-level strategic decisions, can also tell us about new business requirements for this area.

- The 'OP' level represents the operational level, the people who perform the actual tasks of the department. These are the people who can describe the existing business situation accurately, and can identify problems and workarounds to deal with the current procedures. They have information about source documents, bottlenecks and the flow of the work, and are likely to provide ideas about the volume of work (although these need to be treated with caution and should be analysed using quantitative investigation techniques).

Figure 5.1 'STOP', the organisation hierarchy

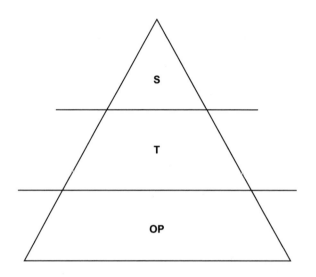

The questioning strategy for the interview will depend upon several factors, including where the prospective interviewee sits in this hierarchy, the objectives for the project and the nature of the issues to be addressed.

Why?
This involves considering why a particular interviewee is to be interviewed and the place of the interviewee in the organisation, as described above. The objectives of the interview may range from the detailed elicitation of business needs to establishing a good rapport and working relationship with a key stakeholder. The forms of questioning and of note-taking will differ significantly between these cases.

What?
This involves considering the information that could be provided by this interviewee and the areas we might explore during the interview.

When? and Where?
These involve considering the venue, timing and duration of the interview. Typically, the interviewee will dictate the exact timing and duration, as this will depend upon availability. Limiting interviews to a maximum length of one hour is a good idea, since:

- The majority of interviewees are busy people and will have trouble finding slots of more than an hour in their diaries.

- It is difficult to maintain concentration and assimilate the information gained in an interview that is longer than one hour; very long interviews can be unproductive.

- The longer the interview, the harder it is to write up the notes accurately.

The 'where' is restricted to three possibilities: the interviewee's place of work, the interviewer's place of work or a neutral third location. The first of these is recommended for a first interview, for the following reasons:

- This is the person's own territory, where he or she feels in charge and less likely to be intimidated.
- The interviewer has an opportunity to observe the working environment and the frequency and nature of interruptions informally.
- The interviewee will have all relevant source documents and screens to hand, instead of maybe forgetting to bring some and thus having to take extra actions after the interview.

Although the best advice is to choose the interviewee's place of work, interviewing people at their desks in an open-plan office may be distracting or intimidating. If this is likely to be the case, it is often helpful to see whether a quieter meeting room or area is available for the actual interview. Subsequent meetings, once there has been an opportunity to establish rapport, may be arranged at any mutually convenient location.

Conducting the interview

It is important to structure interviews to gain the maximum benefit from them. A standard structure of opening, body of interview and closure, as shown in Figure 5.2, provides a helpful means of organising the interview while also providing flexibility.

Figure 5.2 The structure of an interview

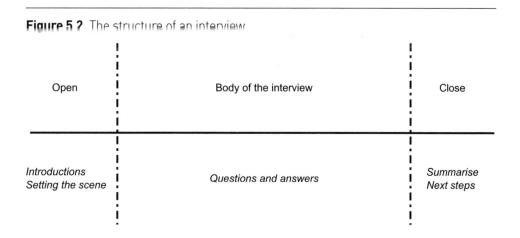

The opening

In addition to making personal introductions, it is also important that the analyst makes sure the interviewee understands the purpose of the project in general and the interview in particular. Ideally the interviewee should know this already, but such knowledge cannot be relied upon. Explaining the context also helps to put interviewees at ease and will help them to provide the relevant information. It is important to make sure that the interviewee has received the agenda and to clarify any points that they wish to raise.

Body of the interview

The main part of the interview is where the facts and issues are uncovered. It is useful to think about how you are going to structure this. A good approach is to begin by obtaining a context for the information that this interviewee can provide. Once you have a context, you can structure the interview by examining each area separately and in detail. This will enable you to consider the issues, and the impact of those issues, in each area and to uncover any specific problems and requirements.

It is essential to take notes during the interview. Even those who have an excellent memory will not remember everything discussed during an interview. If the purpose of the interview is to understand a current procedure, a good way of taking notes can be to draw a diagram, such as an organisation structure or a flow chart. If the purpose is to discuss a number of broader issues, including needs for the future, a mind map is a useful way of noting what has been said and also, if it is drawn up as part of the preparation, provides an easy visual check on what has been covered and further areas for discussion. This can be important since, however well you have structured your questions in your preparation, conversations always take unexpected paths and diversions. It is easy for analysts to feel that they have lost track of where they are in the plan.

Closure

It is equally important to close the interview properly. The analyst should:

- Summarise the points covered and the actions agreed.

- Explain what happens next, both following the interview and, beyond that, in the project. We will usually want to advise interviewees that we will send them a copy of the written-up notes, so that they can check for any errors.

- Ask the interviewee how any further contact should be made. This is a small point, but it will be invaluable later if we need any additional information or clarifications.

Following up the interview

It is always a good idea to write up the notes of the interview as soon as possible – ideally straight away and usually by the next day. If it is not possible to write up the notes immediately, you will find this task easier if you read through them after the interview and extend them where they are unclear. Once the notes are completed, they should be submitted to the interviewee for confirmation that they reflect accurately the substance of what was discussed. After they have been approved, they should become a formal part of the project documentation and be filed accordingly.

Observation

Observing the workplace and the staff members carrying out their work is very useful in obtaining information about the business environment and the work practices. There are several different approaches to observation, depending upon the level and focus of interest. It is important that, before any work is observed, the people being observed should be reassured that the objective is to understand the task, not to judge their performance. Care is needed if you want to observe a unionised worksite. In this situation it is important to ensure that approval is also gained from the trade union representatives and that any protocols are observed.

Advantages and disadvantages of observation

The views of the stakeholders involved in a project may have been sought during interviews, but in order to really obtain a feel for the situation the analyst needs to observe the workplace and business practices. Apart from collecting actual facts, it is also possible to clarify areas of tacit information and hence increase your understanding. This has two advantages:

- You will have a much better understanding of the problems and difficulties faced by the business users.
- It will help you to devise workable solutions, fitted to the working environment, that are more likely to be acceptable to the business.

Conversely, being observed can be rather unnerving and the old saying 'you change what you observe' needs to be factored into your approach and findings.

Formal observation

Formal observation involves watching a specific task being performed. There is a danger here of being shown the standard practice without any of the everyday variances, but it is still a useful tool for understanding the environment. It is important that the staff members being observed are prepared beforehand, and that they understand that you are watching them in order to understand the tasks, and not, as many will fear, that you are assessing their own competence and performance. Self-consciousness can influence how staff members perform, and a lack of preparation will serve to accentuate this problem. If staff members perceive the analyst as having been sent by management, they are more likely to perform the task according to the rulebook, rather than in the way that, perhaps, it has evolved over time.

It is perfectly acceptable to ask people being observed about aspects of the sequence they are following, so long as:

- The question does not sound critical of the way the person is working, either in choice of words or in tone of voice.
- It does not distract from their performance of the job.

Protocol analysis

Protocol analysis involves asking business staff members to perform a task and to describe each step as they perform it. This is a way of eliciting skills that cannot be expressed in words alone. A similar approach is used when learner drivers are taught during the first driving lesson: rather than being lectured in a classroom on how to begin moving a car into traffic and then having to trying it for real, they learn by watching the task being both performed and explained simultaneously and then performing it for themselves. The higher the level of unconscious skill involved in a task, the harder it is to describe in words alone. The 'performing and describing' approach of protocol analysis helps analysts to gain greater understanding.

Shadowing

Shadowing involves following a business user for a period such as one or two days in order to find out what a particular job entails. This is a powerful way of understanding a specific user role. Asking for explanations of how the work is done, or the workflow sequence, is a good way of clarifying some of the taken-for-granted aspects. The longer the analyst spends shadowing a user, the better the rapport they can build over the time and the better chance there is of capturing the additional details that may not be uncovered in a single 45-minute interview. Shadowing key staff members is a useful addition to a more structured investigation approach such as interviewing, since it provides a visual context for the processes that have been, or will be, described.

Ethnographic studies

Ethnographic study is, sadly, beyond the budget of most projects, but would yield high returns if it could be achieved. It comes from the discipline of anthropology, and involves spending an extended period of time, possibly several months, in the target environment. The rationale for such an extended study is that eventually the business community becomes used to the observer's presence and behaves naturally and authentically. This provides a basis for gaining an in-depth knowledge and understanding of complex business systems and uncovering tacit knowledge that is embedded in the business practices.

Workshops

Workshops provide an excellent collaborative forum in which issues can be discussed, conflicts resolved and requirements elicited. As a result they may be used at many different points during the project. Workshops are especially valuable when time and budgets are tightly constrained and several viewpoints need to be canvassed.

Workshops are also a useful forum for carrying out other activities, such as analysing the quality of a requirements set before it is formally documented. This aspect is explored further in Chapter 9.

Advantages and disadvantages of workshops

The many advantages of using workshops include the ability to:

- **gain a broad view of the area under investigation:** having a group of stakeholders in one room will allow the analyst to gain a more complete understanding of the issues and problems;

- **increase speed and productivity:** it is much quicker to have one meeting with a group of people than to interview them one by one;

- **obtain buy-in and acceptance for the project or business initiative:** when stakeholders are involved in such collaboration, not only will they be more open to any business changes or features that result but they are more likely to be champions of the change;

- **gain a consensus view or group agreement:** if all the stakeholders are involved in the decision-making process, there is a greater chance that they will take ownership of the results.

However, these advantages are only possible if a workshop is well organised and run. The means of achieving this are discussed in the rest of this section.

Although workshops are extremely valuable, there are some disadvantages to using them, including:

- Workshops can be time-consuming to organise. For example, it is not always easy to get all the necessary people together at the same time.

- If the workshop is not carefully facilitated, it may happen that a forceful participant can dominate the discussion. In extreme cases such a participant may be able to impose a decision because the other members of the group feel unable to raise their objections.

- It can be difficult to ensure that the participants have the required level of authority – which sometimes means that decisions are reversed after the workshop has ended.

Preparing for the workshop

The success or failure of a workshop session depends in large part upon the preparatory work done by its facilitator and its business sponsor. They should spend time before the event planning the following areas:

- **The objective of the workshop:** this has to be an objective that can be achieved within the time constraints of the workshop. If it is a sizeable objective, the duration of the workshop will need to reflect this, possibly running to several days. In this case, the objective should be broken into sub-objectives, each of which is the subject of an individual workshop session. For example, a two-day workshop may be broken into four sessions, each of which is focused upon a particular sub-objective.

- **The people to be invited to participate in the workshop:** it is important that all stakeholders interested in the objective should be invited to attend or be represented. It is the facilitator's responsibility to ensure that all stakeholders are able to contribute, which may mean performing many of the key tasks by using breakout groups or other techniques and reporting back to a plenary session to collate the individual results.

- **The interests of each participant:** the facilitator should carry out research, perhaps conducting a short meeting with each participant in order to appreciate each one's concerns and viewpoint. These may include any worries about participant behaviour or fears of being ridiculed or overridden. The facilitator has to ensure that all participants' views are voiced and considered during the workshop.

- **The structure of the workshop and the techniques to be used:** these need to be geared towards achieving the defined objective and should take the needs of the participants into account. For example, a standard brainstorming session may not work very well with a group of people who have never met before.

- **Arranging a suitable venue:** this may be within the organisation's premises, but it is sometimes useful to use a neutral venue, particularly if the issues to be discussed are contentious or there is a danger that participants could be interrupted by colleagues or managers who want to call them away.

Facilitating the workshop

The workshop should start by discussing the objective and endeavouring to secure the participants' buy-in. It is often helpful here to get the business sponsor to open the workshop and hence show a commitment to the process. During the workshop the facilitator needs to ensure that the issues are discussed, views are aired and progress is made towards achieving the stated objective. The discussion may range widely, but the facilitator needs to ensure that it does not go completely off the track and that everyone has an opportunity to express his or her concerns and opinions.

A record needs to be kept of the key points emerging from the discussion. This is often done by the facilitator keeping a record on a flipchart, but it is better practice to appoint someone else to take the role of scribe during the workshop. The presence of a scribe allows the facilitator to concentrate fully on the process and the participants. One of the key elements of facilitation involves watching non-verbal behaviour to identify members of the group who may be feeling unhappy or unable to make their points. If the facilitator is spending a lot of time scribing, such cues can be easily missed.

At the end of the workshop, the facilitator needs to summarise the key points and actions. Each action should be assigned to an owner and allocated a timescale for completion.

Techniques

There are two main categories of technique required for a workshop (Figure 5.3): techniques for discovery and techniques for documentation.

Discovery techniques are those that help the facilitator to elicit information and views from the participants. It is vital that the facilitator considers which techniques would be most suitable for a particular situation and group of participants. Examples of useful techniques are:

- brainstorming (sometimes known as idea storming), where the participants are asked to call out ideas about a given item, all of which are written on a flipchart or whiteboard where they can be seen by all of the participants, and any evaluation of the ideas is suspended until everyone has finished making suggestions;
- round-robin discussions, where the workshop participants are asked for their ideas in turn;
- brainwriting, or exercises using Post-it notes, where participants write down ideas that are then collated and grouped;
- stepwise refinement, where we take a statement or idea and keep asking 'Why?' to every answer given until we think we have got to the heart of a problem, idea or situation.

- the use of smaller 'break-out' groups to work on stories and scenarios for a particular process, to be fed back to a plenary session – a powerful way to manage a large workshop where there is a range of skills and knowledge.

Figure 5.3 Workshop techniques

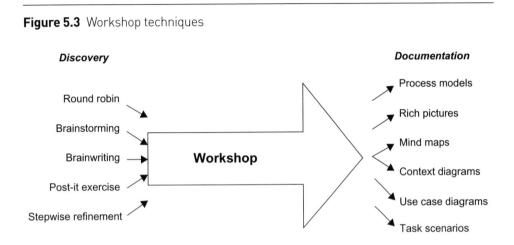

A variety of documentation techniques are suitable for use in a workshop. Several useful diagrammatic techniques are explored during the course of this book, including process models, data models, use case diagrams, rich pictures and mind maps. These techniques help the business users to visualise the area under discussion. Text-based documentation may also be required in order to keep records of agreed action points or issues for further discussion. Another approach is to structure the discussion using recognised strategic or business performance analysis techniques. For example, if the workshop is concerned with the implementation of the business strategy, a higher-level approach, such as critical success factor (CSF) analysis can be employed. This will begin by agreeing the critical success factors for the objective, or the part of the organisation, under discussion, and cascade down through the key performance indicators (KPIs) to consider the information requirements needed in order to measure how the CSFs are achieved. This can then lead to the definition of more detailed requirements in areas such as data capture and management reporting.

Following the workshop
After the workshop any key points and actions are written up and sent to the relevant participants and stakeholders. This should be done as quickly as possible, because it will help to keep up the momentum and highlight the need for quick action.

Focus groups
Focus groups tend to be concerned with business and market research. They bring together a group of people with a common interest to discuss a topic. While such a meeting has similarities to a workshop, it is not the same thing. A focus group could be used to understand people's attitudes to any current shortcomings

with the business system, for example the reasons why customers are unhappy with a service. A focus group will be used as part of an information-gathering exercise, but the findings will need to be evaluated and assessed against the strategy and objectives of the organisation. As a result, the findings from a focus group should not be relied upon to produce definitive requirements.

Focus-group participants should represent a sample of the target constituency, whether they be external customers or internal staff gathered from multiple sites and branches. They are given an opportunity to express their opinions and views and to discuss them. In a focus group, unlike a workshop, there is no requirement to form a consensus during the discussion, or for the group to acquire a sense of ownership of any decisions made or solutions identified.

Scenarios

Scenario analysis is essentially telling the story of a task or transaction. Its value is that it helps a user who is uncertain about what is needed from a new business process or system to visualise it more clearly. Scenarios are also useful when analysing or redesigning business processes. A scenario will trace the set of actions that are initiated by a business event and that have to be completed in order to achieve a successful outcome. A definition of a scenario will also include the definition of other aspects, such as the actor responsible for carrying out the task, the preconditions and the postconditions. The preconditions are the characteristics of the business or the IT system that must be true for the scenario to begin. The postconditions are the characteristics that must be true following the conclusion of the scenario.

One of the key strengths of scenarios is that they provide a framework for discovering the exception situations that require alternative paths to be followed when carrying out the task. The transition from each step to the next provides an opportunity to analyse what else might happen or be true. This analysis often uncovers additional information or tacit knowledge. For these reasons scenarios are extremely useful in requirements elicitation and analysis. In addition, they help the analyst to discuss situations that are easily recognisable to the business users because they are based on what actually happens in their work. The defined scenarios also provide a basis for developing prototypes of IT system requirements.

Scenario analysis is also a useful technique for assisting with risk analysis. This is done through the use of what Alexander (Alexander and Maiden 2004) calls 'misuse cases'. The principle is the same as that described above, but it starts with potentially hostile actors.

Advantages and disadvantages of scenarios

Scenarios offer significant advantages to the analyst:

- They require the user to include each step and the transitions between the steps, and as a result remove the opportunity for omissions.
- The step-by-step development approach helps ensure that there are no taken-for-granted elements and many of the problems of tacit knowledge are addressed.

- They are developed using a 'top-down' approach, starting with an overview scenario and then refining this with further detail. This helps the business user visualise all possible situations and removes uncertainty.

- They provide a basis for developing prototypes.

- The scenario definitions are used for preparing acceptance test scripts.

The disadvantages of scenarios are that they can be time-consuming to develop and some scenarios can become very complex, particularly where there are several alternative paths. Where this is the case, you will find it easier to analyse the scenarios if each of the alternative paths is considered as a separate scenario.

Figure 5.4 Process for developing scenarios

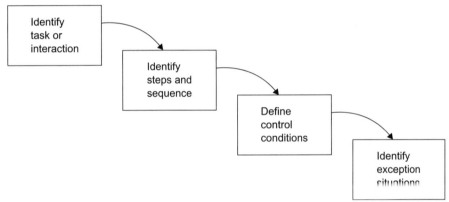

Figure 5.4 shows an overview approach to developing scenarios. It includes the following steps:

- Identify the task or interaction to be modelled as a scenario, and the business trigger or event that causes that interaction to take place.

- Identify the steps that will be carried out during the usual progress of the interaction, and the flow of these steps.

- Define the control conditions that govern the transition from one step to another – the conditions that must be met in order to follow the typical sequence of steps.

- Identify the alternative paths that would be required in order to handle the situations where the control conditions are not met.

This approach establishes a default path for the scenario that assumes no complications, with everything running as expected. This path is often known as the 'happy day' scenario. Scenarios are powerful when eliciting information, because they break down each of the default steps to ask the questions 'What needs to be true in order to continue with this path?' and 'At this point, what might happen instead?'

Once the alternatives have been uncovered the analyst can then ask the question 'What should we do if this happens or this is true?'

Consider an example scenario where a customer wishes to place an order via the telephone. The default steps for the telesales clerk could be:

(i) Enter customer reference number.

(ii) Confirm customer details.

(iii) Record order items.

(iv) Accept payment.

(v) Advise customer of delivery date.

For this scenario to flow in the sequence shown, the control conditions to go from step (i) to step (ii), from step (ii) to step (iii) and so on must be true. For example, the order items recorded in step (iii) must be available if step (iv) is to take place. However, if there were insufficient stock then the next step to be followed would not be step (iv) but an alternative step. There may be several possible actions to be taken following this alternative step, such as:

- delaying order fulfilment until stock arrives;

- allocating a substitute item;

- sending an order and the customer's delivery details directly to the supplier.

All of the possibilities should be explored and documented as alternative paths. These are termed 'extensions' to the default scenario. This approach helps to ensure that all possible situations and exceptions are anticipated.

The example scenario above is described in a generic, abstract way and some users may find this approach difficult to apply to the reality of their work. Another possible approach is to use a 'concrete' scenario, where a specific narrative or story is developed and then tested against the requirements already identified in order to find the gaps. Here is an example of a concrete scenario for a vehicle parts system:

> Turpin Coaches calls with an urgent request for 500 Type 2 gaskets. They are a highly valued – and valuable – customer. They tell the clerk that if we cannot satisfy them, they must go elsewhere. The stock records show that there are 150 Type 2 gaskets available. 400 were allocated to ZED just 30 minutes previously. The ZED order will not be processed for another two hours. The clerk wishes to amend the ZED order.

Using this concrete scenario, we can see that there is a possible extension in that an order may be prioritised and amended, giving rise to alternative paths through the 'take order' scenario. This will require the analyst to record additional requirements to those reflected in the 'happy day', such as the ability to prioritise orders and to amend orders already accepted. Concrete scenarios such as this example are extremely useful in helping to uncover where all of the possible extensions lie. The analyst should set the ball rolling with a prepared 'happy day' scenario that is then used as the basis for a discussion. All of the extensions and resultant requirements that are uncovered are then added to the analysis documentation.

Documenting scenarios
A popular way of documenting scenario descriptions is to develop use case descriptions to support use case diagrams. This technique is part of the UML approach and is a textual method. However, there are a number of graphical methods of documenting a scenario, such as storyboards, activity diagrams, task models and decision tree diagrams.

Prototyping
Prototyping is an important technique for eliciting, analysing, demonstrating and validating requirements. Analysts often complain that the business stakeholders do not know what they want, and that as a result it is difficult to define the requirements. However, it can be very difficult to envisage requirements for the future without having a sense of what is possible. It is much easier to review a suggested solution and identify where there are errors or problems. Prototypes offer a way of showing the stakeholders how the new processes or system might work, and provide a concrete basis for evaluation and discussion. If the business users are unclear about their requirements, using a prototype often releases the blocks to thinking and can result in greater understanding and clarity. Iterative approaches to systems development, such as the DSDM Atern and the Scrum framework, use evolutionary prototyping as an integral part of their systems development lifecycles.

Prototyping involves building simulations of a system in order to review them with the users to increase understanding about the system requirements. Working with prototypes can help business users to visualise the new system and hence give them greater insight into possible requirements. There is a range of approaches to building prototypes. They may be built using the organisation's system development environment so that they exactly mirror the future system. Alternatively, images of the screens and navigation may be built using presentation software packages such as Microsoft PowerPoint, or they may be mock-ups on paper. A quick but effective form of prototyping is to use flipchart sheets, pens and packs of Post-it notes and work with the users to develop paper prototypes. This will enable the users to develop screens, identify navigation paths, define the data they must input or refer to, and prepare lists of specified values that they know will apply. This approach can also be used to develop prototypes of a business process.

There is a strong link between scenarios and prototyping, because scenarios can be used as the basis for developing prototypes that demonstrate how the system will handle the requirements identified in the scenario. As well as confirming requirements, prototyping can often help the users to identify ones that they had not considered previously.

Advantages and disadvantages of prototyping

Prototypes are useful for a variety of reasons, including:

- to clarify any uncertainty on the part of the analysts and confirm to the stakeholders that we have understood what they asked for;

- to help the stakeholders identify new requirements as they gain an understanding of what the system will be able to do to support their jobs;

- to demonstrate the look and feel of the proposed system and elicit usability requirements;

- to validate the system requirements and identify any errors;

- to provide a means of assessing the navigation paths and system performance.

Prototyping has a number of hazards, most of which can be avoided by setting clear objectives for the prototyping exercise and managing the stakeholders' expectations. The hazards include:

- The prototyping cycle can spin out of control, with endless iterations taking place.

- If the purpose of the exercise has not been explained clearly, the business users may think that when they are happy with the mock-up the system is now complete and ready for use.

- User expectations can be raised unnecessarily by a prototype that fails to mimic the final appearance of the system or its performance. A system that is on a standalone machine with six dummy data records to search will be more responsive than a machine that is sharing resources with a thousand other machines on a national network and has over a million records to access. If there is likely to be a delay in the real response time, it is important that you build that into the prototype.

QUANTITATIVE APPROACHES

Questionnaires

Questionnaires can be useful if we need to get a limited amount of information from a lot of people and interviewing them all would not be practical or cost-effective. However, questionnaires are difficult to use successfully and they have to be designed carefully in order to have any possibility of success.

The exact design of a questionnaire depends upon its purpose, but there are three main areas to consider:

Heading section

This is where the purpose of the questionnaire is explained, and where instructions for returning it are given.

Classification section

This is where the details about the respondent that allow the information to be categorised by predefined analysis criteria, such as age, gender or length of service, are obtained. If it is decided that the questionnaire should be completed anonymously, perhaps because it asks some controversial questions, it is important to make sure that the respondents really cannot be identified by other means; otherwise, confidence in the process will be lost and you will be unlikely to get a truthful response, if you receive one at all.

Data section

This is where the main body of questions is posed. It is vital to think carefully about the phrasing of the questions. They must be unambiguous and, ideally, allow for straightforward answers such as 'yes/no', 'agree/neutral/disagree' or 'excellent/satis-factory/inadequate'. It is always better to structure the questions, where possible, so that the range of answers is the same for each group of questions.

We will need to analyse the results once the questionnaires have been returned. If we are sending out a lot of questionnaires, we want to be able to build a summary of the answers and draw conclusions without having to do too much interpretation. The answers must provide clear, unambiguous responses to the questions so that the data can be collated and analysed properly. For example, if you asked 'Have you used our website recently?' and someone answered 'No' would that mean that the respondent:

- is not interested in our products and services and hence has not visited our website?
- didn't know that we had a website?
- is not IT-literate and hence has never used this or any other website?
- last used the website a year ago and does not consider that to be 'recently'?

The key drawback in using questionnaires is that people will find 101 good reasons for not replying, such as:

- They accidentally threw the questionnaire in the bin.
- They were on holiday when it arrived.
- They were very busy when it arrived.
- They didn't realise it was double-sided, and so only completed half of it.

It is very important that the heading section sets out clearly the rationale for the questionnaire, the instructions for its return and, where appropriate, any incentive for completing it. A well-formed heading section will help the respondent to understand why it is important to complete the questionnaire, and as a result will significantly increase the volume that are returned.

Special-purpose records

This technique involves the business users in keeping a record about a specific issue or task. For example, they could keep a simple five-bar-gate record about how often they need to transfer telephone calls; this could provide the analyst with information about the problems with the business process and the scale of those problems. There are difficulties with getting people to carry out this form of survey, the chief of which is that they forget to record the occurrence at the time and then make up the numbers later. Notwithstanding these problems, it can still be useful sometimes to get people to keep such records, for example to show what happens during their working day or how they spend their time. The main advantages of this approach are that it avoids the problems associated with observation and is a more effective use of the analyst's time.

If getting people to keep special-purpose records is to be useful, two important criteria have to be satisfied:

- The people undertaking the recording must be induced to 'buy in' to the exercise. This may be done by persuading them of the need or benefits, but another possibility is that they are instructed to do it by their manager.

- The survey must be realistic about what people can reasonably be expected to record.

Activity sampling

This is a further quantitative form of observation and can be used when it is necessary to know how people divide their work time among a range of activities. For example, how much time is spent on invoicing each day? How much on reconciling payments? How much on sorting out complaints?

One way to find out how people spend their time would be to get them to complete a special-purpose record, but sometimes the results need to have a guaranteed level of accuracy, for example if they are to be used to build a business case. In situations where accuracy is important, activity sampling should be used in preference to special-purpose records or observation. An activity-sampling exercise is carried out in five steps:

(i) Identify the activities to be recorded. This list should include a 'not working' activity, which covers lunch time and other breaks from work. It might also include a 'not related' activity, such as first aid or health and safety officer duties.

(ii) Decide on the frequency and timings, i.e. when and how often you will record the activities being undertaken.

(iii) Visit the study group at the times decided upon and record what each group member is doing.

(iv) Record the results.

(v) After a set period, analyse the results.

The results from an activity-sampling exercise provide quantifiable data about the number of times an activity is carried out per day by the group studied. By analysing that figure against other data, such as the total amount of time available, we are able to calculate the total length of time spent on that activity and the average time one occurrence of the activity will take. This information can be useful when developing business cases and evaluating proposed solutions. Also, it will raise other questions, such as whether the average time is reasonable for a task, or whether it indicates a problem somewhere else in the process.

Document analysis

Document analysis involves reviewing samples of documents to uncover information about an organisation, process or system.

For each document we should analyse the following areas:

- How is the document completed?
- Who completes the document?
- Are there any validations or controls on the document?
- Who uses the document?
- When is the document used?
- How many are used or produced?
- How long is the document retained by the organisation, and in what form?
- What are the details of the information shown on the document?
- Where is the information or data obtained?
- Are other names used in the organisation for any of the items of data?

Document analysis is useful to supplement other techniques such as interviewing, workshops and observation. Samples of the completed documents or system printouts help to provide a clearer picture of how the organisation works in that area, the processes that are followed, and the key items of information used to carry out the work.

DOCUMENTING THE CURRENT BUSINESS SITUATION

While the investigation of the current business situation is going on, the analyst will need to record the findings so as to come to understand the range of issues and business needs. Meeting reports will be produced for each interview and workshop, and this section suggests five diagrammatic techniques that are also useful in documenting the investigation and analysing the situation. These techniques help the analyst to understand the information that has been obtained and to find the root causes of any problems.

Rich pictures

The rich-picture technique is one of the few that provide an overview of an entire business situation. Whereas modelling approaches such as data or process modelling provide a clear representation of a specific aspect of a business system, rich pictures show all aspects. The technique does not have a fixed notation, but allows the analyst to use any symbols or annotations that are relevant and useful.

For this reason, a rich picture can show the human characteristics of the business situation and can reflect areas such as the culture of the organisation. Many problems in the current business system may have originated with the people performing the tasks rather than being caused by poor process design or inadequate IT systems. There could be differing viewpoints, misunderstandings, stress from too many tasks, personal differences with co-workers, dissatisfaction with management or frustration at inadequate resources. Any of these factors could impair the performance of a task, but the traditional analysis models would not be able to record them. A rich picture allows the analyst to document all of the human and cultural aspects as well as process flows and information usage. The unstructured nature of the technique allows the analyst to 'brain dump' the information in a simple, pictorial representation. Its strength is that the process of building the rich picture helps the analyst to form a mental map of the situation and see connections between different issues. The rich picture can also be enriched further as more information about the situation comes to light. Figure 5.5 shows an example of a rich picture for a business system called TrentCars Garage.

Figure 5.5 Example of a rich picture

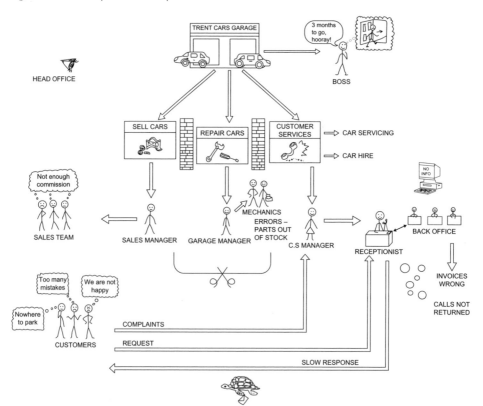

Mind maps

Mind maps are a useful tool for summarising a lot of information in a simple visual form that highlights connections between different ideas and topics. They provide a means of structuring and organising information while, in a similar vein to rich pictures, representing all of the issues that have been uncovered about the situation. The business system or problem under consideration is drawn at the centre of the diagram with the main elements shown as the first level of branches radiating from the central point. Each of these branches is labelled, using as few words as possible, to indicate the nature of the particular area or issue. The branches might represent such matters as particular processes, the equipment and systems used, relationships between the staff who do the job and so on. These branches can then support second-level branches that are concerned with more detailed areas for each aspect of the situation. For example, the branch for equipment and systems might show problems with the printing or photocopying equipment and key failings of the IT systems. A mind map helps structure the information gathered into a recognisable and manageable set of connections. Mind maps are extremely useful in helping analysts to order their thinking, and they work well both on their own and when used in conjunction with rich pictures. The mind map in Figure 5.6 for the TrentCars Garage relates to the rich picture shown in Figure 5.5.

Figure 5.6 Example of a mind map

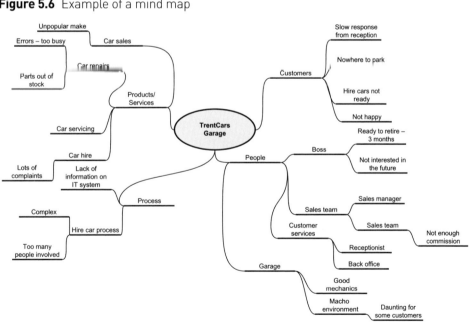

Business process models

In order to understand how a process is carried out, it is helpful to draw a business process model or 'swim-lane' diagram, which shows all of the tasks carried out in a process, the actors responsible for carrying them out and the flow of the process. These models are easy to draw and business stakeholders find them accessible, so they provide a good communication tool between the analyst and the business staff. Business process models are also invaluable as a diagnostic aid since they help identify problems such as delays, bottlenecks and duplicate tasks. They are described in greater detail in Chapter 8.

Spaghetti maps

A spaghetti map is a diagrammatic technique that is used to show the movement and interactions of the stakeholders when performing particular tasks and processes. It is called a spaghetti map because as the movements are drawn the diagram created resembles a plate of spaghetti, with lines crossing back and forth without any apparent formality or design. Spaghetti maps can be drawn up during an observation session, mapping the movements of users across the room to meet different actors or to use equipment such as printers or photocopiers.

Figure 5.7 shows a spaghetti map drawn while observing a clerk in the service department of a garage checking in a car for repair and allocating a courtesy car to the customer. Despite having a computer terminal on her desk, she still

Figure 5.7 Example of a spaghetti map for a garage service section

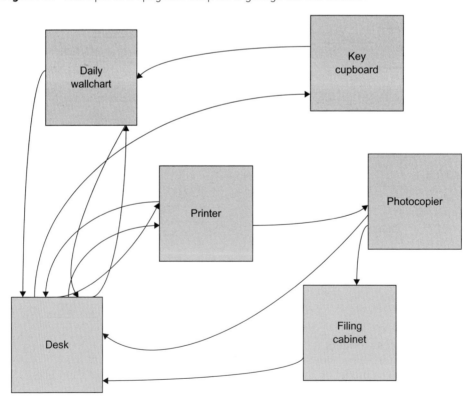

needed to make use of a printer, a photocopier, a filing cabinet and a wallchart in order to perform the task. Their position on the map is similar to their position in the real office. It is easy to see how much of the clerk's time is taken over the course of a day in accessing these different stations. This diagram represents one person executing one instance of a common task, so the scope for efficiency gains is clear.

It is interesting to note that a swim-lane diagram would not show the physical movement required for an actor to carry out a task, so it would not highlight the potential for improvement. The two diagrams together help identify the scope for improvement in the process.

Fishbone diagrams

One of the major objectives in investigating and modelling a business system is to identify where there are problems and discover their underlying causes. Some of these may be obvious, or the stakeholders may be aware of the root causes of their problems. However, sometimes it is only the symptoms that are highlighted by the stakeholders because the causes have proved difficult to isolate. The fishbone diagram is a problem-analysis technique, designed to help understand the underlying causes of an inefficient process or a business problem. It is similar to a mind map in some ways, but its purpose is strictly diagnostic. The technique was invented by Dr. Kaoru Ishikawa (Ishikawa 1990), and the diagrams are sometimes known as Ishikawa diagrams. The technique is also known as root cause analysis. The name of the problem is documented in a box at the right-hand side of the diagram. Stretching out from the box towards the left of the page is the backbone of the fish. Radiating up and down from this backbone are spines; the spines suggest possible areas for causes of the problem. A number of approaches may be used when labelling the spines.

- **the four Ms:** manpower, machines, measures and methods;
- **an alternative four Ms:** manpower, machines, materials and methods;
- **the six Ps:** people, place, processes, physical evidence, product/service and performance measures.

These categories help because they list areas that have been found to be the source of inefficiencies in many business systems. In practice we often consider a range of categories and might combine the most relevant elements from the approaches above, or even define some categories that are particularly relevant to a given project. As with mind maps, the spines have more detailed elements associated with them. Each category along a spine is examined, and the factors within that category that may be affecting the problem are listed. The resultant diagram is shaped like a fishbone – hence the name fishbone diagrams.

It may be necessary to use a variety of investigation techniques in order to uncover the causes of the problem. Facilitated workshops can be useful, particularly as the categories identified on the fishbone diagrams help to give a structure to the workshop discussion. Once the diagram has been completed, we can analyse the results by looking for the key causes of problems. These are the items that are listed several times, since they are the ones that are likely to be having a broad impact upon the situation. They should be considered for rapid action in order to help address the issue promptly.

Figure 5.8 shows an example fishbone diagram for a garage courtesy-car process.

Figure 5.8 Example of a fishbone diagram

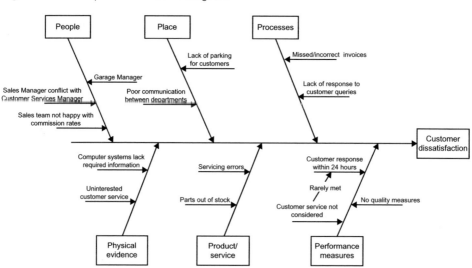

Business needs log

Once the key causes of a problem have been identified, we can begin to consider how the problem may be addressed, and this may lead to the identification of some high-level business requirements. Although more detailed business analysis work will be required in order to produce the formal requirements document, it is important to document these initial requirements. A business needs log helps to ensure that any findings at this early stage are documented and are not lost once more detailed requirements work commences. The areas documented in the business needs log include:

- **key business aims to be met in any new process or system:** for example, a requirement that customers must have one point of contact for any purchases or queries;

- **high-level requirements relating to the functionality of any IT solution:** for example, the ability to access all information recorded about each customer;

- **issues to be addressed:** for example, the need to remove dependency upon certain members of staff;

- **brand-new facilities that must be provided by the solution:** for example, the provision of ad hoc management information on request.

High-level requirements such as those listed above will emerge from the business system investigation and must be logged so that they are not forgotten.

Later they will be analysed and defined in greater detail, but that is not required at this point. An example of a business needs log is shown in Table 5.1.

Table 5.1 Example of a business needs log

Business Need	Source	Comment
1 Booking confirmations must be issued to customers within 24 hours	Customer services manager	Currently confirmations are delayed for up to five days
2 All registered customers must be aged over 18 years	Legal and compliance manager	
3 Discounts can only be awarded on the presentation of a valid promotion code	Marketing director	Some customers have been awarded discounts without stating a discount code

SUMMARY

Any business analysis project will inevitably include the investigation of business situations and requirements. To do this effectively, the business analyst needs a toolkit consisting of a range of investigative and diagrammatic techniques. A key competency required by the business analyst is the ability to appreciate when particular techniques will be appropriate and the skill to apply them effectively.

REFERENCES

Alexander, I. and Maiden, N. (2004) *Scenarios, Stories and Use Cases.* John Wiley & Sons, Chichester.

Ishikawa, K. (1990) *Introduction to Quality Control.* Productivity Press, New York.

FURTHER READING

Alexander, I. and Stevens, R. (2002) *Writing Better Requirements.* Pearson Education, Harlow.

Cadle, J., Paul, D. and Turner, P. (2010) *Business Analysis Techniques*. BCS, Swindon.

Kotonya, G. and Sommerville, I. (1998) *Requirements Engineering*. John Wiley & Sons, Chichester.

Robertson, S. and Robertson, J. (2006) *Mastering the Requirements Process*, 2nd edn. Pearson Education, Boston, MA.

Skidmore, S. and Eva, M. (2004) *Introducing Systems Development*. Palgrave Macmillan, Basingstoke.

Yeates, D. and Wakefield, T. (2004) *Systems Analysis and Design*. FT Prentice Hall, Harlow.

6 STAKEHOLDER ANALYSIS AND MANAGEMENT

James Cadle

INTRODUCTION

Effective stakeholder management is absolutely crucial to the success of any business analysis project. Knowing who the stakeholders are and understanding what it is they expect from the project and delivered solution are vital if they are to remain involved and supportive of the undertaking. One of the major reasons why business analysis projects do not succeed – or do not succeed fully – is poor stakeholder management. The project team does not recognise the importance, or even the existence, of a key stakeholder and the team then finds that its plans are constantly frustrated. On the other hand, if the right stakeholders are identified and managed properly, most obstacles can be cleared from the path. In fact, much of the groundwork for stakeholder management takes place before the business analysis project proper begins – during project inception and initiation – and that work must be revisited constantly during the project itself. The basic steps involved are illustrated in Figure 6.1.

Figure 6.1 Stakeholder management in the project lifecycle

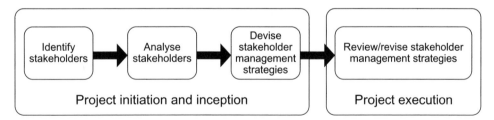

The main responsibility for stakeholder management rests, of course, with the project manager, although in a business analysis project this role may actually be assumed by one of the analysts. However, all team members have important roles to play, in identifying stakeholders, in helping to understand their needs and in helping to manage their expectations from the project.

STAKEHOLDER CATEGORIES AND IDENTIFICATION

As Figure 6.1 illustrates, the first step in stakeholder management involves finding out who the stakeholders are. A good working definition of a stakeholder is 'anyone who has an interest in, or may be affected by, the issue under consideration'. This means, more or less, anyone affected by the project or who may be in a position to influence it.

Of course, each project will have its own distinctive set of stakeholders, determined by the nature of the project and the environment in which it is taking place. However, we can identify some generic stakeholder categories that may apply to many projects, as illustrated in Figure 6.2.

Figure 6.2 Generic stakeholder categories

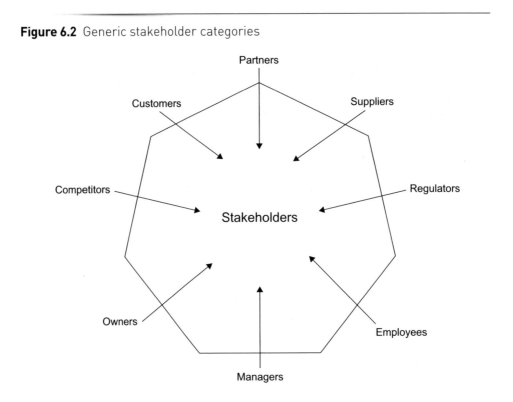

Customers
These are the people or organisations for whom our organisation provides products or services. They are stakeholders because anything we do in the way of change has a potential effect on them. We must consider how to manage that change most effectively so as not to lose customers that we wish to retain. It may be useful to subdivide this general category to reveal more detail about the stakeholders. For example, we may classify them as:

- large or small;
- regular or occasional;
- wholesale or retail;
- corporate or private;
- commercial or public-sector;
- civilian or military;
- domestic or export.

We may even have different categories that we simply label 'good customers' and 'bad customers', however we define these terms.

Partners
These are the organisations that work with our organisation, for example to provide specialist services on our behalf. An example of a partner organisation may be a outsourcing company that provides call-centre services.

Suppliers
These provide our organisation with the goods and services that it uses. Again, we may wish to subdivide them, perhaps into:

- major or minor;
- regular or occasional;
- domestic or overseas.

Suppliers are stakeholders because they are interested in the way we do business with them, what we wish to buy, how we want to pay and so on. Many change initiatives have the effect of altering the relationships of organisations with their suppliers; as with those affecting customers, such changes need to be managed carefully in order to make sure that they achieve positive and mutually beneficial results.

Competitors
Competitors vie with us for the business of our customers, and they therefore have a keen interest in changes made by our organisation. We have to consider what their reactions might be and whether they might try, for instance, to block our initiative or to produce some sort of counter-proposal.

Regulators
Many organisations are now subject to regulation or inspection, either by statutory bodies such as the Office for Communications (OfCom), the Office for Standards in Education (Ofsted) and the Financial Services Authority (FSA), or by professional bodies such as the General Medical Council (GMC) and the Law Society. These regulators will be very interested in making sure that changes proposed by an organisation are within the letter and spirit of the rules they enforce.

Owners

For a commercial business, the owners are just that – the people who own it directly. The business may be, in legal terms, a sole trader or partnership. Alternatively it could be a limited company, in which case the owners are the shareholders. For public limited companies, the majority of shares are held by institutions such as investment companies and pension funds, and so the managers of these share portfolios become proxy owners.

Employees

The people who work in an organisation clearly have an interest in the way it is run and in changes that it makes. In a small firm the employees may be regarded as individual stakeholders in their own right, but in larger concerns they are probably best considered as groups. Sometimes employees belong to trades unions, whose officials therefore become stakeholders too.

Managers

Finally, we have the professional managers of the organisation, those to whom its direction is entrusted. In a large organisation there may be many layers of management, and each may form a distinctive stakeholder grouping, for example:

- board-level senior managers;
- middle managers;
- junior managers;
- front-line supervisors.

As with many aspects of stakeholder management, it is an error to assume that a group such as 'managers' is homogeneous in its views and concerns. Junior managers may well have a very different perspective, and a different set of hopes and fears, from those on the board who take the major strategic decisions.

Other stakeholders

Of course, the groups shown in Figure 6.2 are generic, and in particular cases there may well be other stakeholders. For example, the insurers of an organisation may be interested in any areas that could affect the pattern of risk that is covered. Or perhaps the police might be interested in the law-and-order implications of some actions.

It is important for each project that the identification of stakeholders is as complete as possible, since it will otherwise be impossible to develop and implement effective management strategies for them. It may be useful to conduct some sort of workshop with people knowledgeable about the organisation and the proposed project in order to make sure that the coverage of stakeholders is comprehensive.

ANALYSING STAKEHOLDERS

Having identified the stakeholders, the next step is to make an assessment of the weight that should be attached to their issues. No stakeholder should be ignored completely, but the approach to each will be different depending on their level of interest in the project and the amount of power or influence they have, which determines their ability either to support or to obstruct it.

A simple way of analysing stakeholders is to use the power/interest grid illustrated in Figure 6.3. In using this grid, it is important to plot stakeholders where they actually are, not where they should be or perhaps where we would like them to be. We can then explore strategies for managing them in their positions or perhaps for moving them to other positions that might be more advantageous for the success of our project.

Figure 6.3 Stakeholder power/interest analysis

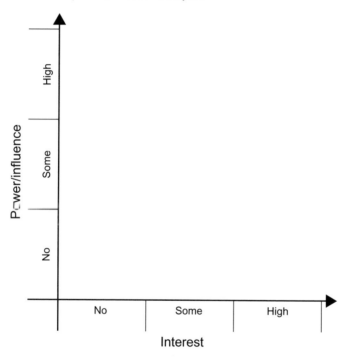

STAKEHOLDER MANAGEMENT STRATEGIES

There are, of course, an infinite number of positions that could be taken on the power/interest grid but it is probably sufficient here to consider the nine basic situations illustrated in Figure 6.4.

No interest and no power/influence
These are stakeholders who have neither a direct interest in the project nor any real power to affect it. For practical purposes they can be ignored as regards day-to-day issues on a project, and there needs to be no special effort

made to persuade them of its benefits. However, as stakeholders do change positions on the map (see the next section), it is probably wise to inform them occasionally about what is going on – perhaps through vehicles such as organisation newsletters.

Figure 6.4 Basic stakeholder management strategies

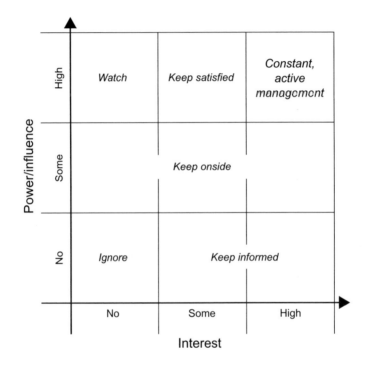

Some or high interest but no power/influence

These groups can be very difficult to manage effectively because, although they may be very directly affected by a change project, they feel powerless to shape its direction in any way. This frustration can result in passive resistance to the change, which, although overcome by positional power, can lead to delay and less-than-optimal results.

The basic management strategy here is to keep such stakeholders informed of what is going on and, in particular, of the reasons for the proposed change. However, this is a rather passive approach, and in most circumstances more effort has to be devoted to 'selling' the project. This can best be done by being as honest as possible about the need for change, by highlighting the positive aspects of the change or the negative consequences of not making it, and by frequent and focused communication of progress.

No, some or high interest and some power/influence

This is a rather varied group. It includes some stakeholders such as middle or senior managers who do have some power or influence but who, because their interests are not directly affected, are not very concerned about the direction a project is taking. Regulators may also fall into this category; they will only start to get involved if some breach of the rules is suspected, at which point they could, in effect, squash an initiative. The group can also include people with more interest in the project but, again, only some power or influence over it.

The best approach with these people is to keep them supportive of the project, possibly by frequent, positive communication with them but perhaps also by involving them more with the project.

No interest but high power/influence

These are probably very senior managers who, for one reason or another, have no direct interest in the project. This may be because it is too small or unimportant for them to bother with or it may be that it is in an area that does not interest them; the group marketing director, for instance, probably will not be concerned about a project to streamline the stationery purchasing procedures. For many purposes, it might be thought that such stakeholders can be ignored, but this is actually a rather risky approach. Our marketing director may, for instance, suddenly get very interested in the stationery system if she keeps getting pens that don't work or can't get hold of any adhesive notes for a conference. So, if a situation arises that might cause them to take a greater interest in the project, we might want to address their needs directly, via one-to-one meetings perhaps, in order to ensure that they do not start to raise concerns or even decide to exert their influence. In some situations it is possible that we may wish to encourage the increased interest of influential stakeholders, for example if we feel that their support would help achieve the project objectives. Where this is the case, we may need to highlight any aspects of the project that will have a direct impact upon the stakeholder's business area; some form of discussion will be required, which, with very influential stakeholders, would typically involve a meeting.

Some interest and high power/influence

These people have some interest in the project – probably an indirect interest caused by the fact that the project is happening within, or affecting, their part of the organisation – and they have real power. The usual stakeholder management strategy here is to keep them satisfied, so that they do not feel the need to take a greater interest in the project. In other circumstances, however, the strategy may be precisely the opposite: to get a stakeholder of this kind more actively involved in the project. For example, if the finance director of an organisation can be persuaded to get positively involved in a project, this involvement will often be a powerful force for success, since the director can make resources available that would otherwise be hard to come by.

High interest and high power/influence

These are the key players, the people who are interested in the project and also have the power to make it work – or not. Often the key players are the managers of the functions directly affected by the project. Initially, it is important to determine whether individual key stakeholders are positive or negative in their attitudes to a project. If they are positive then their enthusiasm must be sustained, especially during a time of difficulty. It is also important to appreciate the concerns and opinions of key stakeholders, and this will need to be taken into account when making any recommendations. For example, if one of the key stakeholders has a particular solution in mind it is important to know about it as early as possible in order to ensure that, at the very least, this solution is evaluated as one of the options. It is also vital that the key stakeholders understand the progress of the project and why certain decisions have been made. These are the people to whom any final recommendations will be presented and who will take the final decisions. They need to be kept informed at all stages of the project so that none of the recommendations comes as a shock to them.

Those key players who are negatively inclined towards a project can be managed in various ways, depending on the circumstances. By far the best approach is to find some personal benefits for them in the proposed course of action. Alternatively, a more powerful counter-force must be found to outweigh their negative influence. This might mean engaging the interest of someone in one of the high-power areas of the grid.

Individuals and groups of stakeholders
An individual customer may not be of much concern to, say, a big supermarket chain. However, if such customers write to newspapers, organise petitions and, perhaps, make a lot of complaints to trading standards officers, they can increase their apparent power considerably. A lot of 'people power' can damage even large concerns considerably and force them into major reversals of course. The classic example of this is the mighty Coca-Cola being forced to reintroduce its traditional Coke in the face of a massive worldwide customer revolt against a new formula. Similarly, individual employees can be marginalised by an organisation, but if they are members of a trade union their power is greater. A single civil servant who objects to a policy may be relatively powerless, but if such people 'blow the whistle' to national newspapers they can cause considerable difficulty.

All of these examples illustrate the dangers of mistaking individual weakness for collective weakness. Stakeholders must be considered not just as individuals but also as potential groups.

Summary of stakeholder management strategies
The basic strategies for stakeholder management are summarised in Figure 6.4. However, individual stakeholders will not fit neatly into one of the nine types, and management approaches must be tailored for each. Also, as we shall discuss in the next section, stakeholders do not stay in the same place over time, and so the ways they are managed must be adapted accordingly.

MANAGING STAKEHOLDERS

Stakeholders' positions on the grid in Figure 6.4 do not necessarily stay in the same place during the life of a project. At the most obvious level, a manager may get promoted from a high interest/low power situation to one of being both interested and powerful. Alternatively, a manager who is promoted into a job with a wider remit may lose interest in a project. The circumstances of an organisation may change, so that, for example, senior managers begin to focus more on IT projects. Or a scandal within a competitor may cause a regulator to take a closer interest in all companies in a sector.

This means that stakeholder analysis must be a continuing activity throughout the project – and even afterwards, to find out what the stakeholders thought of the final outcome. The project team and project manager should be constantly on the lookout for changes in stakeholders' positions and should be re-evaluating their management strategies accordingly. Once stakeholders' initial positions have been plotted, a plan should be drawn up for what to do with each of them and how to approach it. A one-page assessment can be made for each stakeholder, or, if you want to be able to see all stakeholders at a glance, set up a spreadsheet with columns that have the following headings:

Name of stakeholder
It may also be useful to record each stakeholder's current job title as well as the name.

Current power/influence
This is based on the power/interest grid.

Current interest
This is based on the power/interest grid.

Issues and interests
This is a brief summary of what interests each stakeholder and what we believe their main issues with the project are likely to be.

Current attitude
Here we need to devise a classification scheme, perhaps using the following descriptions:

- **champion:** will actively work for the success of the project;
- **supporter:** in favour of the project, but will probably not be very active in promoting it;
- **neutral:** has expressed no opinion either in favour of or against the project;
- **critic:** not in favour of the project but probably not actively opposed to it;
- **opponent:** will work actively to disrupt, impede or derail the project;
- **blocker:** will just obstruct progress, maybe for reasons outside the project itself.

Desired support
Here we record what we would ideally like from this stakeholder, perhaps using a simple scale of high, medium or low.

Desired role

We may wish to get this stakeholder actively involved in the project, perhaps as its sponsor or as part of a steering committee.

Desired actions

What we would like the stakeholder to do, if at all possible, to advance the project.

Messages to convey

This is where we define the emphasis that should be used in any communication with this stakeholder. For example, we might need to identify any issues that are of particular interest to the stakeholder. The 'messages' are likely to be tailored to each individual, so the more we know about the stakeholders and their concerns, the more effective our communications will be.

Actions and communications

This is the most important part of the plan, where we define exactly what actions we will take with regard to this stakeholder. Our action may just be to keep them informed, in a positive way, about the project and progress to date. Alternatively, it may be a more active approach, for example meeting them to engage their interest in the project. Where a strategy has been devised with the aim of changing a stakeholder's position – perhaps to encourage someone to take a closer interest – then its success must also be evaluated and other approaches developed if the desired results are not being achieved. We mentioned earlier that the high interest/high power stakeholders – the key players – require positive management, such as frequent meetings, in order to make sure that they are kept informed about a project and are happy with the approach that we are taking.

STAKEHOLDER VIEWS

Once we have identified and analysed the different stakeholders, we can begin to think about their views with regard to the business system under investigation. It is likely that the stakeholders will have different perspectives on the situation and will feel that the focus should be on different areas of priority. We need to consider the stakeholders' business perspectives, since they can have such a significant impact on the project and can lead to conflicts if they are not addressed. One of the key points is to understand the world views held by different stakeholders, because this helps us to uncover their values and priorities. It is useful to expand upon this by analysing the business perspectives in greater detail. Chapter 7 explores the CATWOE technique, originally devised by Peter Checkland, which is often used to develop business perspectives.

DEFINING STAKEHOLDER INVOLVEMENT – RACI AND RASCI CHARTS

Apart from deciding on the management strategy for the various stakeholders, it can also be very useful in a business analysis project to consider the tasks or deliverables involved, and ask what the involvement of the stakeholders will be for each. A simple and effective method for achieving this is to create a RACI chart, as illustrated in Figure 6.5.

Figure 6.5 Example of a RACI chart

	Project sponsor	Senior user	Business actor (user)	Domain expert	Project manager	Business analyst
R = Responsible A = Accountable C = Consulted I = Informed						
Business case	A	C	I	C	R	C
Project initiation document	A				R	
Interview notes	I	C	C	C	A	R
Notes from workshops	I	C	C	C	A	R
Requirements catalogue	I	C	C	C	A	R
Use case diagram	I	C	C	C	A	R
Use case descriptions	I	C	C	C	A	R
Class diagram	I	C	C	C	A	R

A RACI (responsible, accountable, consulted and informed) chart – more formally known as a linear responsibility matrix – lists the main products or deliverables down the side and the various stakeholders along the top. Where a stakeholders intersect with products, we indicate their involvement with them as follows:

- **Responsible:** This is the person or role responsible for creating or developing the product or performing the task. In Figure 6.5, for example, a business analyst is responsible for creating the interview notes.
- **Accountable:** This is the person or role who will 'carry the can' for the quality of the product or task. The project sponsor, for instance, must ultimately be accountable for the business case for a project.

- **Consulted:** This person or role provides information that is input to the product or task. In Figure 6.5 the senior user, other business actors and the domain expert are shown as being consulted during the interviews and workshops.

- **Informed:** These stakeholders are informed about a product or task, although they may not have contributed directly to it. For example, the project sponsor has the right to be kept informed about any of the products created during the project.

A RASCI chart, as shown in Figure 6.6, uses a similar approach but has an additional category, S, for 'supportive'. This is used when a person (or role) will provide assistance, and sometimes resources, to whoever is responsible for the product or deliverable. For example, in Figure 6.6 the business analyst is shown as supporting the project manager in the creation of the project initiation document and the database administrator supports the business analyst in developing the class diagram.

Figure 6.6 Example of a RASCI chart

	Project sponsor	Senior user	Business actor (user)	Domain expert	Project manager	Business analyst	Database administrator
R = Responsible A = Accountable S = Support C = Consulted I = Informed							
Business case	A	C	I	C	R	C	
Project initiation document	A				R	S	
Interview notes	I	C	C	C	A	R	
Notes from workshops	I	C	C	C	A	R	
Requirements catalogue	I	C	C	C	A	R	
Use case diagram	I	C	C	C	A	R	
Use case descriptions	I	C	C	C	A	R	
Class diagram	I	C	C	C	A	R	S

SUMMARY

Effective stakeholder management is key to the success of any business analysis project. It should begin before the project starts, at the inception stage, and be continued throughout the project – and even afterwards, in order to ensure that the changes are implemented effectively. Although the project manager has the key responsibility in this area, all team members have roles to play. Stakeholders can be assessed in terms of their interest in the project and their power or influence over it, and strategies for managing them actively must be defined in accordance with this assessment.

FURTHER READING

Cadle, J., Paul, D. and Turner, P. (2010) *Business Analysis Techniques*. BCS, Swindon.

Johnson, G., Scholes, K. and Whittington, R. (2008) *Exploring Corporate Strategy*, 8th edn. FT Prentice Hall, Harlow.

Pinto, J.K. (1998) *The PMI Project Management Handbook*. Jossey-Bass, San Francisco, CA.

Stanton, N. (2009) *Mastering Communication*, 5th edn. Palgrave Macmillan.

Turner, J.R. (1998) *The Handbook of Project-Based Management*, 2nd edn. McGraw-Hill, London.

Turner, J.R. and Simister, S.J. (2000) *Handbook of Project Management*, 3rd edn. Gower, Aldershot.

Zuker, E. (1991) *The Seven Secrets of Influence*. McGraw-Hill.

7 MODELLING BUSINESS SYSTEMS

Dot Tudor

INTRODUCTION

Business analysts are usually trying to improve business situations that are seen as being in some way problematic. They begin by making sure that they have a good understanding of the situation under investigation, including all of the issues raised by stakeholders. In Chapter 5 we discussed the techniques that are used to investigate existing business situations and to document the issues that are uncovered. While investigating a business situation, we also identify the stakeholders involved and begin to understand their thoughts and ideas about the situation. In Chapter 6 we described techniques that are helpful when identifying, analysing and managing stakeholders, and considered the issues arising from the stakeholders' different business perspectives. In this chapter we take that a step further, and look at an approach that may be used to examine the stakeholders' views in more detail. There will be different views, different needs, different priorities or even hidden agendas, and it is important that we understand all of them before getting down to defining the new business system. Business analysts often have to take a broader view and consider why an organisation – or part of an organisation – operates as it does and what it is trying to achieve. Techniques for understanding and modelling the 'why' and the 'what' of business systems are the subject of this chapter.

To illustrate why we need to explore the 'why' and 'what' of an organisation, let us consider a business that makes and sells pens. Obviously the purchasers use the pens to write with, but, beyond that, the pen manufacturer could be aiming at different markets. They might be:

- offering well-engineered, reliable but cheap ballpoint pens for sale in bulk to commercial customers;
- creating desirable luxury goods that appeal to affluent and design-conscious buyers.

In the first case the emphasis of the company will be on efficient and effective production and wholesale processes. In the second case there will be an emphasis on stylish design, brand marketing and sales through specialist retailers and good department stores. But which approach should the company adopt?

Of course, the overall direction of the company will – or should – be the subject of the business strategy. But a business strategy, whilst taking business environment considerations into account, is also influenced by the vision that senior management has of the business. Any business analysis project must operate in the light of the core values and beliefs of the organisation in which it is being undertaken. At an organisational level these beliefs are often expressed using the MOST (mission, objectives, strategy and tactics) structure, as explored in Chapter 3. It is important to be familiar with the MOST model for the organisation, since any change must be in support of, or at least not counter to, this expression of organisational intent. However, the MOST reflects the core values of the organisation as a whole, and, even assuming that everyone in the organisation shares these values, which is by no means always the case, there is usually plenty of room for divergences in interpretation and implementation by stakeholders within different departments or business units. We call these divergent stakeholder views 'business perspectives'.

Understanding different stakeholder beliefs is extremely relevant to business analysts and will influence the types of business changes recommended, and, ultimately, the nature of the business processes that are required. Before going on to model the business processes, therefore, we need to be clear about the values and beliefs of stakeholders concerned with implementing the organisation's business strategy. We can use this understanding to develop models of desired future business systems, which we can then assess against the current real-world situation.

SOFT SYSTEMS METHODOLOGY

This whole issue of why an organisation does what it does was the subject of much study by Peter Checkland and a team he led at Lancaster University (Checkland 1981). This work led to the development of the soft systems methodology (SSM). Checkland followed the tradition of systems thinking developed through the work of writers such as Stafford Beer, and proposed that business situations should be considered as systems. He also showed that much previous work in this area had taken a 'hard' approach and had assumed that the goals and objectives of such systems were clear. Such hard systems thinking required the analyst to follow a systematic approach in order to correct problems and thereby make the system more efficient. This contrasted with the reality of business situations, where problems are rarely clear-cut and there is usually plenty of room for differences of opinion about the nature of the business problem, let alone on the question of where suitable solutions might be found.

As an alternative to the hard systems thinking approach, Checkland proposed what he called the soft systems model, the main features of which are illustrated in Figure 7.1.

As shown in Figure 7.1, SSM begins with an investigation into a real world situation of concern. Checkland proposed a technique known as a 'rich picture' to document

Figure 7.1 Checkland's soft systems methodology

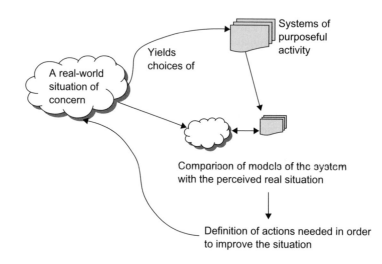

such situations; this technique was described in Chapter 5. The investigation of the situation is followed by speculation about different 'world views', each of which would give rise to a conceptual system that could shape the future for the business situation. These possible systems can then be used to identify opportunities for improvement when they are compared with the situation that exists. The different world views may be derived following discussions with stakeholders or may be conceived by the analysts based upon their views about the situation. In the SSM each view is developed and formulated as a sentence. Checkland named these sentences 'root definitions', but we prefer the term 'business perspective'. Different stakeholders may identify different systems based upon their beliefs and values with regard to the business area in question. The differences between these systems may be considered by examining the models representing the systems and considering where they overlap, where they are in conflict with each other or where gaps exist. This approach can lead to the development of a consensus model, where a desired future system is built; this model can then be used to explore possible improvements to the existing situation.

One important element of Checkland's systems thinking that the business analyst needs to bear in mind is that a system with all of its components working together will have characteristics that are not the characteristics of any one component. These are known as its 'emergent properties', a term that reflects the fact that the whole system is more than the sum of all of its parts. For example, if we consider a car as a system that allows you to travel, the movement along the correct roads at the right speed is an emergent property requiring engine, suspension, steering, the driver and a whole host of other parts in order to be successful. The engine alone could not achieve this; all of the parts individually could not achieve it. The business analyst must be aware of the emergent properties in any recommended business changes, since they may be undesirable as well as desirable.

BUSINESS PERSPECTIVES

The starting point in identifying and analysing business perspectives is the stakeholder analysis that was discussed in Chapter 6. The key stakeholders should be asked how they view, from their own perspectives, the purpose and objectives of the part of the organisation that is within the scope of the change project. For example:

- Bank tellers handling customers' needs in a branch of a bank may see their area of the business as 'a system to provide customers with an accurate and speedy service, whilst maintaining security of cash'.

- A business development manager in the same branch may perceive 'a system to encourage customers and potential customers to use the investment facilities offered by the bank'.

Notice that the bank teller, being faced with customers directly, views the customer service as particularly important, whereas the manager views business development as the main priority. We might consider which perspective is 'right', but it is likely that they both are, and that in studying the bank's business system the analysts must take both into account.

The SSM offers a useful framework for defining and analysing business perspectives, given by the mnemonic CATWOE. The elements of CATWOE are:

- **C = customer:** the beneficiary of the transformation, the recipient of the system's end product or the person or group on the receiving end of its services.

- **A = actor:** those responsible for performing the business activities within the scope of the view being considered. Actors could be within the organisation (in other words, they represent job roles) or they could be outside the organisation, for example business partners such as distribution firms or offshore IT suppliers.

- **T = transformation:** the activity that lies at the heart of the system, transforming the input to the resulting output. It encapsulates the core business processes that are carried out to transform an input into an output of value to the customer.

- **W = *Weltanschauung* or world view:** an encapsulation of the individual's beliefs about the organisation or business system, or in other words their views as to why it exists and what it should be doing.

- **O = owner:** the person, or group of people, who can take major decisions about the business system, who could change its direction or who could in the most extreme case cause it to cease to exist.

- **E = environment:** the conditions and rules under which the system must operate that are outside the control of the owner and that must be regarded as 'givens'. The PESTLE analysis we met in Chapter 3 provides a tool for identifying many of the environmental factors here. Internal business policies may also be relevant if they are to be regarded as fixed and unchangeable.

Let us consider our first banking example again and analyse it using CATWOE:

- **Customer:** people with accounts at the branch, or at other branches of the same bank, who visit the branch to make an account transaction.

- **Actors:** bank tellers; back office staff and branch management.

- **Transformation:** the means of making a change from a state where there are customers who require one or more of a variety of banking services to one where there are satisfied customers who have received appropriate services. This encompasses the provision of bank counter services such as cash deposit and withdrawal, answering account enquiries and setting up standing orders.

- *Weltanschauung:* customers continue to deal through a bank branch, rather than by phone or over the internet, because they value personal service and human contact and find a physical branch convenient.

- **Owner:** the senior management – possibly the chief executive – of the bank. (It is better to identify an individual for this rather than a group, for the sake of clarity about where authority and accountability for the system lies.)

- **Environment:** government policies on banking regulation (P); global banking crisis (E); increasing use of online services (S); electronic funds transfer (T); the attitude of financial regulators (L) and the behaviour of anti-capitalist protesters (E).

When using CATWOE, it is important to begin by understanding the *Weltanschauung* or world view, since this encapsulates the beliefs that underpin the rest of the CATWOE. After this it is useful to define the transformation and the customer, and then to consider the actors, owner and environment.

Checkland's root definition is developed as a sentence that ties the CATWOE elements together. For the example given above, this would be as follows:

> The branch is a system controlled by the bank chief executive (O), where bank tellers, back office staff and branch management (A) provide branch customers (C) who require personal service with bank counter services such as cash deposit and withdrawal, answering account enquiries and setting up standing orders, in order to satisfy their banking needs (T) within constraints imposed by government policies on banking regulation, the global banking crisis, increasing use of online services, increasing electronic funds transfer and increased regulation by financial regulators (E).

Sometimes the perspectives developed for key stakeholders are so different that further progress is impossible. For instance, if one director of a company said that they were in the grocery business but another asserted that they sold stationery, then clearly it would be difficult to get any further in the analysis unless and until these different views were reconciled or one stakeholder was able to over-rule the other. In our experience, however, the differences are more often ones of emphasis and priorities within the same business area. In this case the implications of the perspectives can be developed using business activity models, and these can then be used to consider what the organisation is about and to generate discussion about the nature of any changes.

BUSINESS ACTIVITY MODELS

So what is a business activity model (BAM)? Well, it is not a model of the organisation's business processes; such models are described in the next chapter. A BAM is essentially a 'conceptual model' (the term used by Checkland) that shows the business activities we would expect to see in place, given the business perspective from which it has been developed, in order to achieve the transformation successfully. Developing a BAM therefore requires the analyst to use both analytical ability and creative thought.

We need to ignore – as far as we can – what is actually going on in the organisation now, and instead should consider what ought to be present based on the business perspective. In effect the BAM develops the business perspective, or root definition, to reveal the activities that comprise the system envisaged by the stakeholder. The principles underlying the BAM approach are as follows:

- There will be one BAM for each business perspective.
- A separate BAM is needed to describe each perspective. These will subsequently be overlaid to form a consensus model, possibly covering all relevant perspectives.
- The BAM helps in the analysis of the business situation and the identification of improvements.
- The model is not concerned with who carries out the activities or where they are carried out.

All business systems can be described in terms of five types of business activity and the dependencies between them. These types of activity are:

- planning activities;
- enabling activities;
- doing activities;
- monitoring activities;
- control activities.

We can use these five activity types as a basis for developing a BAM.

Planning activities
These define the rules dictating the type of resources required and how the performance of these resources is to be measured. In a company providing high-quality holidays to customers, the planning activities could include deciding the number of staff required and the skills they should have, deciding the marketing

policy and so on. Within the planning activities, performance expectations should also be set. For example, if we identify a planning activity as 'decide staffing requirements', then we would expect this activity to include metrics (KPIs) for staff numbers and the required skills. If our *Weltanschauung* for this organisation is based upon a belief about customers wanting high-quality holidays then this would affect the decisions made about staffing. Customer service would be important; this might mean ensuring that there are sufficient staff so that customers do not have to wait to be dealt with, and that the staff have excellent customer relationship skills. We would expect these factors to be reflected in the performance targets.

Enabling activities

These ensure that the resources and facilities needed by the doing activities are obtained and deployed. Resources include raw materials, infrastructure, staff and so on. For our travel company, these could include recruiting and training the staff with the required skills, attracting customers, negotiating rates with hotels and so on. The planning activities would influence how the enabling activities are carried out. For example, we would expect the activity 'recruit staff' to take account of the planning decisions about staffing requirements.

Doing activities

These relate directly to achieving the transformation described in the business perspective, and are sometimes also referred to as 'primary task' activities. They contribute directly to the purpose of the business system. In our travel company the transformation required could be 'convert potential holidaymakers into happy, paid-up holiday-goers'. Doing activities to support this would include booking high-quality holidays and supplying detailed travel plans.

Monitoring activities

These collect metrics to check the performance of other activities against the targets, and use the performance expectations set as part of the planning activities. Such activities could include logging enquiries and holidays booked and comparing these with conversion targets, and recording sales against each salesperson and comparing them with individual sales targets. As we are concerned with delivering high-quality holidays, we would also want to monitor the level of customer satisfaction with aspects such as the service provided, the hotels and the airlines.

Control activities

These act on the other activities when monitoring has identified that some action is required. This is usually when performance expectations are not being met, but it could also be when action is felt to be needed, for example if targets are exceeded by a wide margin. Such action may involve changes to any of the activities, including the monitoring activities. For example, if sales targets for a range of products are not being achieved, possible control actions may include reconsidering the price, reviewing the targets or providing additional training to the staff.

Dependencies

In the BAM, activities are connected by arrows. Such arrows represent logical dependency between the activities. This means that for activity B to occur, activity A must have occurred. This relationship allows for the possibility that activity B may be one that happens daily, even though activity A happens monthly.

Modelling notation

The good news here is that there is no universally-agreed notation for creating BAMs, which leaves analysts free to design their own. Soft systems specialists like to use 'cloud' symbols, as illustrated in Figure 7.2, since these emphasise the essentially conceptual nature of the model. However, ellipses, as used in Figure 7.3, are quite acceptable, too.

Figure 7.2 BAM notation using 'cloud' symbols

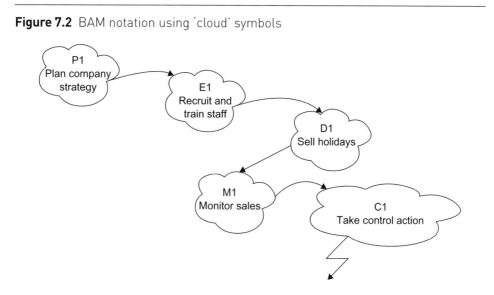

Business activities should be given an identifier, and a title consisting of an imperative verb and a noun – 'do something'. It will be noticed that the control activity in Figure 7.2 has a 'lightning strike' symbol coming out of it. This shows that the actual control action that is taken could feed back anywhere into the model; it might, for instance, involve improving the recruitment process, or changing the way selling is done – or even revisiting the strategy. Trying to model all of these possibilities with individual lines would result in an impossibly cluttered model that would obscure rather than illuminate what the organisation should be doing.

In the more complete BAM shown in Figure 7.3, the travel company's core belief, which underpins the model, is that customers want high-quality holidays that deliver a high level of service. Hence, the monitoring activities focus on checking the level of customer satisfaction, plus the hotel and airline performance, in line with predefined targets. This is in addition to monitoring both sales and profitability levels to make sure that providing high-quality holidays is an appropriate profit-earning strategy.

Developing a BAM

As we have mentioned, creating a BAM involves the use of both business knowledge and creativity on the part of the analyst. The *Weltanschauung* or world view

Figure 7.3 BAM for a travel company

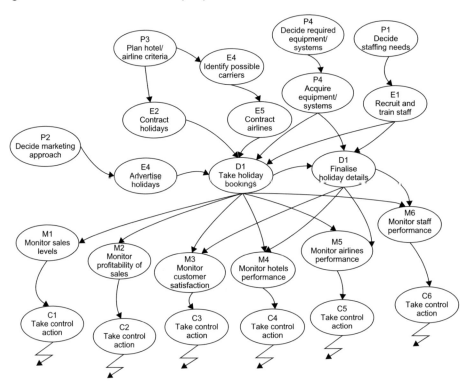

must be kept in mind when building the BAM, since this is the set of beliefs that the model will fulfil. BAMs can be developed in the following way:

(i) Begin by identifying the main **doing activities.** This can be done by referring to the transformation contained in the business perspective. The activities in the BAM must fulfil the need for the transformation.

(ii) Look for **enabling activities** that need to be in place to provide the resources that will allow the doing activities to function.

(iii) Identify **planning activities,** which need to do two things: first, to decide upon the resources to be provided, and second, to define the performance targets that must be met using these resources. You need to consider the *Weltanschauung* to understand the resources that will be required and the performance expectations.

(iv) Add **monitoring activities** to compare actual with planned performance. These monitor the expectations defined by the planning activities.

(v) Add **control activities** to respond to deviations between actual and planned performance.

(vi)   Where environmental constraints are referred to in the business perspective, activities should be added to consider the constraints, (planning activities), to measure performance in relation to them (monitoring activities) and to react to any threat of failure to comply with them (control activities).

(vii) Add dependency arrows between the activities, showing which activities are **dependent** on others.

(viii) Add 'lightning strike' **control** arrows from the controlling activities to indicate the control feedback loop.

Producing a consensus model

The BAMs produced up to this point have each been derived from an individual business perspective derived from a key stakeholder. Potentially, therefore, we could at this point have several BAMs, each representing a slightly different view of the organisation or business system. Our eventual goal is to derive just one definitive BAM of the activities needed by the business, by merging the individual models into one. This model is described as a 'consensus model'.

To arrive at a consensus model, the business analyst must resolve any conflict between the various views that have caused the creation of the separate, different models. In order to achieve this, we must examine the necessity for each activity in each BAM and combine those that are agreed to be necessary by the stakeholders into a consensus model. This is often easier said than done, because all stakeholders have beliefs that underlie their viewpoints, and they genuinely may not be able to appreciate the others' points of view. It may require skilful facilitation to enable each to accept other perspectives as valid.

There are three kinds of consensus that we might consider:

- Global consensus, which assumes there is a neutral model applicable to all organisations of a particular type. For example, all commercial businesses have activities related to purchasing, sales, marketing and finance.

- One hundred per cent consensus, where all the participants readily agree that a given activity, often one that is common to all individual models, is needed.

- Consensus through accommodation, where participants with conflicting viewpoints agree to compromise. The creation of additional activities and/or the modification of existing ones may be necessary in order to achieve this kind of consensus or compromise.

The process of creating the consensus model is best carried out in a controlled and facilitated workshop environment, where views can be expressed openly and conflict resolved in a fair manner. A consensus model workshop should aim to:

- create a tentative consensus model, by combining all individual BAM activities, events and dependencies;

- derive a new, consensus business perspective for the area of study;

- test the tentative model against the new business perspective, adding, removing or modifying activities as necessary, in order to satisfy the consensus view;

- finally, check the consensus model to ensure that it fully satisfies the new business perspective and the objectives of the area of study and the change project.

By deriving a consensus model in this way, we have identified not only areas of agreement but also differences and areas of misunderstanding. The resulting consensus BAM is a powerful and effective tool for communication, focusing on the activities without the clutter of real-world constraints. The development and discussion of this will provide the business analyst with a vehicle for eliciting and clarifying requirements.

BUSINESS EVENTS AND BUSINESS RULES

One way of analysing a BAM is to consider the business events to which the organisation must respond, and the business rules that underpin and constrain the business operations. This information is also very useful when redesigning business processes.

Business events
Business events happen in the real world. For example, customers place orders, suppliers send in invoices and employees resign. All of these events trigger the business system to do something – typically an activity or a series of activities – in order to respond to the event. The approach selected for business activity modelling must have a means of documenting business events and relating them to the activities that they trigger. In effect, a business event tells us when a business activity should be triggered; it sparks into life the process that carries out the activity. Hence, identifying the business events will help us to think about the processes that form the business system response to them.

There are three types of business event to consider:

- **External:** these events originate from outside the boundary of the business system. In our travel company, an external event would be a prospective customer telephoning with a holiday enquiry. Other, less welcome, external events would include a customer arriving at the company's front door with a complaint or one of our chosen hotels going bankrupt.

- **Internal decision points:** these events are usually internal decisions made by business managers. For example, the senior management of the travel firm decides to award discounts for holidays that are to be taken within the next month. This event would be the result of an internal decision rather than an external occurrence.

- **Scheduled points in time:** these are the events that occur regularly. For example, at the start of each day the travel agency staff produce travel documents for holidays that are due to begin two weeks later.

Figure 7.4 Business event triggering activities

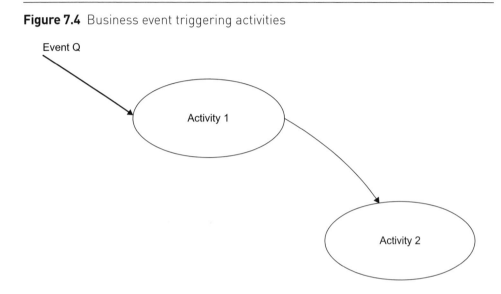

Event Q

Activity 1

Activity 2

In the BAM, events can be recorded as inward arrows that point to an activity but have no source, since they do not originate from another activity. Some business events may trigger more than one activity, and some activities may be triggered by more than one business event. Figure 7.4 shows two activities triggered by one event.

Business rules

For the activities identified in the BAM, there will be rules governing their performance. It is important that these rules are considered when modelling the processing to carry out the activity. Rules are of two main types:

- **Constraints:** these restrict how an activity is performed. They may include laws and regulations and – if these cannot be challenged – business policies.

- **Operational guidance:** these describe the procedural rules that dictate how activities should be performed. An example for our travel organisation would be the guidance on how to calculate discounts on holidays where there is a group booking.

The business rules would emerge in discussion of the activities with stakeholders and should be documented to support the BAM.

CRITICAL SUCCESS FACTORS AND KEY PERFORMANCE INDICATORS

Another useful way of approaching BAM construction is to consider the organisation's CSFs and KPIs.

The CSFs are the things the organisation must be good at in order to succeed, and they therefore provide some insights into the planning, enabling and doing activities that are needed. For example, 'excellent customer service' may be a CSF – in which case the recruitment, training and retention of good customer-service staff may be needed on the BAM.

The KPIs are the things an organisation measures to find out how well it is doing. These may be identified by considering the planning activities in the BAM. Checking up on the KPIs should therefore be reflected in the BAM's monitoring activities.

VALIDATING A BUSINESS ACTIVITY MODEL

The following checklist, derived from the work of Peter Checkland (1981), provides a series of checks to see whether a business activity model is complete and at least internally consistent. The checklist consists of the following:

- **Objectives and purpose (of the system):** these must be explicit.
- **Connectivity:** the activities in the model must all be connected. If they are not, then they represent separate systems.
- **Measures of performance:** these must exist, and expected levels of performance must be set.
- **Monitoring and control mechanisms:** there must be control activities that have the power to change other activities when expectations are not met.
- **Decision-making procedures:** there must be decision-making procedures that will be influenced by the control actions.
- **Boundary:** the extent of the system must be clear and communications across the boundary defined explicitly.
- **Resources:** staff, materials and other resources used by the system must be acquired, allocated, replenished and accounted for.
- **Systems hierarchy:** it should be possible to decompose the system hierarchically based on the scope of control activity. Any business activity should be within the scope of only one control activity. If not, then additional activities need to be introduced to resolve any conflict.

USE OF THE BUSINESS ACTIVITY MODEL IN GAP ANALYSIS

Although the analysis of business problems, and devising solutions, is the subject of other chapters, it is useful to understand how you can use the BAM to identify high-level business problems and issues. The BAM represents a theoretical (conceptual) model of the activities we would expect to find in place given the initial business perspective. When we compare the BAM with the current reality in the organisation, we will find the following:

- Some activities are in place and are quite satisfactory. Therefore, little needs to be done about these, except perhaps to make sure that they are not lost in our proposed changes.

- Some activities are in place but are not satisfactory. This could be because the processes they represent are poor, there are organisational issues associated with them – they are carried out in the wrong department, for instance – or there are problems with the people involved. It could also be that these activities are poorly supported by the current information systems. In any of these cases, there will be opportunities for business improvement.

- Some activities are not in place at all. In this case, there will again be implications for the organisation and opportunities for beneficial change.

SUMMARY

In this chapter we have made a journey that began with understanding that any business situation may be considered from different perspectives. Each of these perspectives is based upon the core values and beliefs held by different stakeholders. By taking into account the differing viewpoints of key stakeholders, we have explored how you might develop a model of the business activities, including the key events and the business rules. We have also explained how you might derive a consensus model encompassing the different stakeholder perspectives, and we have shown how the BAM can provide a powerful analytical tool to identify problems in an organisation and opportunities for improvement.

REFERENCES

Checkland, P. (1981) *Systems Thinking, Systems Practice.* John Wiley & Sons, Chichester.

FURTHER READING

Bowman, C. and Faulkner, D. (1996) *Competitive and Corporate Strategy.* Irwin, Homewood, IL.

Checkland, P. and Poulter, J. (2006) *Learning for Action: A Short Definitive Account of Soft Systems Methodology.* John Wiley & Sons, Chichester.

Checkland, P. and Scholes, J. (1999) *Soft Systems Methodology in Action.* John Wiley & Sons, Chichester.

Rummler, G. and Brache, A. (1990) *Improving Performance.* Jossey-Bass, San Francisco, CA.

Wilson, B. (1990) *Systems: Concepts, Methodologies and Applications,* 2nd edn. John Wiley & Sons, Chichester.

8 MODELLING BUSINESS PROCESSES

Keith Hindle

INTRODUCTION

The business processes are the means by which an organisation carries out its internal operations and delivers its products and services to its customers. In this chapter we will look at techniques for modelling business processes, covering both the organisational view of process modelling and the more detailed business process models.

There are many reasons for creating business process models, including:

- To understand how the existing process works. This can be particularly useful if the process has 'grown' organically (without any real planning) and no one is quite sure what happens currently in response to an event.

- To explain to those working on the process what they do and how their tasks relate to those of others working on the process. Here the process model can be a training aid for new staff and an aide-memoire or reminder for more experienced personnel.

- To help ensure consistency of approach, so that everyone follows the same process. For example, customers' experiences are not wholly dependent on the 'luck of the draw' as to who is dealing with them.

- To identify the problems and weaknesses of an existing business process with a view to developing and implementing an improved one. A model of an existing business process is often called an 'as is' model and the improved one a 'to be' model.

ORGANISATIONAL CONTEXT

A typical organisation has numerous processes, many of which could be improved in some way or other. The costs and benefits of such improvement projects will vary enormously. Before embarking on a business process improvement project, it is useful to examine the organisational context in which the business processes take place. An understanding of the context will also help in understanding how the process is affected by external environmental factors.

The traditional view of a business is based on the specialist functional areas such as sales, accounts and operations. Typically, this is documented on an organisation chart that shows the departments and how they are further subdivided, the reporting lines and the staff who work in the various areas. Individual employees tend to identify with a particular function – 'I work in IT' – because that defines not just the job that they do but also their social group, attitudes and culture.

Figure 8.1 Functional view of an organisation

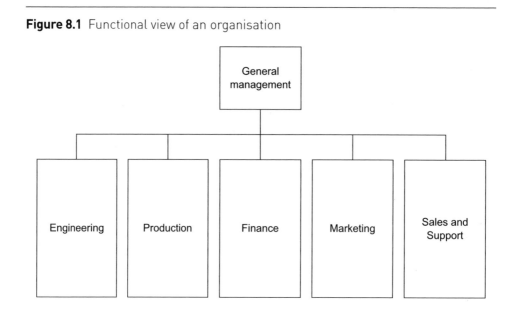

The functional view of an organisation, as shown in Figure 8.1, is very useful for the internal management and staff as a way of seeing how the organisation is structured and where they fit within it. However, there are some limitations with this view. It is predominantly internally oriented, concentrating on the structure of the organisation and the internal reporting lines, aspects that are usually of little interest to the organisation's customers. Moreover, it defines the formal structure, ignoring the unofficial communication and cooperation between staff that can be just as important for success. The functional view is also 'static', since it does not show what the business does over time in order to react to an event such as a customer's request for a service.

The static nature of the functional view contrasts sharply with the process view. The people carrying out the tasks within a process could well belong to several different functions and may need to pass information or products across functional boundaries. For example:

(i)   A customer may first tell a salesperson the details of an order.

(ii) The order is then passed on to warehouse staff, who have to physically make it up.

(iii) The result is then collected by logistics staff.

(iv) The goods are delivered to the customer.

The process view emphasises the need for cooperation between all of the participants if the desired level of customer service is to be achieved. Thinking of the organisation as separate, autonomous departments may erect barriers and create operational difficulties that a more joined-up approach can overcome.

AN ALTERNATIVE VIEW OF AN ORGANISATION

Paul Harmon developed the organisation model, which provides an alternative view of an organisation, representing both the internal processes and the external world with which the organisation operates. The model is often developed in two stages: first the external factors that influence the organisation are considered and then the internal business process is analysed.

Figure 8.2 Organisation model (after Harmon 2007)

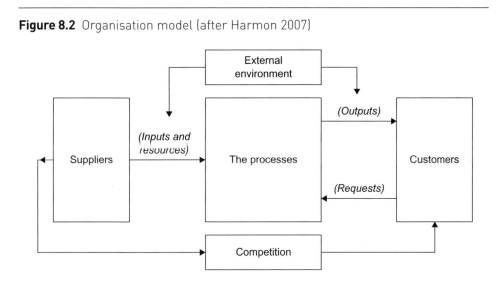

The four areas shown outside the organisation in Figure 8.2 highlight those aspects of the external environment that need to be considered; they define the context in which the organisation operates. These four areas are:

- The suppliers of the resources required by the business processes. This covers not only the supply of physical materials but also external suppliers of finance, people and ideas.

- The beneficiaries of the organisation. While we always include the customers who purchase the products and services within this group, it is also important to take a broader view and include the owners and managers of the organisation. The owners will vary depending upon the type of organisation. For example, in a commercial business there may be shareholders, whereas in a not-for-profit organisation there will be a board of trustees. For each group of beneficiaries we need to know the outcomes that they would like the organisation to deliver. These outcomes are often in conflict with each other; where customers would like prices to be as low as possible, shareholders would like to have high dividends, which they may see resulting from higher prices.

- The competitors operating within the same industry or business domain. Traditionally this is interpreted to mean those other organisations with whom we are competing in specific markets. In the organisational model we extend the concept further by including those organisations with which we are competing for the supply of finance, skilled staff and ideas as well as customers.

- The generic factors that may affect the organisation, such as changing regulation, economics or green issues. These are factors of the type covered by a PESTLE analysis, as explained in Chapter 3.

Analysing the external context shown on the organisation model encourages the business analyst to think carefully about the context for the organisation. For example:

- What resources does it require in order to operate? Are these plentiful or are they in short supply? Against whom is it competing for scarce resources?

- Who are the major competitors for the purchasing customers? What do their processes offer, and can we improve on this?

- What are the factors in the external environment that condition or constrain the way we can operate?

- Who are the owners of the organisation that we need to satisfy? This is not always an easy question to answer; for example, in the case of a state school does this mean the governors? The local education authority? Central government? We may need to consider all of them.

- Who exactly are the organisation's customers? What do they require from it? How demanding are they?

The organisation's business processes need to operate within this external environment. If we are carrying out a business process improvement project it is important to understand this business context, since this will help us determine the changes that will deliver business success.

THE ORGANISATIONAL VIEW OF BUSINESS PROCESSES

Now that we have understood the circumstances in which the business operates, we can turn our attention to what the business does when reacting to the external environment. Bearing in mind that the organisation model is a high-level view of the processes that operate across the entire business, we need to show the end-to-end set of processes that convert the inputs from the suppliers to the outputs for the customers. It is possible to identify the high-level processes by discussion with the staff and managers of the organisation.

Figure 8.3 A process receiving input and producing output

An organisational business process map is formed from a high-level set of activities carried out in order to deliver benefit or value to the customers, as shown in Figure 8.2. Each process receives an input and produces an output, as shown in Figure 8.3.

When building business process models, we can begin by producing a business process map that follows the structure shown in Figure 8.3. An example is shown in Figure 8.4.

Figure 8.4 Outline process map

It is important to distinguish between process maps and business process models. Process maps show sets of related processes in a single diagram. Each process set is shown as a box, and the arrows between them show their interdependencies. Business process models show a more detailed view of each of the processes within a higher-level set.

It is useful to begin by considering:

- the core operation at the heart of the entire process, for example 'take bookings' or 'sell goods';
- the processes that provide input to the core process, for example 'schedule events' or 'make goods';
- the processes concerned with delivering products or services to the customer, for example 'issue event confirmation' or 'deliver goods';
- any sales, marketing or customer-service processes.

The process map in Figure 8.5 shows the processes for the internal lending library of a consultancy company. The library provides a service to in-house staff ('Loan item'). The 'Loan item' process cannot take place unless the person requesting the loan is a registered borrower.

Figure 8.5 Process map for a library service

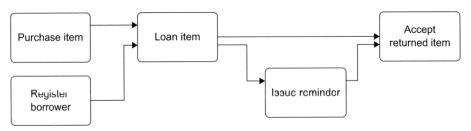

Although we will not have full details about each process at this point, we can find out the events that trigger the process, the customer of that process and the results required. For example, if we consider 'Register borrower':

- The process will take place each week, on receipt of information from HR detailing all the staff changes. This will allow the library both to add and to delete borrowers.

- The customers will be the members of staff who are registered and the HR department, which wants new employees to be added and employees who have left to be deleted.

- The results required are the successful addition or removal of employees, possibly within a prescribed timeframe.

Once a loan has been made, the subsequent process would normally be 'Accept returned item', but failure to return the item within the specified time period would result in the process 'Issue reminder'.

The overview process map is extremely useful when the analyst starts to model a particular process. It helps to identify the boundaries of each process by showing where the process begins and where it ends. If we use the example of the lending library, the 'Issue reminder' process concludes with the sending of the reminder; it does not include the acceptance of the returned item. If we consider the 'Loan item' process, the customer here is the borrower, and the process objective is achieved when the borrower has successfully completed the loan transaction. The measures applied to this process will typically be concerned with the speed and accuracy of the loan transaction.

An alternative approach to building a process map is to look at the products and services, and consider what processes are required to deliver them.

Michael Porter's value chain is a useful technique here because it helps us to structure our thinking and possibly identify areas of process that we may have missed. The generic value chain is shown in Figure 8.6.

Figure 8.6 Porter's value chain

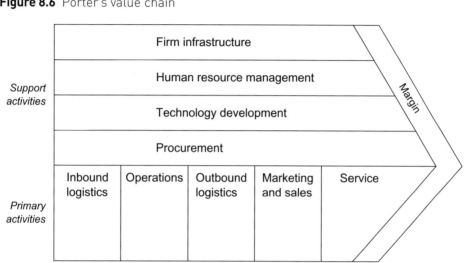

The value chain provides a means of analysing the activities performed by an organisation. It identifies key areas of primary and support activity that will be required to deliver value to the organisation's customers and potentially differentiate the organisation from its competitors. We can use the concept of a value chain to develop high-level process maps for the organisation. Figure 8.7 identifies the value chain activities for a manufacturing organisation, using each of the primary activity sections of the value chain.

When using the value chain, it is usually easiest to start with the operations – the core activity of this value chain – and then consider the other areas. In the example in Figure 8.7, we have a manufacturing organisation and the primary operations activity is 'Make products'. However, we can only do this if we obtain raw materials, so that is the inbound logistics activity. The outbound logistics activity concerns delivery to the end customers. In the marketing and sales area, the organisation needs to promote products and take orders. Finally, the service activity involves providing support to customers, presumably by answering queries and dealing with complaints.

VALUE PROPOSITIONS

The definition of the value chain assumes that we understand the customers who purchase our goods and know what products or services they want. A value

Figure 8.7 Example value-chain activities for a manufacturing organisation

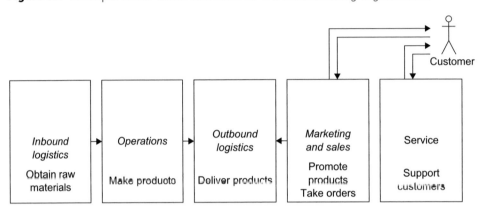

proposition is a definition of an organisation's product or service that will demonstrate to customers that we understand and can satisfy their needs. Moreover, it differentiates organisations from their competitors. Unfortunately, many organisations produce poor value propositions that are bland descriptions of their products rather than being closely aligned with the needs of their customers.

In order to overcome the problem of inappropriate value propositions, Kaplan and Norton, the architects of the balanced business scorecard, have identified the main attributes that make up successful value propositions. These are the drivers that lead to increased customer satisfaction, acquisition and retention. The proposition attributes cover three areas:

- product/service attributes that define the product itself;
- customer relationship aspects;
- image and reputation aspects.

The elements of a value proposition are illustrated in Figure 8.8.

Figure 8.8 Elements of a value proposition

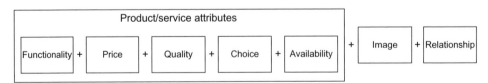

The product attributes are:

- functionality, or what the product does;
- the price that we charge for the product;
- quality, or how well the product performs;
- choice: whether we simply provide a standard product, or whether it can be tailored to the specific needs of the customer;
- availability or timing, for example how quickly we can respond to customer requests, and whether we introduce new products at the most appropriate time.

The customer-relationship aspects will influence how a customer feels about purchasing from the organisation. For example, a supermarket chain may want to emphasise convenient access to their stores as well as knowledgeable staff who have the interests of the customer as their first consideration.

The image may relate to the product, and may be built up through extensive advertising and promotion to suggest that the product has desirable attributes. Alternatively, an organisation may develop an image relating to the customer. For example, a fashion retailer may use advertising to promote an attractive 'typical' customer. Effectively, their message to their customers is 'Buy our clothes and be as attractive and successful as the image in the advertisement'.

It is useful to understand value propositions because they define what the organisation needs to deliver to its customers – and the business processes are the delivery mechanisms for organisations.

An organisation can differentiate itself in three ways, by:

- being the most efficient;
- having the best products;
- providing the best customer service.

Efficiency here means having high volumes, low costs and hence low prices, as, for example, budget airlines do. Having the best products implies high quality but also innovation and the ability to introduce new products before the competition does. Companies such as Apple spring to mind here. High levels of customer service rely on flexibility, which allows the product to be adaptable to the exact needs of the customer, as well as staff that have the attitudes, training and freedom to understand and react to changing customer needs. The clearest examples are at the expensive end of the leisure industry, where suppliers promise to exceed their customers' needs.

When conducting a business process improvement project, having an understanding of the value proposition adopted by the organisation helps analysts to understand the focus and objectives of the business processes. For example, where an organisation prides itself on excellent customer service the processes delivering the service need to be designed to ensure that this is what is delivered.

An alternative view of the value proposition is to consider the customer's perspective. Customers usually know what they expect and will survey the industry to find the organisations that will meet their needs. An understanding of the customers' value proposition helps us to consider how this aligns with the organisational value proposition and can illuminate areas of the business processes that would benefit from improvement.

BUSINESS PROCESS MODELS

A business process is triggered by a business event and includes five key components: the tasks that make up the process, the process flow, the decision points, the actors that carry out the tasks and the outcome of the business process. Unfortunately there is no universally agreed set of terms in business process modelling, and the terms 'process', 'activity', 'task' and 'step' are often used interchangeably. For the sake of simplicity, we have adopted the following conventions here:

- 'Process' refers to an entire set of activities, starting with a triggering event and ending with some output being delivered.

- 'Task' refers to an activity within the overall process that is usually carried out by an actor at a single point in time.

- 'Step' refers to the activities carried out within an individual task. It is useful to show just the tasks on the process model rather than each individual step, because this helps with the readability and clarity of the model. Task descriptions, where the steps within each task are stated, can then be produced.

Developing the business process model

There are many standards for modelling business. Two of the most popular are the UML activity diagram technique and the Business Process Modelling Notation (BPMN). Business process models are often called 'swimlane diagrams' because the 'swimlanes' form a key element of the models. Here we will use the notation and structure from the UML activity diagramming technique to build swimlane diagrams. BPMN also provides a notation and structure for modelling business process.

The swimlane diagramming technique includes the following elements:

- the overall layout;
- the symbols used;
- the sequencing of the symbols;
- the naming of the tasks.

To build a business process model we first identify who takes part in the process. This enables us to identify the business 'actors' or 'roles'. Actors may be individual people, a group of people or an organisation, or an IT system. The tasks carried out

Figure 8.9 Business process model for 'Loan item' process

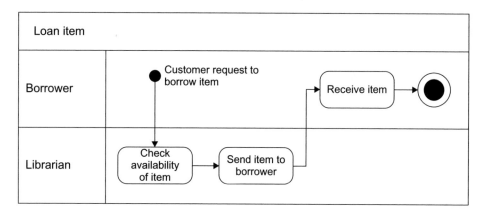

by each actor are shown in a separate band, or 'swimlane', and arrows are used to show the flow of the work between the different swimlanes. Swimlanes usually appear on the diagram in a sequence that follows the actors' involvement in the process, although it is an informal convention that the customer swimlane is placed at the top. As a result, the action on the model goes from left to right on a horizontal layout, following the time axis, and from top to bottom as the different actors get involved. These left-to-right and top-to-bottom flows mirror the way in which many people read text, at least in the western world, and tend to be intuitive.

The diagram in Figure 8.9 shows the expanded process 'Loan item'. This process involves two actors, the borrower and the librarian, so we have two swimlanes. We place the borrower (or customer) at the top of the diagram because this is usually where the process begins or ends. The start and end points of the process are shown clearly, the former with the named event and the latter with the bullseye symbol. The first task takes place when the borrower contacts the librarian, who checks whether an item is available for loan. Once the librarian has carried out the check, the process moves to the next task, 'Send item to borrower'. The final task occurs when the borrower receives the item.

This diagram can be expanded further to show the tasks performed to deal with a request for an item that is unavailable. Figure 8.10 shows the decision point, the alternative flows and the additional task required to handle this situation. The alternative paths that could be taken are controlled by a diamond symbol (the decision point). The circumstances under which the process takes each route are indicated by placing a 'guard expression' in square brackets next to the flow lines.

The action that follows 'Reserve item' will be carried out in the 'Accept returned item' process, shown on the higher-level model (see Figure 8.5). Within that process there is a check each time a borrower returns an item. The check is done in order to determine whether or not another borrower has reserved the item. The librarian will recognise that an item is on the reserved list, and will trigger the 'Send item to borrower' task in the 'Loan item' process in order to issue it to

Figure 8.10 Business process 'Loan item' with alternative paths

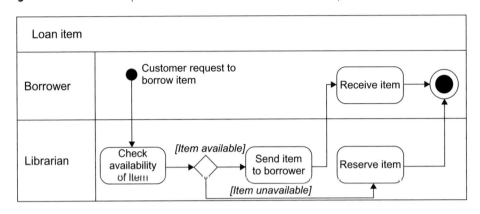

the reserving borrower. This flow can be added to the process model, as shown in Figure 8.11.

Figure 8.11 Business process model with link from another process

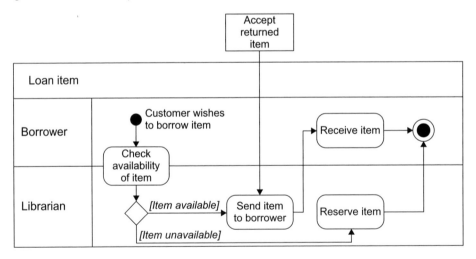

It is always good practice to use a limited set of symbols on a business process model. This will help communication, since the model will require minimal explanation when discussing it with business stakeholders. An important convention concerns the naming of business processes and tasks. The read-ability of the model is enhanced if each process and task is named according to a standard approach. It is best practice to construct the process or task name using the verb–noun format; the name should also describe what the process or task does. Where possible use specific verbs, avoiding words such as 'manage' or 'handle'. 'Find book' is a good example; it is specific, clearly describes what activity is carried out and indicates what the situation is after the task has been completed – the book has been found. 'Handle payment' is not specific enough; by the end of the task the payment may have been handled, but what does that mean?

A major advantage of a business process model is that all of the actors can easily see their contributions to the overall process. As discussed earlier, we are trying to provide a summarised view of the business process at this stage of the analysis. As a result, the tasks reveal minimal detail. A rule of thumb is to show a separate task whenever there is a piece of work done by an actor at a particular point in time. Each task should be shown as a single action, in which the actor receives an input from the preceding actor and hands over to the succeeding actor. The flow of work from one actor to another is known as a 'handoff'. It is important to analyse where these occur since handoffs often cause problems. This is discussed in more detail later in this chapter.

The swimlane diagram shows the work carried out within the business process, including actors and the flow of the work. This may be sufficient to identify problems with the 'as is' process, but often we have to go into more detail in order to really understand how the process works and what is going wrong. A more detailed approach is to analyse each task (or box) shown on the business process model. We might consider the following aspects for each task:

- the trigger or business event that initiates the task;
- inputs to the task, including perhaps the trigger and probably also other information that is required to carry out the task;
- outputs from the task;
- costs relevant to this particular task;
- measures and standards applicable to the task;
- a detailed breakdown of steps within the task;
- business rules to be followed in performing the task.

Documenting these aspects will help in the analysis of the task and the identification of any problem areas or opportunities for improvement. A textual description may suffice for many tasks, but where the steps and business rules are more complex a diagram, such as a flowchart or a UML activity diagram (without swimlanes), will be more useful.

This multilevel approach to business process modelling will necessitate an iterative approach to the analysis. As the analysis of the lower-level tasks reveals more detail, it is inevitable that the higher-level business process models will have to be updated.

ANALYSING THE BUSINESS PROCESS MODEL

Analysing handoffs

Business process models help us to identify problems with the existing process before producing a replacement process. While the version that represents the existing process is called the 'as is' process model, the version that represents the new, improved process is called the 'to be' model.

As mentioned earlier, 'handoffs' are a frequent source of problems in business processes. Figure 8.12 shows two handoffs, one from the manager to the clerk and the other from the clerk to the manager. The task 'Calculate results' has two handoffs in this diagram, one preceding it and one succeeding it.

Figure 8.12 An example of handoffs on the high-level process model

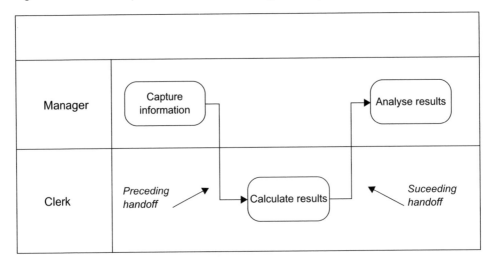

Clear representation of handoffs is a major advantage of this diagramming technique when we are trying to improve processes. Handoffs account for many of the problems experienced by traditional processes, because they can cause delays, communication errors and bottlenecks to occur. For example, once a piece of work arrives at its destination it may have to wait in a queue until an actor is free to deal with it. Analysis of 'as is' processes commonly shows that transactions spend more than 80 per cent of the elapsed time simply waiting. It has even been estimated that in some processes the transactions are being actively processed for less than 10 per cent of the elapsed time, with more than 90 per cent of the time spent in transit or in queues. Queues form at handoffs because the two actors have not synchronised their work. In some situations attempts to optimise work in one task can actually make the performance of the whole process worse. For example, batching of transactions will help a particular task to be carried out more efficiently, but the delay caused by waiting for the batch to build up may slow down the overall progress.

A further cause of delays at handoffs is inadequate resource capacity to handle the throughput. Queues can behave in an odd way, especially when the transactions are coming in a random fashion. Queuing theory tells us that attempts to increase the utilisation of the workers under these circumstances will cause the queues to build up dramatically. The production system on the shop floor of a factory is a specific example of a process in which the queues are very visible. In this case, queues of physical components may be seen as they progress through the different machine operations that make up the production process. Although a process in a bank, for example, may seem very different from one in a factory, they both face the same kinds of problems where handoffs occur.

There are other problems with handoffs that are often caused by a transaction going from one system to another. The systems here could be large information systems or small spreadsheets developed by individuals. The result is that the data within the transaction needs to be reformatted to suit the needs of the receiving software. This not only takes time and effort but can also introduce errors, and subsequent correction of the errors takes up additional time and resources. Handoffs, and the problems they can cause, are a major source of inefficiencies in processes, so addressing the handoffs can be a key to business process improvement.

Piecemeal modifications

Another reason for problems with 'as is' processes is that they may have been in use for some considerable time. During this period, they may have been changed in a piecemeal fashion to react to changing business needs. Little, if any, effort may have been spent examining the process as a whole, and as a result there are significant inefficiencies and inconsistencies. When analysing business processes it is important to look for problems that have arisen over time, such as.

- **Duplication of work:** some tasks may be carried out even though they duplicate other actors' tasks or record the same information.

- **Lack of standardisation:** previously, organisations were less aware of the need for effective processes, and hence there was less emphasis on carrying out processes in a standard way. Remote locations such as branch offices and depots were allowed flexibility in the way in which they interpreted and implemented their processes. This may have worked in a decentralised business, but if there is now greater control and centralisation, all of the different parts of the business are expected to operate in an integrated fashion.

- **Inconsistent measurement or control:** the business process approach has increased the emphasis on measuring the standard of work and the service provided to customers. Where a process has developed over time the measures may not be relevant, or they may be inconsistent with other measures.

IMPROVING BUSINESS PROCESSES

Improving the business process is about removing the problems that have been identified in the 'as is' process. It is also about challenging the assumptions upon which the current process is built, which may be limiting the process. In this section we describe some commonly used approaches to improving processes.

Simplify the process
Simplifying a process can be achieved by eliminating unnecessary parts. Certain tasks within a process may have been required when the process was first introduced, but might now have become redundant as a result of changes to the business. For example, reports may still be produced although nobody uses them any more. Eliminating these tasks not only reduces the running costs and resources used by the process; it also reduces the handoffs and their delays.

Another example of simplification is where a number of tasks carried out by different actors are combined into a single task for one actor only. As well as reducing the number of handoffs, this can result in other improvements such as a reduction in errors. There is also greater scope for giving the actor an extended, more meaningful task to carry out.

Remove bottlenecks
Bottlenecks result when there is a mismatch in the capacities of related tasks. For example, we have a mismatch if task A can handle 100 transactions per hour and these are passed on to task B, which can only deal with 90 transactions per hour. In this example it is easy to see that the resources needed by task B will have to be increased. However, real-life processes are often very complex and hence require detailed analysis to identify such capacity mismatches. In these cases sophisticated process modelling tools can be useful, because they provide simulation facilities that help us examine the performance and resource requirements of proposed process designs.

Change the sequence of tasks
'As is' business processes often reveal their origins. Although they may be supported by computer-based information systems now, often they are merely updated versions of the original clerical version of the same process. Unfortunately, the processes may have unwittingly and unnecessarily carried through the limitations of that approach. Typically, there was only one copy of a paper transaction, which meant that only one person could be working on the information at any one time. As a result, the process tasks are sequential, even though there might be no logical dependency between them. Modern workflow technology can free us from this limitation. Even if the transaction starts life in paper form, it can be scanned and electronic copies can be sent to several actors simultaneously, so long as they are able to work independently. As a result, the elapsed time for the overall process can be reduced significantly. This is only one example of the way technology can be used to carry out tasks in different ways. Another example is the use of computer systems in order to automate the flow through a process as much as possible.

Redesign the process
A business process could be completely redesigned. A good approach to this is to identify the business event that triggers the process and its required outcome. Then focus on identifying the tasks required in order to work from the business

event towards the required outcome. Finally, add in the actors to carry out the tasks. This approach will help create options for the redesigned process, some of which may not be practical or suitable. However, the open-minded approach can cause the analyst to question existing practice and assumptions, and can often be extremely useful in building 'to be' processes.

Redefine process boundaries

Our final approach to improving an 'as is' process is to redefine the boundary of the process. This may involve extending or reducing the activities carried out by the organisation. This is a common approach adopted by many organisations, where they outsource tasks or even entire processes to other specialist organisations. A variant of this approach is to redefine the boundaries of processes so that external stakeholders undertake tasks in place of the organisation's employees. Facilities offered by internet access can enable such boundary redefinition, for example by replacing order-processing staff with an online booking system or providing access to electronic documentation rather than providing printed documents.

Business processes are complex – something we realise when we try to understand and improve them. Although we can examine the flow through a process and determine how that can be supported by an IT system, there are many other factors that can affect the success of a process. Most processes involve people, and there are many reasons why individuals do not work at peak efficiency. Maybe they have not been trained properly to carry out their task. Perhaps they do not understand how their task fits into the overall process, so when something unusual happens, they cannot deal with it. Perhaps staff motivation is poor. It is important, therefore, to ensure that the processes, the people and the organisation structure work in harmony in order to optimise performance.

PROCESS MEASUREMENT

When we are designing an improved business process, we must define not only what the process does but also how well that processing is to be carried out. The importance of measurement is illustrated by the oft-quoted statement 'You can only manage what you can measure'. If we want the actors carrying out tasks to achieve the required levels of performance, we need to define what the performance measures are and ensure that the actors carrying out the work are advised of them. When defining performance measures, one of the fundamental points to recognise is that there are two perspectives on performance measurement: measurement for internal management purposes and measurement by external customers. Organisations sometimes create difficulties when they concentrate on their internal measures at the expense of customer concerns.

Internal measures

Internal measures are often derived from organisational objectives, critical success factors and key performance indicators. These measures are usually defined first at the organisational level, then at departmental level and then at the operational level. The operational measures should support all of the higher-level measures, right up to the organisational level. The problem with internal measures is that they are often focused on what the organisation wants to achieve and not on what the customer values. For example, the organisation may set 'low cost of operation' as a critical success factor for itself and there may be key performance indicators defined that specify which aspects of cost should be measured. However, when related performance measures are defined for the business processes, it is possible that the focus on costs can create problems for the delivery of the service to the customer.

External measures

The other aspect of performance measurement is concerned with what the customer expects to have delivered. One way of thinking about this is to consider what it is that each customer group will value about the deliverables it receives from the organisation. Having identified this, we can then think about the performance measures that we need to apply internally in order to achieve what our customers require. The three major areas to think about are:

- the time it takes to complete a process or task;
- financial measures, such as costs and prices;
- the quality measures that are concerned with accuracy and effectiveness.

It is important to consider all three areas when improving a business process. If a task is likely to take too long, there will be consequential effects in other parts of the business process, leading to poor customer service. If an organisation charges for a particular service but the cost of the process that delivers the service is greater than the amount charged, then the organisation is going to run into financial difficulties at some point. A failure to consider the performance measures related to quality can lead to the delivery of inaccurate information and poor customer service.

Process and task measures

One of the key issues for performance measures is to understand the customers' expectations. The customer has an expectation of the organisation's performance in delivering the product or service. Internally, the process may be made up of several individual tasks, each of which will need to be allocated performance measures. These performance measures need to work collectively to deliver the product or service within the overall performance measure for the process. Figure 8.13 demonstrates this principle by showing our 'Loan item' example with a timeline added. This timeline shows that the first task, 'Check availability of item', must take place within two working days of receiving the request from the customer. The second task, 'Send item to borrower', must take place within a further two working days. The customer must receive the item within a further one working day. These are the internal performance measures, but they need to be aligned with the external expectation. If the external performance measure, the customer view, is that

Figure 8.13 An example of a business process with a timeline

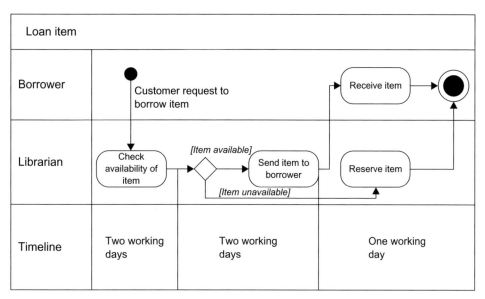

the item will be received within five working days then the internal measures are fine. However, if the customer is expecting the item within two working days then these internal measures are likely to ensure that the customer's expectations will not be met.

The performance targets set for a particular process have to be in alignment with the expectations of the customers. If we design a process that results in a service that does not meet customer expectations, then the likelihood of losing customers is very high.

Estimating the timeline for a process is difficult. It will depend on a range of factors, including:

- the length of time taken by each task within the process;
- the resources available to support the tasks;
- the number of transactions to be processed and how this varies over time;
- the variety and mix of different transaction types;
- the amount of reworking caused by errors;
- the delays and queues at each of the handoffs;
- the quality and productivity of the staff;
- other work that could interrupt the process.

Some process modelling software provides performance information by using data on these factors to simulate the behaviour of the process. The value of the simulation results depends on the accuracy of the assumptions and data fed into the model, but the information gained can be very helpful when designing the process and identifying the performance targets.

Cost and time estimates are interrelated, so similar issues apply when setting financial performance measures. The longer the tasks within the process take, the more resources are required and hence the higher the cost. There may also be trade-offs; in order to reduce time, we may be able to increase the expenditure on resources. However, it is important to consider how much the resource will cost and whether or not the reduced time or the higher performance will justify that extra expenditure.

Performance issues

Measures and targets need to be chosen with care, especially when managers are given incentives to achieve those targets. Targets will change the way people behave – that is what they are designed to do. It is possible that the behaviour could be inappropriate if we have not thought the implications of the targets through. For example, sales staff are often set sales targets on the assumption that more sales are good for the business as a whole. However, this may not be true if the increased sales are achieved by lowering prices too much. This is an example of sub-optimisation, where seemingly better performance in one part of the business can result in poorer performance for the business as a whole.

SIX SIGMA

An alternative approach to process improvement is embodied in the Six Sigma approach, developed by Motorola in the 1980s and based on ideas from statistical process control. First used in manufacturing industries in the reduction of product defects, it is now used in a range of organisations including those in the pharmaceutical industry, local authorities, food processing, hospitals, the military, logistics, NASA and financial services. Its purpose is to eradicate performance deficiencies in processes that are critical to achieving customer satisfaction. These processes might include complaint handling, order fulfilment or delivering a package to a customer's house. To achieve process improvement, Six Sigma follows a five-step approach: define the problem, measure the data, analyse the problem, improve the process by removing the root causes of the problem, and then introduce controls to prevent the original problem from reoccurring and to maintain the benefits of the changes made. In Six Sigma language this is the 'DMAIC' approach.

Let us assume that we are Global Deliveries PLC and that we are getting an increasing number of customer complaints about the non-delivery or late delivery of packages; incomplete deliveries against acknowledged orders; packages delivered to wrong addresses and very bad performance from the offices in Denver, Brisbane, Glasgow, Calgary and Swindon. Following the DMAIC approach, we would carry out the following activities:

- **Define** the problem. What is going wrong? Is it one problem or many? What is the visible evidence? Where is it and where does it come from? How serious is it? Is it organisation wide or localised? What will be done about it? What is the objective of this investigation?

- **Measure** the data. This means identifying the symptoms. Do they occur all the time or from time to time? Produce a map of the process that is producing the problem. Concentrate on the symptoms doing the most damage.

- **Analyse** the results so far. Be creative and prepare theories about the causes of the problems. Document the theories and test them. Identify the root causes.

- **Improve** the process. Assess alternative improvement methods. Design and test the chosen method. Implement the chosen method.

- **Control** the new process and monitor its effectiveness.

Six Sigma can therefore be seen as a very methodical and structured approach to process improvement that uses data and measurement to identify where the most business benefit can be obtained through such improvement. The aim is to reduce errors, so that all processes meet or exceed customers' expectations and there are no more than 3.4 defects per million occurrences. In the Global Deliveries PLC example this would translate into performance that delivers the right package to the right place at the right time 99.997 per cent of the time!

SUMMARY

An organised, structured approach to business process improvement will be beneficial for both the organisation and the business analysts carrying out the work. We have described an approach using an organisational view of processes that is then developed further into more detailed business process models. Business process models can be used for many purposes, including business improvement and staff training, but if they are to be useful it is important to produce clear, easily understood diagrams and well-structured supporting documentation.

REFERENCES

Harmon, P. (2007) *Business Process Change*, 2nd edn. Morgan Kaufmann, Boston, MA.

FURTHER READING

Burlton, R. (2001) *Business Process Management: Profiting From Process*. Sams Publishing, Indianapolis, IN.

Hammer, M. and Champy, J. (2001) *Reengineering the Corporation: A Manifesto for Business Revolution*, 3rd edn. Nicholas Brealey Publishing, London.

Hammer, M. (1996) *Beyond Reengineering: How the Process-centred Organization is Changing our Work and our Lives.* HarperBusiness.

Rummler, G. A. and Brache, A. P. (1995) *Improving Performance: How to Manage the White Space on the Organization Chart,* 2nd edn. Jossey-Bass, San Fransisco, CA.

Sharp, A. and McDermott, P. (2001) *Workflow Modeling Tools for Process Improvement and Application Development.* Artech House, Boston, MA.

USEFUL WEBSITES

Business Process Management Group: www.bpmg.org

Business Process Management Initiative. www.bpmi.org

9 GATHERING THE REQUIREMENTS

Malcolm Eva

INTRODUCTION

> When I actually meet users ... I find that they certainly have needs, but that
> these do not appear in an organised form at all. The needs come out in a rush,
> a mixture of complaints, design decisions, interface descriptions, current
> situations, and from time to time specific human–machine interface require-
> ments. It is sometimes possible to isolate chunks of this as definite functions.
> In short, there seems to be a gap between theory and practice. Theory says that
> on the one hand we'll find people who state what they want, and on the other,
> people who make things to please the first bunch of people. Instead, all the
> people and tasks and documents seem to be muddled up together.
>
> Alexander and Maiden (2004)

Most analysts involved in defining user requirements will probably recognise
Ian Alexander's description. Requirements, apparently regarded by business users
as the uncomplicated area of a new systems development, are actually the most
problematic aspect. And yet, as we see below, the time allocated is often far less
than for the other phases. Requirements engineering is the information systems
industry's response to the problem of requirements for new IT/IS systems not
being met and, indeed, not being offered clearly in the first place. Tight timescales
and tight budgets – both the result of constraints on the business – place pressures
on the development team to deliver a product. However, without sufficient time to
understand and define the requirements properly, the product that is delivered on
time may not provide the solution that the business thought was requested. Applying the process of requirements engineering should help to rectify these problems.

THE PROBLEMS WITH REQUIREMENTS

Studies carried out into IS project failures over the last 30 years tell a common
story. The problems highlighted have included the following:

- A large proportion of errors (over 80 per cent) are introduced at the
  requirements analysis stage.

- Very few faults (less than 10 per cent) are introduced at the development stage – developers' programming of things is right, but they are frequently not programming the right things.
- Most of the project time is allocated to the development and testing phases of the project.
- Less than 12 per cent of the project time is allocated to the requirements analysis phase.
- There is poor alignment of the developed system to business strategy and objectives.
- There is poor requirements management.

These findings are particularly significant because the cost of correcting errors in requirements increases dramatically the later they are uncovered during the development lifecycle. And yet the study quoted above identifies requirements analysis as the most error-prone stage of the development lifecycle.

Typical problems with requirements have been identified as:

- lack of relevance to the objectives of the project;
- lack of clarity in the wording;
- ambiguity;
- duplication between requirements;
- conflicts between requirements;
- requirements expressed in such a way that it is difficult to assess whether they have been achieved;
- requirements that assume a solution rather than stating what is to be delivered by the system;
- uncertainty amongst business users about what they need from the new system;
- business users omitting to identify requirements;
- inconsistent levels of detail;
- business users and analysts taking certain knowledge for granted and failing to ensure that there is a common understanding.

The first point often results from a lack of terms of reference for the project. Clearly defined terms of reference are essential to ensure that everyone involved in defining the requirements understands the objectives, scope and constraints within which the project is to be carried out. A useful mnemonic for the terms of reference is OSCAR. This stands for:

- **Objectives:** of which both business and project objectives should be defined;
- **Scope:** the aspects to be covered, typically defined by specifying the activities and deliverables of the project;

- **Constraints:** the budget, timescale and standards to which the project must adhere;
- **Authority:** the business authority for the project, ensuring that there is an ultimate arbiter to handle any conflicts between business users and their requirements;
- **Resources:** the people and equipment available to the project.

The difficulty associated with taking some knowledge for granted is by no means trivial and, in a world of new business practices, business processes and technology, by no means uncommon. The business analyst is the person who must help the staff members visualise precisely what they need the new system to do, and then help them to articulate this.

Another source of difficulties for the business analyst is recognising the different stakeholder viewpoints. Depending upon their roles in the organisation, one person might see the business system as revolving around the product, another may think in terms of finding a marketing solution and a third may see the system as being customer focused. All three are describing their perceptions of the same system, but each sits in his or her own silo, looking at the business from that one viewpoint. It is up to the business analyst to draw the threads together in order to view the system as a whole and to meet all three perspectives as well as possible.

The philosopher Wittgenstein proposed an ambiguous animal in his *Philosophical Investigations* (1953) that illustrates this point well. The view of the animal is of its head in profile, showing two long protuberances which look like a bill – or could they be ears? – and a dimple on the other side of its head. The animal's eye is unambiguously visible in the centre. If the creature is viewed as looking to the left, it is clearly seen as a duck with a bill; if it is seen as looking towards the right, however, it is clearly a rabbit with its long ears. What it is not, though, is both together. Wittgenstein named this ambiguous animal a duckrabbit, to make its identity clear.

The business analyst will encounter many duckrabbits during his or her career: a sales director who sources products to satisfy customer demands sees the company as a sales organisation, while a finance director who has invested heavily in an in-house manufacturing capability will see a manufacturing organisation. They are describing the same company, but one sees a duck and one a rabbit. Is the company there to provide satisfaction to its customers (a duck) or to sell its manufactured products (a rabbit)? The analyst or requirements engineer needs to understand all of these valid perspectives – each is a *Weltanschauung*, as described in Chapter 7 – to be sure of capturing more than a one-sided view. Recognising the existence of a duckrabbit, or simply multiple *Weltanschauungen*, helps to anticipate scoping issues and potential requirements conflicts before they arise.

Another problem that business analysts face is an apparent inability on the part of the business users to articulate clearly what it is they wish the system to do for them. Some users, perhaps due to uncertainty, may even be reluctant to state their requirements. Very often they are deterred from doing so because the nature of the requirement is not susceptible to a straightforward statement. These issues may be due, at least in part, to the problem of tacit knowledge; we shall explore some of them in the section on 'Requirements elicitation' on page 157.

A PROCESS FOR REQUIREMENTS ENGINEERING

Just as 'software engineering' suggests a more structured and scientific approach to the development of software than is implied by the older term 'programming', requirements engineering encapsulates a more disciplined and rigorous approach to the requirements process. The business analyst must understand and document requirements thoroughly in order to avoid the mistakes identified in the previous section. In order to achieve this rigour, the analyst should follow a process or road-map that includes all of the key steps required to develop a rigorous requirements document. Figure 9.1 illustrates the requirements engineering process, which provides such a road-map.

Figure 9.1 Requirements engineering process

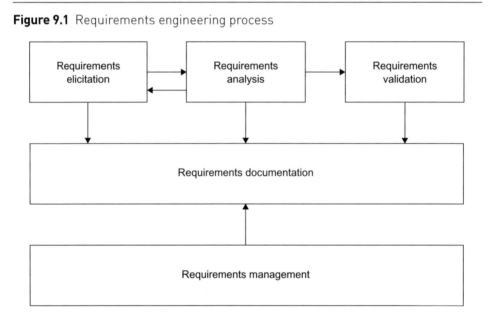

Requirements elicitation is concerned with gathering information and requirements from the business stakeholders. Requirements analysis focuses on examining the gathered requirements in order to identify those that overlap, are in conflict with others or are duplicates. When we gather requirements from the users their explanations often lack clarity and completeness, as recognised by the comment from Ian Alexander quoted at the beginning of this chapter. Before the requirements are formally entered into a requirements catalogue, the business analyst needs to list them and subject them to careful scrutiny in order to ensure that they are well formed. As a result, this activity also highlights any areas for further elicitation. In requirements analysis the business analyst has a gatekeeper role, ensuring that only those requirements that pass the scrutiny will be entered in the document.

Requirements validation involves the external stakeholders reviewing the requirements in order to agree and 'sign off' the requirements document. The requirements catalogue is one part of the full requirements document, which also contains models of the business processes and IT system. This document should be analysed and checked by the business analyst for completeness and consistency. Once the document is considered to be complete, it must be reviewed by business representatives and confirmed to be a true statement of the required system; at this point the document is said to be 'signed off'. During this stage the reviewers examine the requirements and question whether they are well defined, clear and complete. The review will be similar to that undertaken in the analysis stage, but this time it is the business stakeholders who will carry out the checks rather than the analysts. The process of requirements validation is explained more fully in the final section of this chapter.

There are two other aspects that complete the requirements engineering work: requirements documentation is concerned with the development of a well-organised requirements document, and requirements management covers the activities needed in order to manage changes to the requirements. Changes occur throughout the business change and solution development lifecycles, and procedures have to be in place to deal with them. Whatever the reason for them, the business analyst must record, analyse and act on the changes, and hence ensure that every requirement is fully traceable from its initial recording to sign-off during user acceptance testing. Chapter 10 discusses the development and structure of the requirements document, the issue of traceability and the use of computer aided software engineering (CASE) tools to support requirements management. Approaches to developing the IT system models that are included in the requirements document are described in Chapter 11.

ACTORS

There are some participants we would always expect to see in the requirements process. They represent two broad stakeholder groups: the business and the project team.

The business representatives
The business is represented by the project sponsor, the domain expert and the business users.

The project sponsor represents the business in ensuring that business objectives are met. The sponsor has the following responsibilities:

- to agree the project initiation document that approves the requirements engineering study;
- to deliver the specific and agreed business benefits predicted in the business case;

- to make funds and other resources available for the project;
- to accept the deliverables at the end of the project;
- to approve and sign off the requirements document as a true statement of the business needs;
- to rule on any conflicting requirements where the business analyst cannot negotiate agreement.

The role of the domain expert (or subject-matter expert) is to give high-level advice on the requirements. Particular situations when this may be relevant are when:

- the requirements cover more than one business function;
- the requirements relate to a redesigned business process;
- the organisation wishes to introduce a new product that the company does not yet fully understand;
- the organisation wishes to adopt the latest industry best practice.

The domain expert brings breadth of understanding to the process, and should have experience and knowledge of industry best practice. This person's level of knowledge of the domain should help analysts distinguish between what the business and the project need and what a particularly forceful individual user wants. A domain expert may be either an internal expert or an external consultant brought in for the duration of the project. While an external domain expert can bring in fresh views and insights from industry, drawing on best practice as used elsewhere, there are some risks associated with their use:

- They may not understand well how this particular company works, and its specific culture. This might make their preferred approach to the solution inappropriate.
- They may be unaware of political undercurrents in the organisation that can affect the project's success or failure.
- They may be regarded as outsiders, and so be resented by internal workers who feel they, too, have the right expertise.

The business users are the individuals or groups who will need to apply the new business processes and use the new IT system. They comprise the group for whom the solution is designed. They are required to describe current procedures and documentation, highlight any difficulties they experience with current processes and identify new requirements for the system. They should be able to help the business analyst to define the requirements in detail by providing specific, clear information. They will be able to assist with the definition of non-functional requirements that apply to their tasks, although some aspects may need management involvement. For example, decisions about archiving information and the duration for the retention of data are likely to require the involvement of middle or senior managers. The business user community members are likely to perform several roles, each of which needs to be considered when analysing the requirements. One of these might be the 'customer' role. This will arise for any IT systems that are accessible by the end customer, for example where an internet-based system is to be developed and implemented. In this case care needs to be taken to ensure that the requirements are gathered accurately and that appropriate techniques, such as the use of focus groups, are employed in order to acquire the relevant information.

The project team

The project team is represented by the project manager, the business analysts and the developer.

The project manager is mindful of the need to meet the business requirements and satisfy the business imperatives that drive the project. The project manager will report to the project sponsor, and will be concerned to:

- break the project down into identifiable and measurable pieces of work, each with its deliverable;
- allocate the pieces of work to competent people to perform;
- schedule the tasks with their start and end times, recognising dependencies between tasks;
- monitor the progress of the various tasks and be alerted to any likely slippage;
- take any corrective action should there be slippage or risk of non-completion of a task for any reason.

The business analysts will be responsible for carrying out the requirements engineering work. Their key objective is to ensure that the requirements are well documented and complete and align with the business objectives. Working closely with the business staff, they gather and analyse the requirements and are responsible to the sponsor for the quality of the requirements document.

Many organisations assign the project manager role to the business analyst on a project, but this can be problematic because the two roles call for different aptitudes, priorities and skills. There may also be conflicting priorities and interests to be reconciled, which will be problematic if one individual is assigned both of these roles.

The developer will be able to check the technical feasibility of some of the requirements and help the analyst appreciate the implications of some of them. The developer will be able to produce prototypes from the requirements to help the business users visualise more clearly what they have requested, so as to help them confirm the analysts' understanding of the requirements.

REQUIREMENTS ELICITATION

In the early days of systems analysis, this activity was often known as 'requirements capture'. The word 'capture' implies the existence of discrete entities called 'requirements' that were readily available to be spotted and caught. In those days most IT projects were concerned with developing systems that would perform the tasks then being carried out by people, mostly clerical staff. To some extent, each task performed by a person could be regarded as a requirement, or a set of requirements, to be delivered by the system – so requirements capture was not an unreasonable term for the process.

Nowadays the rationale for developing or enhancing IT systems includes a need to help the organisation gain a competitive advantage, to support new business processes or to support a business process re-engineering exercise. The more straightforward approach of using the current procedures as a basis has declined, and hence there is a strong likelihood that the business users will not be at all clear about what they need the system to provide. The term 'capture' is less suited to the reality of today's business world, and has been superseded by 'elicitation'.

Whereas earlier methods placed the onus on the business user to identify the requirements, requirements elicitation is a proactive approach to understanding requirements. It involves drawing out the requirements from the users and helping them to visualise the possibilities and articulate their requirements. The requirements emerge as a result of the interaction between analyst and user, with much proactive elicitation on the part of the analyst.

Tacit knowledge

When we are developing a new system, the business users will pass on to us their explicit knowledge: the knowledge of procedures and data that is at the front of their minds and that they can easily articulate. By tacit knowledge we mean those other aspects of the work that a stakeholder is unable to articulate or explain. The term derives from the work of Michael Polanyi (1966), whose thesis is succinctly expressed in the maxim 'We can know more than we can tell'. In understanding requirements we must be aware of a number of elements of tacit knowledge, and recognise them when we encounter them.

Some common elements of this unspoken knowledge that cause problems and misunderstandings are:

- **Skills:** explaining how to carry out actions by using words alone is extremely difficult. For example, consider how you might convey the correct sequence of actions that would be necessary in order to turn right at a roundabout on a dual carriageway. This would include every touch or release of the pedals in the correct sequence, every check of the mirror, every gear change and every turn of the wheel with the degree of turn. To build an automated vehicle that could travel along roads without a driver, one would need all of this information to be specified in detail. In practice, however, an experienced human driver would not be able explain it accurately during an interview, largely because drivers perform the task without having to rationalise each step;

their bodies and limbs 'know' what to do without the intervention of conscious thought. If we needed to document this process, we would have to select a requirements elicitation approach that would help to uncover information about these automatic actions. Protocol analysis is a powerful way to explore these unconscious skills and gather the information to document them. This technique involves the expert performing the task in discrete steps, talking through each step while making it, and repeating this two or three times. This is an approach often used where skills are taught, for example when children are taught to tie shoelaces, learner drivers shown how to drive a car and apprentices taught to use machines.

- **Taken-for-granted information:** even experienced and expert business users may fail to mention information or clarify terminology, and the analyst may not realise that further questioning is required. This issue has been identified as a cause of many systems failures. It has also been termed 'not-worth-mentioning' information, which highlights that it is not through malice or intention that the user fails to reveal some aspect of the procedure or documentation; it is simply that to users it is so obvious that they take the analyst's familiarity for granted. The fact that the analyst then fails to ask a question on that aspect simply confirms to them that to talk about it is unnecessary. The gap in our understanding may not emerge until the stage of user acceptance testing or even after implementation, and this may be costly and complex to correct.

- **Front story/back story:** this issue concerns a tendency to frame a description of current working practices, or a workplace, in order to give a view that appears more positive than is actually the case. The business user may do this in order to avoid reflecting badly on the staff or the organisation. An analogy could be the swan gliding gracefully across the smooth surface of a lake (front story) while below the surface its feet are paddling frantically (back story) to sustain the gentle momentum. This problem may occur if the analysts are perceived to represent management, and as a result may be given the favourable front-story version of how the business or department works. It is clearly important then that we build good working relationships with the business users and encourage them to trust us, so that we are able to obtain details of the back story: the reality of the business operation.

We should be most suspicious of a front story when we are told that an operation runs very smoothly without any problems, and that if there are problems they are always easily dealt with. We might also be concerned if we are told that the customers of that process are always very happy with the results. While this could be the case it is always sensible to probe a little deeper and ensure that there is quantifiable data to support the assertion. The saying 'If it sounds too good to be true, it probably is' is often found to reflect reality in organisations. Analysts must avoid seeming sceptical about what they have been told – after all, success lies in building a rapport with key stakeholders and earning their trust. Nonetheless, the true story – the 'back story' – will in all probability give a different picture. Work shadowing, observation of the working environment and process modelling are all techniques that help to clarify what really happens.

- **Conceptualising requirements:** if the study is required to examine a new business system and there is a lack of expertise and knowledge in the organisation, it is very difficult for the business stakeholders to imagine what they require the solution to offer. We cannot ask them to demonstrate any existing processes or procedures, and yet it is important that we draw from them precisely what they need the solution to provide. Although the information about the business context, for example the business strategy or the legal constraints, will provide a degree of understanding, it is extremely difficult to define a more detailed definition of the requirements. A good approach is to help the users visualise for themselves how the business processes could work and what IT support they will require. Providing a visual representation will enable the users to consider and articulate their requirements more clearly. Approaches that would help with this include exploring possibilities in a workshop, using business scenarios and story-telling workshops or enlisting the developers to build some initial prototypes to show what the IT system might offer and how it might look.

- **'Your finger, you fool!':** this is based upon an apocryphal story and tells about a 17th-century European explorer who landed on an island and asked a native inhabitant the name of a prominent mountain. He pointed at the landmark he was asking about, but the islanders did not recognise the gesture of pointing to distant objects; the inhabitant assumed that what he was being asked to identify was the outstretched finger. This illustrates the difficulty when an outside party assumes that there is a common language and that the common norms of communication apply. In such situations cultural and language differences may create many possibilities for confusion, so we should consider whether an extended investigation might be required. An ethnographic study can be an extremely useful technique in such situations, although it will require an extended period of time and a great deal of effort. However, without a detailed investigation approach the analysts cannot be sure that they have sufficient understanding and knowledge to be able to define the business requirements. Without this, the scope for misrepresentation of the situation can grow considerably.

- **Intuitive understanding, usually born of considerable experience:** decision-makers, such as those working in medical diagnosis or geological surveys, are often thought to follow a logical, linear path of enquiry while making their decisions. In reality, though, as individuals acquire decision-making skills and technical knowledge, the linear approach is often abandoned in favour of intuitive pattern recognition. Ask specialists why they made a particular judgement and you may be told about the logical steps, but there will often be a point where the logic ends and intuition takes over; this is where knowledge has been applied at a tacit level rather than explicitly.

With the exception of 'front story/back story', which is more of a reluctance to tell than an inability to articulate, these issues all occur because of the application of an individual's tacit knowledge. However, there are situations where an organisation possesses tacit knowledge and it is also important that this is recognised and understood. Examples of organisational tacit knowledge include:

- **Norms of behaviour and communication:** these evolve over time in every organisation. Any new process or system that threatens to conflict with these norms may face resistance.

- **Organisational culture:** the culture of an organisation can be expressed through the behaviour of the management and staff. The analyst needs to consider what the behaviour says about the culture of the organisation and ensure that this is taken into consideration when considering any business changes.

- **Communities of practice:** these are discrete groups of workers who may be related perhaps by task, by department, by geographical location or some other factor. They have their own sets of norms and practices, distinct from those of other groups within the organisation and not reflected in the organisation as a whole. A community of practice is likely to have its own body of tacit information, which the members of the community understand well and are not accustomed to sharing openly. If a systems development project involves cross-functional requirements, or is company-wide, then understanding the various communities of practice is an important part of the elicitation.

Table 9.1 shows types of both tacit and explicit knowledge.

Table 9.1 Types of tacit and explicit knowledge

	Tacit	Explicit
Individual	Skills, values, taken-for-granted knowledge, intuitiveness	Task definitions, job descriptions, targets, volumes and frequencies
Corporate	Norms, back story, culture, communities of practice, organisation history	Procedures, style guides, processes, knowledge sharing repositories, manuals, company reports

Tacit knowledge can be made more explicit. To do this we need to use techniques that assist business users to articulate their tacit knowledge. Once they have done this, we need to make the knowledge explicit by documenting it and disseminating it to the other members of the project team.

Requirements elicitation techniques

There are a number of techniques available to the analyst to help elicit tacit knowledge and requirements from all levels of the organisation. The most common and accessible ones are discussed in Chapter 5.

Figure 9.2 Tacit to explicit knowledge

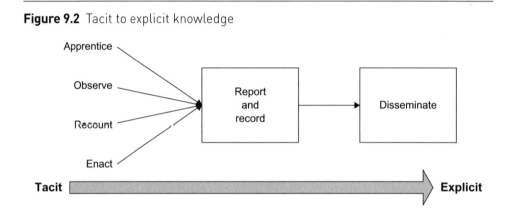

The process for eliciting tacit knowledge shown in Figure 9.2 identifies approaches for uncovering tacit knowledge. They include:

- **Apprentice:** shadowing or protocol analysis;
- **Observe:** observation;
- **Recount:** story-telling or scenarios;
- **Enact:** prototyping or scenario role-play.

Table 9.2 Techniques and knowledge types (after Maiden and Rugg 1996)

Technique	Explicit knowledge	Tacit knowledge	Taken for granted	Front/ back story	Skills	Future requirements
Interviewing	√√	√	√	√	√	√
Shadowing	√√	√√	√√	√√	√√	√
Workshops	√√	√√	√√	√	√	√√
Prototyping	√√	√√	√√	√	√√	√√

(Continued)

Table 9.2 *(Continued)*

Technique	Explicit knowledge	Tacit knowledge	Taken for granted	Front/ back story	Skills	Future requirements
Scenario analysis	√√	√√	√√	√	√	√√
Protocol analysis	√√	√√	√√	√	√√	√

It is important that business analysts have a toolkit of techniques so that they can tailor their approach when eliciting requirements. Table 9.2 matches some of the most popular elicitation techniques with the knowledge types that a business analyst is likely to have to handle. This mapping of techniques to knowledge types provides a good indication of where certain techniques can be particularly useful and where they can still be useful but to a lesser extent.

BUILDING THE REQUIREMENTS LIST

As we uncover the requirements from our various business stakeholders, we need to document them. This is best done in two distinct passes: building the requirements list and, later, developing an organised requirements catalogue. The business needs log, described in Chapter 5, is an input to, and complement to, the requirements list. The development of the requirements catalogue is described in Chapter 10.

The requirements list is quite simply what it says – a list containing every requirement that has been stated or elicited. The list tends to be an informal document and can be presented using three columns, as shown in Table 9.3.

The requirements list is begun following an initial interview or workshop and is developed further as more requirements are identified. The requirements identified at this stage will not be well formed and their level and scope will vary considerably; some may be detailed and specific whilst others will be defined at an overview level only or may represent several potential require-ments. The requirements list helps to ensure that everything that is raised is documented and its source identified.

Table 9.3 Example requirements list

Requirement	Source	Comments
1. The company needs to reduce the amount of paper moved between departments.	I. Morris	Real requirement? See 5, as well
2. The system must capture customer payments	I. Morris	
3. The customer file must be password protected.	F. Drake	Non-functional? Is this a solution?
4. We need the information quicker.	J. Keen	Quantify – what information? What timescale? What is wrong with current?
5. We must record customer details, and be able to amend them and delete old customers.	J. Keen	Need breaking into three requirements?

REQUIREMENTS ANALYSIS

Once a set of requirements has been elicited and entered in the requirements list, the next step in the requirements engineering process can begin: analysing the individual requirements.

Requirements analysis is concerned with ensuring that all of the requirements identified during the elicitation stage have been developed into clear, organised, fully documented requirements. The separation of requirements elicitation from requirements analysis is one of the strengths of requirements engineering. The analysts are encouraged during elicitation to gather information, uncover tacit knowledge and identify requirements; during analysis, the analysts examine the results of this work in detail in order to develop the requirement documentation that will take the project forward. Requirements analysis requires a high degree of logical thought, organisation and rigour if the documentation is to be of the required standard. In this instance, the analyst takes the role of a gatekeeper in order to ensure the quality of the requirements. Only those requirements that are clearly stated, unambiguous, atomic, feasible, aligned with the project objectives, not in conflict with any other requirements and not overlapping with or duplicating other requirements will be documented.

As this work is carried out many additional questions will be raised, and you may need to investigate the requirements further using requirements elicitation techniques. Thus an iterative cycle of requirements elicitation and analysis develops.

Requirements analysis includes the following aspects:

- **Categorisation of the requirements:** as a first pass at the analysis, the requirements should be categorised into specific types. There are four major types of requirements: general, technical, functional and non-functional. These types are described in detail in Chapter 10. Further subgroupings may be by more detailed sub-categorisation, business area or function, or possibly by use case. Grouping requirements helps with the analysis because the analyst is able to examine the related requirements as a coherent group.

- **Applying a series of filters** in order to ensure that the requirements are well defined.

Requirements filters

The following filters should be used to examine the requirements and build a well-formed, clearly documented requirements set:

- **Checking for overlapping or duplicate requirements:** once requirements that cover a similar area are grouped together, it is much easier to find the duplicate or overlapping ones. Where there is duplication, the requirements should be merged; where there are overlapping requirements, they should be either merged or separated into distinct requirements.

- **Unravelling multiple requirements:** some requirements may have been listed that cover a number of different aspects rather than stating just one requirement. It is important that these grouped requirements are split into individual, atomic requirements. An example of a grouped requirement is: 'Reservations clerks must be able to record a booking. They must also be able to amend or cancel bookings.' In fact there are three requirements here, each potentially having its own priority and acceptance criteria. Therefore each of them needs to be documented.

- **Necessity checking:** all requirements should be aligned to the business and project objectives. They should also address a problem rather than a symptom of a problem. If a proposed requirement does not support these criteria then it is likely that it is not really a requirement.

- **Feasibility evaluation:** all requirements should be evaluated to see whether they would be feasible. There are three aspects to feasibility – technical, business and financial. Technical feasibility is concerned with the availability of technology to fulfil a requirement. Business feasibility concerns the likely level of acceptance of the requirement by the business. Financial feasibility involves considering how expensive it would be to meet the requirement and whether the expense is justified. Imagine a client asking an architect to build a large swimming pool into a new house design without increasing the cost.

This would not be acceptable. However, business stakeholders sometimes ask for additional features without appreciating the cost implications. Sometimes a manager asks for information to help with a decision, which at first seems reasonable but later turns out to involve building a very sophisticated decision support system or expert system at a cost far exceeding the original budget.

- **Removing conflicts:** some requirements may contradict or conflict with others, such that only one of them may be implemented. When such a conflict is identified the business analyst is responsible for helping to negotiate a resolution. Sometimes necessity checking will resolve a conflict if one of the requirements is directly aligned with the business objectives. However, if the sources of the requirements are adamant and there is no room for compromise or discussion, then the decision will need to be passed to the sponsor or even escalated to the project board.

- **Checking for solutions:** on examination, a requirement may not be some thing that the business needs to happen or to be addressed, but may instead be a predetermined solution. Business stakeholders often express a requirement in terms of the solution rather than in terms of what the business needs. For example, a requirement may dictate that a specific software package should be used rather than expressing the business requirements to be addressed.

- **Confirming quality:** all requirements should meet the quality criteria and should be:

  - **Clear:** the requirement must be expressed in clear language, avoiding vague adjectives and adverbs and using precise verbs and nouns. It is also important to avoid terms such as 'and', 'but', 'except' and 'until', since each of these suggests that there is more than one requirement.

  - **Concise:** the requirement must be described concisely.

  - **Consistent:** the requirement must not contradict other requirements.

  - **Relevant:** the requirement must be within the scope of the project.

  - **Unambiguous:** the description of the requirement must not contain any ambiguity. We need to consider the problems of terminology and jargon. Common sources of confusion involve the use of synonyms (two words used to mean the same thing) and homonyms (the same word used to mean different things). If two people who read the requirement have a different mental picture of what is being asked for, it is ambiguous.

  - **Correct:** the requirement must describe something that is required.

  - **Testable:** the requirement should be described in such a way that the solution may be tested in order to confirm that the requirement has been met.

  - **Traceable:** information about the requirement must enable the traceability of the requirement.

There are several potential outcomes that follow from this exercise. The possible actions are:

- Accept the requirement as it stands and document it in full in the requirements catalogue.

- Reword the requirement to remove jargon and ambiguity.

- Merge duplicated or overlapping requirements and reword them.

- Take unclear, ambiguous or conflicting requirements back to the business users for clarification.

Requirements that are in conflict, unrealistic or out of alignment with the business objectives still need to be recorded in the requirements catalogue in order to ensure that an audit trail is kept of all requirements raised and any subsequent action taken. This does not mean that they will be implemented in the new system – that decision comes later – but that they should be considered for implementation. The structure and format of the requirements catalogue is described in Chapter 10.

Once all of the requirements have been grouped and analysed, it is useful to carry out a final, further check. The analyst needs to examine each requirement on the list to check that they are well formed and SMART (specific, measurable, achievable, relevant and time-framed).

VALIDATING REQUIREMENTS

Once the analysts have completed the analysis activity and have deemed the requirements document to be complete and correct, the business representatives need to confirm that the document provides an accurate statement of the requirements. A review group is formed that will be responsible for checking the requirements document and confirming its suitability. Once the reviewers have been identified, the requirements document should be issued for review.

The review group must include representatives from the key stakeholder groups, with different representatives to review different aspects of the requirements. The reviewers should include the following representatives:

- The business sponsor should review the document to ensure that the requirements are all in alignment with the business objectives and do not address areas that are outside the scope of the project.

- The business owners of the individual requirements, or their representatives, should review the requirements to ensure that they express the business needs clearly and correctly, without ambiguity. It is the business representatives' responsibility to be satisfied with the requirements before accepting them, and this is their last opportunity.

- The domain expert should review the requirements to ensure that they reflect correct business practice.

- The developers should review the requirements to ensure that they are technically feasible.

- The testers should review the requirements to ensure that they are testable.
- Project office representatives should also attend the review meeting in order to ensure that the requirements are compliant with business standards and policies, and that correct quality review procedures have been followed.

The group may meet to discuss the requirements document in a formal review meeting, have a virtual meeting in which comments are submitted electronically via a shared forum or possibly provide individual responses via email. A formal meeting or shared forum provides an additional aspect to a document review, since the reviewers are aware of the comments from the entire group, which provides an opportunity to consider other perspectives. The use of individual emails tends to provide a more limited review approach because there is a lack of shared review and comment. However, it is still a valuable review approach and is preferable to no review. Whichever approach is taken to the review, there are two important roles to be filled: there should be a chairperson, who is responsible for controlling the review, and a business analyst, who is responsible for providing information about the requirements document or possibly presenting it to the review meeting.

A common problem during requirements validation concerns the size of the document that is to be reviewed. Where the requirements document is large it is a good idea to review it in sections. If the requirements have been grouped by business area, it is possible to conduct a set of shorter review meetings. Only relevant stakeholders can be invited to review each section of the document, which will help to save time for everyone.

There are three possible outcomes to a review:

- The requirements document is confirmed as a satisfactory statement of the business requirements. Once the document has been agreed, it is said to be 'signed off'.
- The requirements document requires some amendments and, once these have been completed, can be signed off by the review chairperson, who is typically the business sponsor.
- The requirements document requires significant reworking and should be reviewed again once this reworking has been carried out.

Once the document has been signed off, any subsequent changes will be subject to formal requirements management. This is described in Chapter 10.

The outcome of the review should be an agreement that the entire requirements document is complete, consistent, conformant and a true reflection of what the business requires to be delivered.

SUMMARY

Requirements engineering is the approach by which we ensure that the process of understanding and documenting the business requirements is rigorous and that it ensures the traceability of each requirement. This process comprises the stages of elicitation, analysis (which feeds back into the elicitation) and validation. All of these contribute to the production of a rigorous, complete requirements document. The core of this document is a repository of individual requirements that is developed and managed during the requirements engineering process. Where organisations place insufficient emphasis on defining requirements this is to the detriment of the implemented solutions and can leave business stakeholders unable to do their jobs effectively. Requirements engineering is an approach by which we can deliver solutions that truly meet business needs.

REFERENCES

Alexander, I. and Maiden, N. (2004) *Scenarios, Stories and Use Cases*. John Wiley & Sons, Chichester.

Maiden, N.A.M. and Rugg, G. (1996) ACRE: selecting methods for requirements acquisition. *Software Engineering Journal,* **11**, 183–192.

Polanyi, M. (1966) *Tacit Knowledge in Managerial Success*. University of Chicago Press, Chicago.

Wittgenstein, L. (1953) *Philosophical Investigations*. Blackwell, Oxford.

FURTHER READING

Alexander, I. and Beus-Dukic, L. (2009) *Discovering Requirements: How to Specify Products and Services*. John Wiley & Sons, Chichester.

Alexander, I. and Stevens, R. (2002) *Writing Better Requirements*. Pearson Education, Harlow.

Cadle, J., Paul, D. and Turner, P. (2010) *Business Analysis Techniques*. BCS, Swindon.

Gause, D. and Weinberg, G. (1989) *Exploring Requirements: Quality before Design*. Dorset House, New York.

Hay, D. (2003) *Requirements Analysis*. Prentice Hall, Upper Saddle River, NJ.

Kulak, D. and Guiney, E. (2004) *Use Cases: Requirements in Context,* 2nd edn. Pearson Education, Boston, MA.

Robertson, S. and Robertson, J. (2006) *Mastering the Requirements Process,* 2nd edn. Pearson Education, Boston, MA.

Skidmore, S. and Eva, M. (2004) *Introducing Systems Development*. Palgrave Macmillan, Basingstoke.

Yeates, D. and Wakefield, T. (2004) *Systems Analysis and Design*. FT Prentice Hall, Harlow.

10 DOCUMENTING AND MANAGING REQUIREMENTS

Debra Paul

INTRODUCTION

This chapter is concerned with two of the key elements of requirements engineering: documenting the requirements that have been gathered and managing those requirements in such a way that they are communicated to stakeholders and can be traced through the business change process. Documenting requirements clearly is vital to the success of a project. Projects fail because they lack good requirements definition.

THE IMPORTANCE OF DOCUMENTATION

There are many reasons for needing good documentation. First, it enables communication within the project team and provides a basis for ensuring that all of the related requirements are consistent with each other. Second, the documentation provides the business managers and staff, who are the sources and owners of the requirements, with a firm basis for validating that the documentation accurately records what they need the solution to provide. Third, any further work to develop and test the business solutions will use the documentation as input to these activities. The requirements documentation will define what the solution is to do, and the acceptance criteria required to test the solutions will be defined. The requirements documentation is also used after the implementation of the business solution, for example in the maintenance of IT systems and during benefits realisation.

THE REQUIREMENTS DOCUMENT

Structure
The requirements document has to provide the basis for the solutions to be delivered to the organisation, so it needs to be well formed and clear. The business managers and staff have to review the documentation in order to ensure that the descriptions of the requirements reflect their needs and that the analysts have correctly interpreted and understood the information provided to them.

One of the key approaches to supporting the review of the documentation is to ensure that it is well structured. The requirements document needs to provide all of the information that the reviewers require in an easily understandable and digestible form. A well-structured document will help to improve the accessibility of the information in it. The requirements document may be partitioned by business area or for specific groups of stakeholders. Whatever the basis used for partitioning, an organised requirements document will make reviewing much easier and help to ensure that the agreed requirements are accurate.

Content of the Requirements Document

The requirements document should contain the following sections, as represented in Figure 10.1:

Figure 10.1 Contents of a requirement document

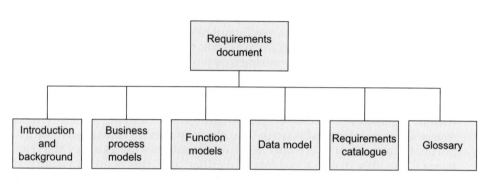

- **Introduction and background:** this section should set out a description of the business situation and drivers for the project. It serves to clarify the objectives and scope of the work and ensure that all stakeholders are aware of the business context for the requirements.

- **Business process models:** typically, the requirements will involve changes to the business processes. In addition, any software solution must support the business processes. This section is where the 'to be' process models should set out the vision for the new processes. If required, the 'as is' processes that are to be revised may also be included here.

- **Function models:** diagrams showing the functionality of the proposed software solution may be included here. Types of diagram often used here are context diagrams and use case diagrams. These models provide an excellent introduction to the functionality of the required solution because they give a complete overview of it, and they provide a means for structuring the requirements catalogue. Context diagrams and use case diagrams are described in Chapter 11.

- **Data model:** a data model is relevant where the requirements document is to be defined at a level of detail such that it can be used to build a software solution or evaluate an off-the-shelf package. If the requirements catalogue contains lists of data within individual requirements, these lists are extremely difficult to review and evaluate for correctness. Also, the structure of the data and the ways in which different groups of data need to relate to each other cannot be defined easily within a textual description. A data model provides a far superior view of the data and enables the analyst to consider the exact business rules and requirements to be met by the solution. Two data modelling techniques, entity relationship modelling and class modelling, are described in Chapter 11.

- **Requirements catalogue:** the information about each individual requirement should be documented in the requirements catalogue. The catalogue is the key component for the audit trail of the requirements because it is the central repository of information relating to the identification, cross referencing and source of the requirements. This document is described in more detail below.

- **Glossary of terms:** one of the key quality characteristics for the requirements document is to ensure that it provides a clear definition of the requirements so that it can be read, understood and agreed as easily as possible. However, within any organisation there will be terminology that is understood by the people working in a particular area, and often this terminology is very precise in conveying information. As a result, it is important that the requirements are able to use this terminology, but this can present a problem for the analysts and reviewers who lack familiarity with it. A glossary of terms overcomes this problem and provides a central source of terminology definitions. The glossary may be created just for a particular project, or there may be an organisation-wide glossary that can be used, possibly in a reduced form. In either case, this is an important component of the requirements document and will be used throughout the business change and software development lifecycles.

This is not an exhaustive list, and many organisations include other areas in their templates. For example, a list of assumptions or decisions made can often be found in a requirements document.

THE REQUIREMENTS CATALOGUE

When requirements are initially elicited they are not organised, and it is only once the requirements analysis activity takes place that they are structured and formed into an organised set. There are a number of ways of organising requirements, but, fundamentally, a hierarchical approach will provide the easiest structure for navigating and reviewing the requirements. Figure 10.2 shows the four types of requirements: general, technical, functional and non-functional. These categories provide a useful overview structure for a requirements catalogue.

This hierarchy structures the requirements into four discrete areas, based upon their types. These are described below. At the next level, the hierarchy uses other subdivisions to categorise the requirements. For example, within the functional requirements all of the requirements relating to reporting may be grouped together. Alternatively the use cases may be utilised as a mechanism to group requirements.

Figure 10.2 Types of requirements

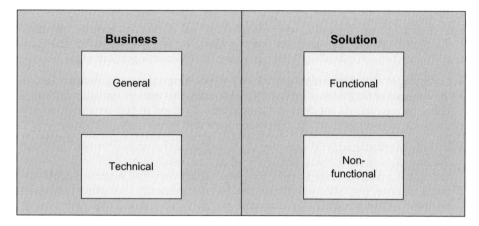

Types of requirements

Within each of these areas there are several specific categories of requirement that should be considered in further detail. We can use these categories as an aide memoire to ensure that areas of requirement are not missed. As discussed in Chapter 9, tacit knowledge is a major issue when eliciting requirements, and the categories of requirement provide a useful basis for asking specific questions about areas that the business staff may not consider relevant or that are taken for granted. Figure 10.3 shows the key categories of requirement for each of the types identified in Figure 10.2.

General requirements

These are the requirements that define business policies, standards and needs. These requirements are often very broad in scope and can have an impact upon a number of different areas. Many general requirements apply to entire business change programmes, and sometimes to all of the change initiatives under way across the organisation. There are specific sub-categories of general requirements:

- **Business constraints:** these cover aspects such as budget, timescale and resources.

- **Business policies:** these cover aspects such as standards and business policy decisions (often known as business rules). These policies and standards ensure consistency of operation across the organisation.

- **Legal:** these are the requirements that state relevant legal and regulatory constraints. Some of these, for example the Data Protection Act, may relate to organisations in many business sectors. Others, such as the Financial Services Act, may be specific to a business sector or an industry.

- **Branding:** these requirements are concerned with the image and style to be promoted for the organisation. Typically there will be branding documentation, for example a style guide, which will set out factors such as logos, key words, language and colour requirements. This documentation will ensure that a consistent brand and image are established across all forms of communication deployed by the organisation. The style guide will set out the look and feel of any systems and documents used within the course of the organisation's work.

- **Cultural:** these requirements relate to the type of culture required within the organisation. They may set out the vision for the organisation, the approach taken to dealing with customers or the management style.

- **Language:** many organisations have specific language requirements because they are operating across international boundaries and in multiple languages. These requirements set out the languages to be used in the organisation and the ways of communicating with customers and other organisations.

- **Business continuity:** the ability of the organisation to continue to function in the face of various threats, natural and as the result of human activity, is very important and gives rise to various disaster-recovery and business-continuity requirements. For example, there may be requirements that state how quickly an organisation should be operational, possibly in a limited way, following a business-continuity incident. Business-continuity requirements may include those designed to prevent a disaster affecting the organisation to any great extent – for example, the need for duplicate installations – as well as contingency requirements that will be needed should a disaster occur. There are likely to be several non-functional requirements associated with the business-continuity requirements, for example in the areas of backup and recovery.

Figure 10.3 Categories of requirements

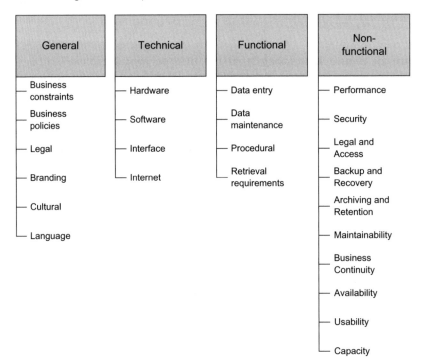

Technical requirements

These are the requirements that state the technical policies and constraints to be adopted across the organisation. They apply to a range of change projects. The specific sub-categories of technical requirements are:

- Hardware requirements covering aspects such as the make and model of hardware equipment to be used in the organisation. These requirements may cover the IT hardware but can also include equipment relating to the work of the organisation, such as production or general office equipment.

- Software requirements covering areas such as operating systems, software package applications, networking and communications software.

- Interoperability requirements that cover the standards for communicating between systems where they are required to exchange data. These requirements may also need to be specified where systems need to communicate with other technical equipment such as printers. The interfaces may be with systems and equipment operated within the organisation or by other, external organisations.

- Internet requirements, which relate to the technical policies governing the organisation's use of the internet and web-enabled services.

Functional requirements

The functional requirements are those that set out the features that any solution should provide. The features that appear in these requirements may be incorporated in a resulting IT system solution, but this is not necessarily the case. Some of the requirements may prove to be too costly or time-consuming, in which case alternative means of delivering them will need to be considered – or they could be dropped altogether. This is a key use for the requirements catalogue, because, whereas the general and technical requirements tend to have a certain longevity, the functional requirements can be subject to frequent change, particularly as they are elaborated upon. As a result, they need to be well documented so that they can be tracked through the development and delivery of the business solution. When eliciting and investigating functional requirements it can be useful to consider several kinds, as follows:

- **Data entry requirements:** these are concerned with gathering and recording the data that is required in the solution.

- **Data maintenance requirements:** these handle changes to the data used within the solution.

- **Procedure requirements:** one of the key sources of error in a business solution occurs where the detailed business rules to be applied during working procedures are not understood well. These requirements need to be defined clearly so that they can be adopted accurately within the solution. Techniques such as those involving decision trees or decision tables can be very useful in documenting these requirements.

- **Retrieval requirements:** these requirements are concerned with requests about the data, and include the provision of specified reports and responses to enquiries. Management and operational information requirements can be numerous and wide ranging. If so, it can be useful to consider these requirements as a separate area of functionality when structuring the requirements catalogue.

Non-functional requirements

The non-functional requirements are concerned with how well the solution will operate, and answer questions such as 'How quickly will it respond?' and 'How easy will it be to use?' There are several areas of non-functional requirement to consider. They are:

- **Speed of performance:** these requirements concern the speed with which a transaction should be processed. For example, if a customer wishes to order some goods or to place a booking, this kind of requirement would define the speed of the processing that is done to handle this.

- **Level of security:** the majority of organisations handle information and data of varying levels of confidentiality. These requirements identify the security levels required for the organisation's information and data. The security levels are likely to differ for different types of information or data. Some will be highly confidential and will require extremely rigorous security; other kinds may still be confidential while being subject to less security. The storage requirements for the information and data may also be defined here.

- **Access permissions and constraints:** these requirements are usually related to the security requirements because they define the stakeholder groups and their levels of access to the information and data. The access permissions will state which stakeholders are able to carry out which transactions, for example which stakeholders are allowed to delete the details held for a customer or to pay an invoice from a supplier. The requirements relating to the provision of functions to implement the access permissions will be documented among the functional requirements.

- **Backup and recovery:** the requirements for secure storage and access to information are also linked to these requirements. While it is important to guard against confidentiality breaches, retaining data is also vital, particularly with the rise of remote storage and cloud computing. The backup and recovery requirements define the policy for protecting against the loss of data and information.

- **Archiving and retention:** the retention of data and information within an organisation may be subject to internal policies or external legal regulations. These requirements define aspects such as the duration of the retention, the nature of the archiving methods and the approaches to be taken to the disposal of information and data.

- **Maintainability:** these requirements concern the approaches to be taken to maintaining the solution. These will include aspects such as servicing, problem investigation and correction.

- **Availability:** these requirements concern the timeframe during which a solution must be available to stakeholders. For many web-enabled systems, a requirement is likely to be 24/7 (24 hours a day, 7 days a week) availability. However, other solutions may not require this level of availability or there may be some aspects that can accept a lower level. For example, a telephone enquiry service may need to be available from 8.30 am to 6.00 pm each day but should be supplemented by a recorded message service outside these hours.

- **Usability:** this area concerns the ease with which a stakeholder can learn, apply and use new processes and systems. It is a critical aspect of many IT solutions, in particular because of web-enabled information and purchasing services offered by many organisations. Whereas internal business stakeholders can be trained to use new processes and systems, this will not be possible for external stakeholders such as customers. Ease of learning and use is therefore very important. There are many criteria that can be defined for usability requirements, including speed in learning to use the system and ease of navigation (for example, the number of clicks needed to obtain information).

- **Capacity:** these requirements cover areas such as the volumes of data and information to be stored, the volumes of transactions to be processed and the number of stakeholders to be supported.

The non-functional requirements are areas that are often left until later or even dismissed at an overview level without clear thought and analysis. This can be a critical error. There are numerous apocryphal tales of organisational disasters – or near-disasters – resulting from such relaxed thinking. Public-sector organisations have been criticised heavily for losing confidential data or for making it accessible when it should not have been. However, private-sector organisations are not necessarily any better at this. Some commercial organisations have promoted new services and then not had the capacity in terms of staff and systems to handle the level of interest generated. Some websites providing online information and services are either shockingly unusable or simple but tedious. How often have you entered account data, only to be told after submitting it all that you have made a simple error and now have to re-enter the entire set? How often have you left an organisation's website in frustration at the lack of assistance and the time required to complete a simple enquiry? In a competitive business world, organisations cannot afford either legal transgressions or business mistakes. It is often the work of the business analyst that can put in place the processes and systems to overcome them.

Hierarchy of requirements

Requirements are related to each other. Some general and technical requirements refer to business policies that are elaborated and expanded in the non-functional and functional requirements. Understanding the hierarchy of requirements helps ensure that the requirements are consistent and coherent. When we define a functional requirement the business context and basis that underpins and supports it is clear. When eliciting non-functional requirements, the business and technical policies help give insights into why these requirements are necessary at the level of performance stated.

As an example, UK data protection legislation defines eight principles to be adopted by any organisation that stores personal data. This requirement will be elaborated further in the non-functional requirements, with definitions of the security levels required for specific sets of data and information, and in the requirements concerning access restrictions and data backup and recovery. Further, the functional requirements that define the data and information requirements will be linked to the security and legal requirements for this area.

The hierarchy of requirements, linking functional and non-functional requirements back to the general and technical business requirements, provides a means of tracing the original business need for them. This helps when considering the priority of the requirements, the timescale for delivery and the possibility of dropping a requirement.

Documenting a requirement

Each requirement should be documented in order to define clearly what is required. A standard requirements catalogue template should contain the entries described below.

- **Requirement identifier:** the unique identifier allocated to the requirement. This is often a code that is linked to the type of requirement. For example, the technical requirements may be allocated identifiers T-n, such as T-001, T-002, and so on. The identifier will also include a version number, including a 'draft' version number to be used when the requirement is still to be reviewed and agreed. Example identifiers might be 'G-006v0-1' to indicate a general requirement in its first draft version or 'F-028v2-0' to indicate a functional requirement in its second reviewed and agreed version.

- **Requirement name:** the name allocated to a requirement. This is a short descriptive phrase that indicates what the requirement concerns.

- **Requirement description:** a clear definition of the requirement. Initially the description may be at an outline level, and it will be elaborated in more detailed versions of the requirement documentation. When describing requirements it is good practice to adopt the structure:

  (i)   actor (or user role);

  (ii) verb phrase;

  (iii) object (noun or noun phrase).

An example functional requirement is 'The receptionist shall be able to view the customer name, address and telephone number'. An example general requirement is 'The solution shall comply with the provisions of the Data Protection Act, 1998'.

- **Source:** the originating person or information source for the requirement. This might be the name of a stakeholder, or it could be a reference to a document containing information relevant to the project. For example, a stakeholder may have identified the requirement during an interview or other discussion, or there may be an earlier document – such as a project brief or feasibility study – that includes some of the business requirements.

- **Owner:** the business stakeholder who can make decisions regarding the requirement. Typically this will be the business manager responsible for the business function or department, who has the authority to approve the definition of the requirement.

- **Author:** the analyst who has elicited and documented the requirement.

- **Type of requirement:** the category to which this requirement belongs. It may be sufficient to indicate whether the requirement is general, technical, functional or non-functional – although it may not be necessary to state this if the identifier includes a reference to the type – or the type of requirement may be defined at sub-category level. For example, a requirement may be 'general, legal'.

- **Priority:** the level of priority of the requirement. The approach used here varies between organisations but can also vary between different projects within an organisation. Sometimes a straightforward system of high, medium or low priority is used, with the organisation deciding the implications of each level. Sometimes priorities are described in some detail, as in 'mandatory', 'desirable' and 'nice to have'. The DSDM Atern method defined a richer approach to prioritisation by using the mnemonic MoSCoW. This is particularly suitable where several increments of a business change solution are to be implemented or an evolutionary development approach is to be taken to a software solution. The acronym stands for:

  o **M – must have:** mandatory in the first increment – absolutely essential;

  o **S – should have:** mandatory but may be deferred (for a short period) to the second increment;

  o **C – could have:** desirable but may not be implemented due to time and budget;

  o **W – won't have this time:** identified as a requirement to be deferred until a later stage. There may be several reasons why a requirement is deferred. Some requirements are recognised as ones that need further consideration and that would cause delays to some of the mandatory requirements if they were to be implemented in the first increment. Others may require a later implementation for business reasons. This might be because a requirement concerns an element of the business strategy that is due to be put into operation at a later point, or it could be because of an anticipated legal change.

- **Business area:** the name of the business area to which the requirement belongs. This might be the name of the business function or department. If a more detailed approach is considered to be useful, the name of the business process or use case may appear here.

- **Stakeholders:** the job roles or names of any stakeholders with a particular interest in the successful resolution of this requirement, and the details of their interest. Identifying stakeholders and their interests for each requirement provides a useful prompt to the business analyst to ensure that all relevant stakeholders' interests have been covered and, later, satisfied.

- **Associated non-functional requirements:** the specific non-functional requirements that may be associated with some functional requirements. For example, there may be a business customer service policy that guarantees a speed of response to information requests. As a result, the functional requirement about accessing customer account information may have a non-functional requirement concerning performance response time associated with it.

- **Acceptance criteria:** the criteria that will enable the business staff to agree formally that the requirement has been met. For each requirement, we should consider how we can check or measure whether the requirement has been met.

- **Related requirements:** the identifiers of any requirements that are related to this requirement. They may be related for several reasons: there might be a higher-level business requirement that provides further business information or justification for a functional or non-functional requirement, there might be non-functional requirements concerning areas such as usability or security that affect functional requirements or vice versa or there might be other requirements that concern a similar general, technical, functional or non-functional area. The identifier for each of the related requirements should be listed here.

- **Related documents:** the identifiers for any documents that provide further information about this requirement. These could be part of the project documentation, such as the project initiation document, or business justification documents such as the business case. Another form of documentation that may be linked to the requirements is the set of modelling documents that have been created for the business change project. Some of these models may be contained within the requirements document. However, it is still useful to show where there are requirements that are related to them.

- **Comments:** additional comments that the analyst finds it useful to record for a particular requirement.

- **Rationale:** the business justification for the requirement. The rationale entry for a requirement may be cross-referenced to specific benefits in the business case.

- **Resolution:** the outcome of this requirement. There are several possibilities here because a requirement may be implemented, deferred for consideration in a later increment, merged with another requirement or dropped. The resolution field will be used to record the decision and its timing.

- **Version history:** the history of the requirement through the different versions that have been created. Each version should also record the reason for the change and a reference to the change-control documentation.

However, producing a full definition for each requirement will be extremely time-consuming and could result in wasted effort in some situations. The level of detail of the definition will depend upon several factors, including:

- the stage of the analysis – whether it is an initial view of the requirements or a more detailed requirements specification;

- the nature of the solution, for example whether it is a business process change or an IT system replacement;

- the priority of the requirement, which is an essential piece of information that will help to prioritise the requirements work (for example, if a requirement is allocated a W priority, the detailed work should be deferred until the point where it is to be included in the solution);

- the approach to be adopted in order to deliver the solution – for example, evolutionary system development or off-the-shelf software purchase.

Some aspects of a requirements catalogue definition will emerge earlier than others. Initially, we may only document the identifier, name, description, source and author. However, once more detailed requirements analysis has been performed, additional aspects such as owner and priority will be defined. After the requirements catalogue has been structured and duplicate or overlapping requirements removed, features such as the related requirements will be stated. Cross-referencing to other documents or models may be done late in require-ments analysis. The resolution of a requirement may only be entered once the requirements have been validated, and this could be subject to change if a MoSCoW prioritisation approach is used.

The requirements catalogue is a central document throughout a business change project. It records what is required, business justifications, sources of information and a rich network of connections. The level of the descriptions needs to be suffi-cient for the purpose rather than over-engineered for any eventuality. Sometimes the business stakeholders are unable to provide the precise requirements in extensive detail, and the approach that will deliver the requirements needs to take account of this. In this situation the description still needs to be clear about what is required but may not contain the complete set of details. Sometimes the busi-ness staff have decided what is needed but some of the finer detail, particularly concerning the way the requirement will ultimately be delivered, may still be open for discussion. In this situation, the requirements catalogue should be clear about what is required and leave the further detail to be explored using approaches such as scenarios and prototyping.

Figure 10.4 shows a sample entry from a requirements catalogue.

MANAGING REQUIREMENTS

A failure to understand, document and manage requirements often lies at the heart of problems with business and IT system change projects. While a struc-tured, well-defined set of requirements will provide an excellent basis for a change project, problems can still occur if the requirements are not traceable. The traceability of requirements is a critical quality characteristic. There are two forms of traceability: 'backwards from' and 'forwards to':

- 'Backwards from' traceability involves the ability to trace the source of a requirement from any later point in the business change or software development lifecycle. It answers the question 'What was the source requirement for this feature of the solution and who raised it?' We need to be able to identify where a requirement originated so that we can seek clarifica-tion from the source where necessary. This is particularly important when requirements are in conflict or there are conflicting views as to the priority of a requirement.

Figure 10.4 Requirements catalogue example

Requirements catalogue					
Project ID and name: TrentCars Sales Improvement Project					
Author:	Date:	Version:	Status:	Page:	1
J Williams	02/09/10	0.1	In development	of	1
Requirement ID		G-001v0.1			
Requirement name		Compliance with Data Protection Act			
Business area/domain		Sales, Servicing, Customer Services			
Source		L. Stevens, Customer Services Manager			
Owner		W. Brown, Managing Director			
Priority		M			
Type of requirement		General			
Requirement description		The solution shall comply with the eight principles of the Data Protection Act, 1998.			
Associated non-functional requirements		See related requirements.			
Acceptance criteria		Users without authorised access to personal data shall be advised that they do not have the authority to access the data and shall not be allowed access to the data.			
Justification		Legal requirement. Non-compliance could result in the receipt of an enforcement notice from the Information Commissioner's Office or the Information Commissioner's Office could impose a financial penalty on TrentCars.			
Comments					
Related documents		Memo from W. Brown 'Data Protection Act compliance' dated 12/06/08. Information Commissioner's Office website www.ico.gov.uk			
Related requirements		N-005 Data Access Restrictions; N-110 Data Security			
Resolution		To be implemented in phase 1			

- 'Forwards to' traceability involves the ability to identify any requirement and track where it has been further developed and ultimately implemented. It answers the question 'What happened to this requirement?' and should show that each requirement has been resolved satisfactorily.

Requirements management is essential if requirements are to be traceable. There are several elements involved in managing requirements, as shown in Figure 10.5 and described below.

Figure 10.5 Elements of requirements management

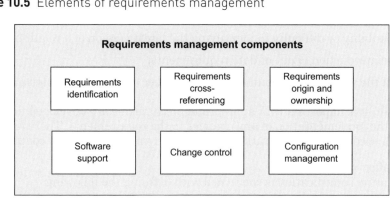

Requirements identification
Each requirement needs to be identified uniquely so that any reference to it corresponds to only one requirement.

Cross-referencing
All related requirements and documents should be cross-referenced so that further elaboration or information concerning a requirement can be accessed easily. During requirements management, the cross-references provide the basis for impact analysis of proposed changes. They allow the analyst to identify which requirements are related to the one that is the subject of the change and to consider whether the change will affect the other requirements.

Origin and ownership
The source identifies the origin of the requirement. This is the person or the document to which the requirement's 'backwards from' traceability should lead. Whether it is a person or a document, the source will be able to provide additional information about, and justification for, the requirement. When we are considering changes to the requirement the source can help to clarify the impact of the change and, as a result, help with the decision about it.

The owner typically has responsibility for the business area affected by the requirement, and will need to make decisions about the requirement. It is important, therefore, that this person is involved as the change project unfolds. The owner will be a key stakeholder should any proposed changes arise that will affect the requirement, either directly or indirectly (via related requirements). In addition, fundamental business changes such as budget reductions or timescale changes may cause requirements to be discontinued, reprioritised or delayed. The owner will be the senior person in the decision-making process for the requirement, and will have the ultimate authority concerning it.

Configuration management

Configuration management is concerned with controlling any changes made to project deliverables, such as documents, in order to ensure that the changes are made in a disciplined manner and traceability is sustained. Without effective configuration management the requirements document can become inaccurate, as the following problems can occur:

- impossibility or difficulty in identifying the latest version of a requirement;

- the reintroduction of out-of-date requirements;

- use of the wrong set of requirements for further development or testing work.

As a result, it is important that appropriate mechanisms are developed to manage the implementation of any changes to the requirements. There are two key areas to consider: configuration identification and configuration control.

Configuration identification

Configuration identification is concerned with defining the following:

- The deliverables to be brought under configuration control. These are known as the configuration items (CIs). During requirements management, the deliverables will include the individual requirements' catalogue entries, the composite set of entries that form the requirements catalogue, the models that elaborate and define the requirements and the requirements document. There should also be a structure showing how these configuration items relate to each other.

- The identifier and version numbering scheme to be applied to the CIs. As discussed previously, each requirement has a unique identifier. If we are to control the other configuration items, each of them will also need one. The requirements catalogue, for example, will require an identifier. Where a CI has been identified and has an identifier, it will also require a version number, and the approach to be adopted for allocating version numbers will need to be defined. Version numbers will apply to all the different CIs. For example, while an individual requirement will have a version number, so will the whole requirements catalogue within which the requirement sits.

Configuration control

There will also need to be a process for controlling the CIs and ensuring that they are not changed without formal approval and version numbering. This is typically called a version control process. There are several elements to this.

First, a CI is created in draft form. While the item will have an identifier, the version number will need to indicate that the CI is still in draft form. One approach is to number initial drafts using the format $0.n$. For example, a draft requirement catalogue entry with an identifier T-007 could be numbered T-007v0.3, indicating that this is the third draft version of the technical requirement numbered 007.

Second, as described in Chapter 9, requirements validation is carried out in order to review and agree the requirements documentation. At this point the CIs that describe the requirements are said to be 'baselined'. This means that they are brought under configuration control and cannot be changed by anyone without following the formal configuration management procedure. When a CI is brought under configuration control it is allocated a version number reflecting its base-lined status. Using our example above, the technical requirement would have the identifier/version number T-007v1.0. Sometimes it can be useful to baseline a requirements document prior to requirements validation, when rigorous requirements analysis has been carried out and a formal approach to change control is felt to be beneficial.

Third, once a CI is baselined, no changes can be made to the content without the approval of the configuration manager. All of the CIs should be stored in a secure area so that they cannot be accessed and revised at will. If a change to an item is approved, the configuration manager releases it for revision. Once the item has been amended and the revised version brought under configuration control, the new version is renumbered. In our example the requirement would now be allocated the number T-007v2.0.

Configuration management in an agile environment

Configuration management needs particular consideration when an agile development approach such as DSDM/Atern or Scrum is used. Because these approaches tend to embrace change and explore requirements using prototyping approaches, much of the information about the requirements will be defined within the prototypes rather than the requirements documentation.

While the high-level requirements documentation should be relatively stable, the prototypes that are used to elaborate and implement the requirements are likely to change regularly. Having been baselined reasonably early in the development project, the requirements document will provide an audit trail for the high-level requirements. However, baselining and controlling the versions of the prototypes will also be important if the requirements are to be managed.

There are several possibilities for baselining the prototypes during agile software development, including:

- **Baselining every prototype before demonstration:** this has the virtue of clarifying the version that has been demonstrated to the business users.

- **Baselining daily:** this is highly disciplined but can prove onerous and unnecessary.

- **Baselining at the end of a timebox:** this is fine if the timeboxes are reasonable short – a few days, perhaps – but less sensible with longer timeboxes or, for example, the 30-day 'sprints' used within Scrum.

Each baselined prototype is placed under configuration control, since this is the only way to ensure that the up-to-date version of the prototype is used. The CI will consist of the actual prototype, the tests run on it and the record of the users' comments. Thus, as the prototypes are developed and refined, a complete audit trail is created of the changes made and – very importantly – why they were made.

Change control

Changes occur frequently on projects. This may be because of external factors such as legal or regulatory changes or competitive forces, or may result from internal changes, for example in strategies, policies or people. As a result, any requirement may be subject to change during a project. Having accepted that changes will happen, requirements management should include a process to handle these changes. The stages of this process are as follows:

- **Documenting the proposed change:** the change should be documented on a 'change request' form stating who raised the change, a description of it and a justification for requesting it.

- **Consulting the stakeholders:** each change request should be sent to representative stakeholders to assess the impact of the proposed change, including the effort it will take to make the change and the corresponding cost.

- **Deciding on the change:** the change request and the impact assessment should be reviewed by the designated approval authority. If the change has been approved for implementation, the CI is released by the configuration librarian so that the change can be applied and the new version created. The combination of the configuration management and change control approaches provides a means of creating a version history for the requirements documentation. Each change that has been applied to the requirements is documented with an explanation of why the older version was changed to create the new version. Over time a complete audit trail will be created, explaining what actions were taken, why this was done and when.

Software support

Most requirements documents contain so many requirements that it is not possible to manage the set of documentation, cross-references and versions manually, so an automated tool is usually required. Such a tool should provide the following features:

- **Documentation creation and storage:** this will require editing tools that provide facilities such as word processing and modelling. Further, some tools provide document management capabilities that incorporate functions such as the publication of documents for access by authorised stakeholders, allowing online reviewing and revision tracking.

- **Secure storage and access:** if the documentation is to be placed under configuration control, it will be essential for there to be restricted access to the individual documents.

- **Documentation linkage:** the cross-references between documents will need to be recorded and related documents accessed easily. This will help in requirements management activities such as impact analysis and the tracing of version histories.

- **Version numbering:** the tool should manage the allocation of identifiers and version numbers to configuration items.

Some specialist toolsets provide a range of features, including those listed above, designed to support rigorous and efficient requirements management. Some may be integrated tools, providing functionality that supports later activities such as code generation and testing. However, many organisations use automated tools that are not designed specifically for requirements management and may only offer generic features such as diagram creation and word processing. Such software can offer the key functionality required for requirements management but will require a great deal of manual activity rather than giving automated support.

CONCLUSION

Well-defined and traceable requirements are absolutely key to a successful business change project. The requirements document needs to be structured clearly so that a rigorous requirements validation can be conducted by the reviewers. Traceability of the requirements is also critical if the business is to be able to confirm that its needs have been met and all decisions regarding the requirements are to be transparent and auditable.

FURTHER READING

Cadle, J., Paul, D. and Turner, P. (2010) *Business Analysis Techniques*. BCS, Swindon.

Robertson, S. and Robertson, J. (2006) *Mastering the Requirements Process,* 2nd edn. Pearson Education, Boston, MA.

Skidmore, S. and Eva, M. (2004) *Introducing Systems Development.* Palgrave Macmillan, Basingstoke.

Withall, S. (2007) *Software Requirements Patterns.* Microsoft Press, Redmond, WA.

Yeates, D. and Wakefield, T. (2004) *Systems Analysis and Design.* FT Prentice Hall, Harlow.

11 MODELLING REQUIREMENTS

Debra Paul and James Cadle

INTRODUCTION

This chapter introduces some of the most commonly used techniques for modelling requirements for IT systems. These techniques are used to analyse and specify requirements during systems development. Models are extremely useful in helping to clarify understanding and, if cross-checked with other models, ensuring the completeness of the analysis. A model shows only one view or perspective of a system, but it shows this view very clearly. This induces the analyst to ask further questions, often those that have not been identified previously. The techniques we describe here have been selected from two distinct approaches to systems modelling: use case diagrams and class modelling from the unified modelling language (UML) and entity-relationship modelling from the family of structured, data-driven approaches. The selected techniques model two distinct views of the IT system: the functions that the system will provide and the data to be stored within the system.

MODELLING SYSTEM FUNCTIONS

The saying 'one picture is worth 10,000 words' applies directly to the definition of IT system requirements. It is extremely difficult, if not impossible, to write textual statements that are completely unambiguous. However, this is not the case with a model that has been drawn using defined notational standards; every box or line makes a clear statement about the system under investigation. Some models are more easily understood by business users than others. The view of a system that is often most accessible to business users depicts the 'functions' that will be provided and the 'actors' who are involved in using those functions. A function may be defined as a set of actions that the business users want the IT system to support in order to achieve a specific goal. For example, a function might be 'Record customer'; the actions here would include the following:

- Accept the customer details.
- Validate the customer details.
- Store the customer details that have been entered.

In the UML a use case is something that an actor wants the IT system to do; it is a 'case of use' of the system by a specific actor and describes the interaction between the actor and the system. Each use case will have a stated goal and will contain a description of the actions that the system must perform in order to achieve this goal. The use case model will consist of a diagram showing the actors, the use cases and the associations between them, plus a set of use case descriptions. The following elements are found in the use case diagram:

- **Actors** are whoever or whatever expects a service from the system. They are usually user roles but may also be external systems or time. On the use case diagram, actors are shown interacting with the use cases. As they are external to the system and outside its control, defining the system actors and the use cases they are associated with helps in defining the system boundary. Actors are usually shown as matchstick figures, but if the actor is another system it can be shown by a rectangle with an <<actor>> stereotype before the name of the system. Some analysts prefer to show all actors, including the job roles, as rectangles because business users can feel that matchstick figures trivialise the diagrams. Time can also be an actor and may be shown as a rectangle or matchstick figure.

- Each **use case** is shown as an oval and represents a function that the system will perform in response to a trigger from the actor. We use the 'verb–noun' convention to name use cases, for example 'Set up project' or 'Book room'.

- **The system boundary** is indicated by drawing a large box around all of the use cases but with the actors outside the box. This clearly illustrates the boundary of the system and is very useful when agreeing the scope of the system.

- **Associations** indicate which actors will need to interact with which use cases. Lines are drawn linking actors with the appropriate use cases.

The use case diagram in Figure 11.1 shows part of a project control system. We might create a diagram such as this during a workshop or following some interviews with the business users

---

Figure 11.1 A use case diagram for a project control system

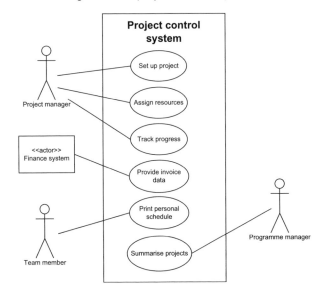

Use case diagrams are particularly helpful during a workshop because they are so easily understood by business users and provide an excellent framework for the discussion. The detail of the interaction between an actor and a use case is documented in a use case description. This lists the steps that take place during the interaction and is usually a textual description. The detail of any processing carried out within the use case may be documented using a variety of techniques. For example, we could use activity diagrams from the UML or other more established techniques such as decision tables.

The <<include>> and <<extend>> constructs

When exploring the use cases, it often emerges that some processing elements are repeated. For example, in the project control system many of the use cases start by identifying the project concerned. As it stands, the steps involved in identifying the project would have to be included in each use case and a great deal of duplication would result. Instead of this, the project identification elements can be written as a separate use case and then 'included' in a number of others. This is represented in Figure 11.2 where the

---

Figure 11.2 Use case diagram showing <<include>>

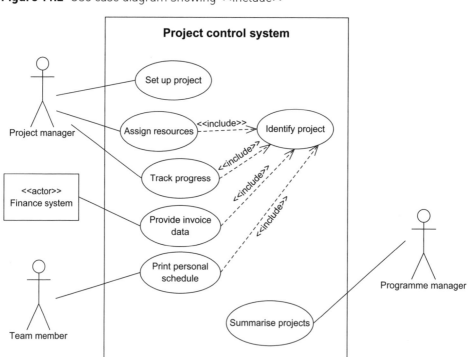

<<include>> stereotype is shown on a dotted line with an arrowhead pointing to the included use case.

It may also emerge during more detailed investigation and specification that there are some optional elements to the use cases that require a significant amount of processing and may be so large that they overwhelm the original use case. In this situation, a separate use case can be created to 'extend' the original use case. For example, after the project manager tracks progress, he or she may also print a progress report; in Figure 11.3, this has been split off into a separate use case. The new use case is said to 'extend' the original use case. This type of association is shown by a dotted line with an arrowhead that points back to the original use case.

The <<include>> and <<extend>> concepts allow use cases to be connected to each other. This is the only way in which use cases are linked, as these diagrams are not intended to show the flow – or sequence – of the processing.

Figure 11.3 Use case diagram showing <<include>> and <<extend>>

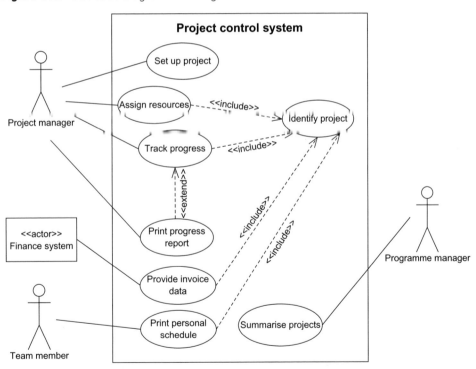

MODELLING SYSTEM DATA

Modelling the data to be stored within the IT system is essential. A data model allows the stakeholders who will need to use the system or obtain information from it to agree on the data that will be recorded and retrieved. It will also provide the basis for the database design in a bespoke development or help in the evaluation of a packaged application. Data modelling is a useful tool for the business analyst. It helps the analyst better understand the data required to support process improvements and provides a mechanism for communicating the data requirements forward into the design and building of an IT system. The entity relationship modelling technique is used extensively to model the data to be held in IT systems. The UML approach to modelling data, known as class modelling, is also widely used. In this chapter we look at both of these techniques.

Entity relationship diagrams

Whether they are computerised or not, organisations require clear and accurate knowledge of the data structures that underlie their information requirements. Data is the raw building block of all information systems, and the objective of data modelling is to express this structure in a concise and usable way. Data modelling is concerned with identifying and understanding:

- the data items (attributes) that the organisation (or system) needs to keep;
- the grouping of the attributes (into entities);
- the relationships between entities.

The notation we use here is from the information engineering approach, pioneered by James Martin (Finkelstein and Martin 1981). It is used in various analyst support tools.

An entity is something that the enterprise recognises in the area under investigation and wishes to collect and store data about. An entity might be:

- physical, e.g. an order, a customer or a supplier;
- conceptual, e.g. a booking or an appointment;
- active, e.g. a meeting or a course.

Entities are represented on the model by boxes. Each entity has a meaningful name, normally a noun, which is always singular. It is important to distinguish between the 'entity type' and the 'entity occurrence'. For example, if the entity type is 'Book' then the entity occurrence is a specific instance of a book, such as *Business Analysis or Data Analysis for Database Design*. The physical equivalent of an entity type is a table, and that of an entity occurrence is a record. We usually talk about 'entities' as an abbreviation of 'entity types' but refer specifically to entity occurrences. Individual occurrences of an entity must be uniquely identifiable. For example, each 'Customer' or 'Order' must have a unique identifier such as 'account-number' or 'order-number'.

Attributes

Entities contain and are described by attributes (or more accurately attribute types). For example, the entity 'Book' might be described by the attributes 'title', 'author-name', 'publisher' and 'price'. Attributes may also be called data items. An attribute's physical equivalent is a field. A specific entity occurrence should be uniquely identifiable by the value of an attribute or combination of attributes. For example, a 'Member' may be identified by the attribute 'member-number', or a specific 'Book' be recognised from the combination of the two attributes 'author' and 'title'. This identifying attribute or combination of attributes is termed the key to the entity. The initial entities and some attributes will be identified from the interview notes, documents and observations made in the fact-finding and investigation of the current system. Existing file or database content and information needs also give pointers to system entities and their attributes.

Relationships

A relationship is a relevant business connection between two entities. A relationship is represented on a data model by a line linking the associated entities. Relationships may be:

- one-to-many (1:m);

- one-to-one (1:1);

- many-to-many (m:m).

One-to-many relationships

Relationships are often of the degree one-to-many (1:m). For example, an employee is allocated to one office, but each office must have one or more employees allocated to it. We represent this as shown in Figure 11.4. Here the notation of a 'crow's foot' is used to indicate that an 'Office' is related to one or many 'Employee's. At the other end of the line, a solid line indicates that an 'Employee' is related to exactly one 'Office'. In a simple order-processing entity model there appears to be an obvious 1:m relationship between 'Customer' and 'Order'. A customer will place one or many orders, but a particular order will only be placed by only one customer.

Figure 11.4 Diagram showing one-to-many relationship

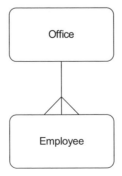

One-to-one relationships

If we were looking at a system to hold data about a company, its offices and the employees working in the offices, and each office was allocated to only one employee while each employee was allocated to only one office, then the relationship between 'Office' and 'Employee' would be one-to-one. Similarly, in the system shown in Figure 11.5, an 'Order' is related to one 'Invoice' and an 'Invoice' is concerned with only one 'Order'. The relationship between the two entities is exactly one-to-one. A solid line is used to indicate this.

Figure 11.5 Diagram showing a one-to-one relationship

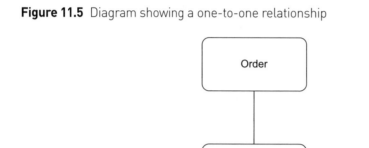

One-to-one relationships are not permitted in some data-modelling approaches and, where this is the case, it is usually suggested that the two entities should be merged. If this happens, one of the identifiers is selected to identify the merged set and the entity is named accordingly. An identifier is the attribute or set of attributes used to identify an entity; the one that is created first is usually used to identify the new entity created from the merged entities. If the 'Order' and 'Invoice' entities from the example above were merged, the identifier for the 'Order' entity would be likely to be the one chosen, since an 'Order' is created before its 'Invoice'.

Optionality

More detailed information about the business rules that underpin the data model is represented by including optionality in the relationship between two entities. The optionality of a relationship describes whether the entities at both ends of it must always coexist or whether one of them can exist without the other. Where there is no optionality and both entities must always coexist, the relationship is drawn using a solid line. In the examples in Figures 11.4 and 11.5, the entities are joined by a solid line. This indicates that both entities must exist and that neither can be stored in the system without the other being present; this is sometimes called a fully mandatory relationship. Another example of this type of relationship is shown in Figure 11.6. In this case, each 'Order' input to the system must always have at least one 'Order line', and each 'Order line' must be related to exactly one 'Order'.

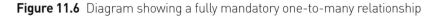

Figure 11.6 Diagram showing a fully mandatory one-to-many relationship

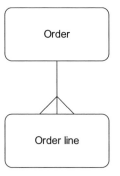

The complete opposite of a fully mandatory relationship occurs where a relationship is fully optional. This means that both entities can exist completely independently of one another. In the example in Figure 11.7 the relationship is shown by a dotted line. This indicates that an order can be placed without a customer call being made and a customer call need not result in an order.

Figure 11.7 Diagram showing a fully optional one-to-many relationship

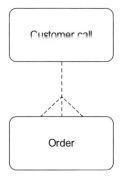

The remaining two alternatives show how relationships need to be analysed in two directions: from the 'one' end of the relationship, known as the parent or master entity, to the 'many' end of the relationship, known as the child or detail entity. The first situation is where a parent entity can exist without any child entities but a child entity must have a parent. In the example in Figure 11.8 we can see that a customer may not have placed any orders as yet, but an order must always be placed by a customer.

The second situation is the opposite of this, where the parent entity must be linked to at least one child but the child entities can exist without a parent. The example

Figure 11.8 A mandatory parent entity with optional child entities

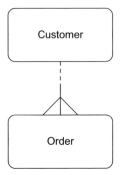

in Figure 11.9 shows that an order need not be related to any complaints but a complaint must concern at least one order.

Figure 11.9 An optional parent entity with mandatory child entities

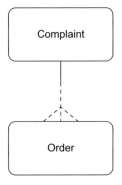

Many-to-many relationships

Many to many (m:m) relationships occur frequently. For example, as shown in Figure 11.10, an employee may be contracted to work on one or more projects and a project may have one or more employees contracted to it.

Many-to-many relationships are normally decomposed into two 1:m relationships with the definition of an additional link entity. Figure 11.11 shows how the link entity 'Contract' has been added so that the many-to-many relationship can be removed. The extended structure shows that an employee is linked to one or more contracts and a contract is for exactly one employee, while a project is linked to one or more contracts and a contract is for exactly one project.

This allows all of the contract details with which an individual employee is associated to be accessed as detail entity occurrences. It also allows access

Figure 11.10 Diagram showing a many-to-many relationship

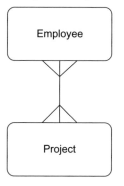

from the project entity to all of the contracts associated with a specific project occurrence. Attributes of the original relationship, for example 'date employee contracted to the project' and 'duration of each contract', can now be recorded as attributes of the link entity. Note that the name of the link entity is normally the noun form of the verb that described the relationship, and thus the contracted relationship is replaced by a 'Contract' entity.

Figure 11.11 Diagram showing a resolved many-to-many relationship

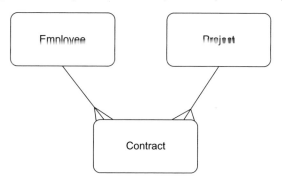

If we look at an order-processing example, there appears to be a many-to-many relationship between the entities 'Product' and 'Order'. An order may be for more than one product, and we would expect most products to be ordered more than once, so they would appear on more than one order. This is solved by introducing a link entity, 'Order line', that has one-to-many relationships with both of the original entities. This structure will be shown as part of the extended example in Figure 11.14.

Many-to-many relationships can be problematic for at least two important reasons:

- They may mask omitted entities. Two examples have already been given above.
- Most database management systems (DBMSs) do not support many-to-many relationships.

Relationship names

The nature of the relationship between two entities is clarified by relationship naming and identification. A relationship link phrase is constructed from the perspective of each entity. In the example in Figure 11.12, a sales region is responsible for zero, one or more customers.

Figure 11.12 Named relationship between entities

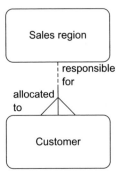

This reads from the 'Sales region' end as:

Each sales region is responsible for zero, one or more customers.

and from the 'Customer' end as:

Each customer is allocated to exactly one sales region.

Figure 11.13 Exclusive relationships

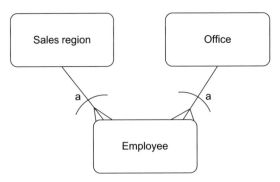

Exclusive relationships

In an exclusive relationship, the participation of an entity occurrence in one relationship precludes it from participating in another. This is indicated by an exclusivity arc (Figure 11.13).

In Figure 11.13, the diagram uses the exclusivity arc notation to show that:

- each employee must be allocated to one and only one sales region or to one and only one office;
- each office is occupied by one or more employees;
- each sales region has one or more employees.

Figure 11.14 An entity relationship diagram for a sales system

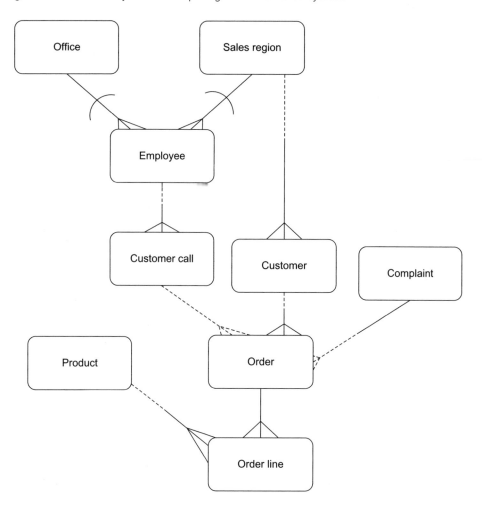

The exclusive relationship may extend to more than two alternatives. For example, if the employee could be allocated to a sales region, an office or a data centre, there would be three entities related to 'Employee' and the exclusivity arc would extend across all three relationships.

Entity relationship diagram for the sales system
If we put the above examples together we can build an entity relationship diagram that reflects the data requirements for our system. This is shown in Figure 11.14.

Alternative notation
There are many notations used when modelling data. Class modelling from the UML is one such alternative and is described below. A further alternative uses horizontal lines to indicate 'one' and circles to indicate optionality. Examples using this notation are shown in Figure 11.15.

Figure 11.15 Alternative data modelling notation

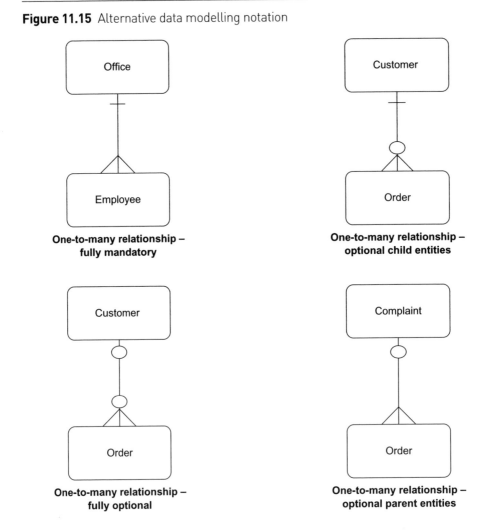

One-to-many relationship –
fully mandatory

One-to-many relationship –
optional child entities

One-to-many relationship –
fully optional

One-to-many relationship –
optional parent entities

CLASS MODELS

A class model shows graphically the **classes** in a system and their associations with each other. These models have similarities to entity relationship diagrams and apply many of the same principles. In a business system a class model captures information about the particular things involved in the organisation's operations, for example projects, customers and team members for a project-control system.

Objects

An **object** is something about which we wish to hold data, because that data is needed within the system we are analysing. For example, an object might be account number NX112G AK506 and we may wish to hold the following information about this object:

- Account number: NX112G;
- Name: Mr H. Hillman;
- Credit limit: £8000;
- Amount payable: £3500.

Objects are sent messages that invoke some kind of a response from them, typically causing them to change data. For example, a message might be sent to the object 'NX112G' telling it to change Mr H. Hillman's credit limit.

Classes

To build a model of the system data we consider classes of objects rather than individual objects. We explained earlier the difference between entity types and entity occurrences. Similarly, in object class modelling we have classes that provide the generic definition of the data items or attributes, and objects that are the instances of a particular class. Thus account 'NX112G' is an object of the class 'Account'. The class 'Account' has attributes such as 'accountNumber' and 'creditLimit' and, as we saw above, the object 'NX112G' has values associated with these attributes. When we define a class we also include **operations** to which it is subject. For an 'Account' these might include 'updateCreditLimit' and 'recordAmount'. All of the 'Account's in the system will contain these attributes and be subject to the same operations. A class, therefore, is a template for its object instances in the same way as an entity type is the template for its entity occurrences. Every object is an instance of some class that defines the common set of features (attributes and operations) that are shared by all of the objects in that class.

In the UML, classes are represented by rectangular boxes with three sections (see Figure 11.16). The name of the class is shown in the top part and is a noun. The first letter is capitalised. Examples are 'Account', 'Payment' and 'Transaction'. If the name is more than one word long, then the words are joined and each is capitalised in the class name, for example 'OrderLine'.

The **attributes** – the individual items of data about the class – are stored in the middle section. The attribute names are usually given in lower case with constituent parts starting with capital letters. The first letter of the attribute name is not capitalised. Examples are 'name', 'dateLastPayment' and 'creditLimit'.

Figure 11.16 Definition of the class 'Account'

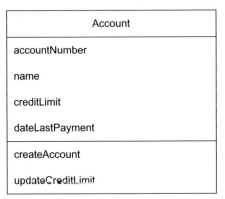

Account
accountNumber
name
creditLimit
dateLastPayment
createAccount
updateCreditLimit

Operations are stored in the bottom part of the class and are invoked by messages being sent to the class by other classes. It is usual to name an operation in the class with the same name as the message that invokes it. The detailed content of the operation – what the class will do when that operation is invoked – will be defined in the **method** associated with the operation; this is usually left to the later stages of the development process.

Attributes held within a class are only accessible to the operations of that class, because they are hidden from all other classes in the system. This is known as encapsulation and is an important principle of the object-oriented approach. Another part of the system that needs to access or modify the data of that class has no need to understand how it is structured. It just sends a message, and the receiving class responds appropriately.

For example, in Figure 11.16 the object class 'Account' has the operation 'update-CreditLimit', which may take place when the customer requests a new credit limit. To enable this to take place a message is sent to the object 'Account' to 'updateCreditLimit', and the parameters of 'accountNumber' and 'newCredit Limit' are also sent so as to indicate the account in question and the new credit limit amount. In the class 'Account' we have defined an operation that is also called 'updateCreditLimit' to respond to the message of the same name. This operation has been specified as 'Replace creditLimit with newCreditLimit', and it uses the value passed in the message to update the credit limit on the appropriate account.

Associations

As in entity relationship modelling, we now need to establish how different classes are linked to each other and the nature of these connections. We call the connections between classes 'associations'. For instance, a 'Project' class must have an association with a 'ProjectManager' class so that the system will be able to list the projects for which a manager is responsible. Figure 11.17 shows this association.

Figure 11.17 An association between two classes

We have already said that classes interact and that this is done by the messages moving along the association lines defined in the class model. If there is no association between classes, then they cannot communicate directly.

The class model reflects the business rules that will govern the classes and the operations performed upon them. Multiplicity is used to show the business rules for an association between classes. For example, the multiplicity of the association shown in Figure 11.18 indicates that a project manager may manage many projects but an individual project may have only one project manager.

Figure 11.18 An association with one-to-many multiplicity

The multiplicity entries can be extended to show the minimum and maximum values in the association. This is shown by using two dots between the minimum and maximum values. For example, the asterisk in the example in Figure 11.18 is a simplification of the range 0..* and the '1' is a simplification of 1..1.

The 'JobSheet' to 'Task' association shown in Figure 11.19 shows that an instance of 'Task' has an optional association with 'JobSheet'. In addition, this shows that,

Figure 11.19 An association with one-to-zero-to-one multiplicity

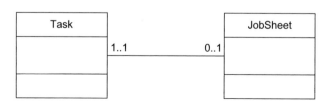

although there may be no 'JobSheets' associated with a 'Task', there is also a maximum of one 'JobSheet' for a given 'Task'.

In the example in Figure 11.20, the class 'Employee' has a mandatory association with 'Allocation' (which is the assignment of someone to a project). There must be at least one instance of 'Allocation' for each instance of 'Employee' (though the asterisk indicates that there is no upper limit). An allocation is for only one 'Employee'.

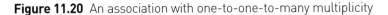

Figure 11.20 An association with one-to-one-to-many multiplicity

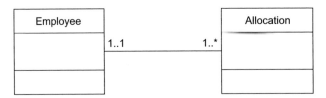

In some circumstances the actual minimum and maximum values may be defined. For example, if we assume there is a business rule that no more than 20 people can be allocated to a project, this would be modelled as shown in Figure 11.21.

Figure 11.21 An association with one-to-one-to-20 multiplicity

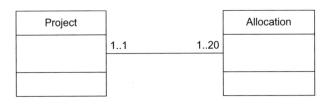

The class model supports associations where the multiplicity is many-to-many. For example, Figure 11.22 shows that a project may have many project managers and each project manager may control many projects. Should this happen, it is likely that it would occur over a period of time. The zeros on this diagram indicate that a project manager may be newly appointed and thus not yet have been allocated a project, and that a project may be set up without the name of the project manager being known.

In some circumstances the association between the classes also holds information. If we consider the example in Figure 11.22, we would probably want to know which project manager was in charge of a project during a particular period.

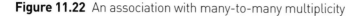

Figure 11.22 An association with many-to-many multiplicity

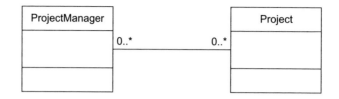

To do this we create an **association class** called 'Assignment' to hold the start and end dates for each project manager. Figure 11.23 shows this additional class.

In this example there is only one instance of the class 'Assignment' for each combination of 'Project' and 'ProjectManager'. If there were more than one – for example, if project managers could be reassigned to projects they had previously left – then it would be necessary to convert this association class into a class in its own right.

Figure 11.23 An association class

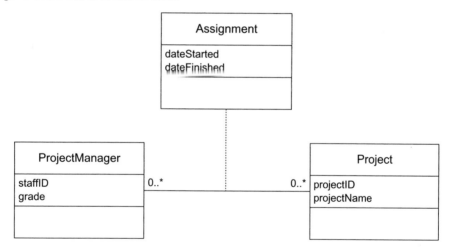

Generalisation and inheritance

The 'ProjectManager' class that we have been considering has been defined for the narrow requirements of a project control system. However, we now suppose that during analysis it turns out that the organisation also needs to keep information on contracts – managed by account managers – and more information on job roles in general.

Some of the data kept for 'ProjectManager' and 'AccountManager' will be common to the more general class 'JobRole', whereas some will be specific to the two existing classes. It also appears that, whereas some operations are common to all job roles, some are only relevant to project managers or account managers. The UML handles this situation through a concept known as generalisation, and this is illustrated in Figure 11.24.

Figure 11.24 A generalisation structure

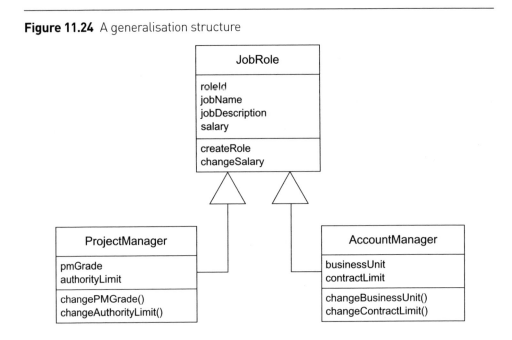

Both specialisations are said to **inherit** the attributes and operations of the generalisation. So the class of 'JobRole' has the attributes 'roleId', 'jobName', 'jobDescription' and 'salary'. 'ProjectManager' has 'pmGrade' and 'authorityLimit' in addition to the 'JobRole' attributes and, similarly, 'AccountManager' has the additional attributes of 'businessUnit' and 'contractLimit'.

SUMMARY

This chapter has provided an introduction to some of the key techniques used to model system requirements. The benefit of using models is that they provide an unambiguous view of the system, albeit from one specific perspective. Another benefit is that these views may be compared and cross-checked. For instance, we might develop a use case diagram and cross-check it against a model of the data in order to identify any gaps such as missing data items or use cases. The models also help to generate further questions and to improve our understanding of the business requirements and the business rules to be implemented in the system.

REFERENCES

Finkelstein, C. and Martin, J. (1981) *Information Engineering*. Savant Institute, Carnforth, Lancs.

FURTHER READING

Arlow, J. and Neustadt, I. (2005) *UML 2 and the Unified Process: Practical Object-oriented Analysis and Design*. Addison-Wesley, Boston, MA.

Cadle, J., Paul, D. and Turner, P. (2010) *Business Analysis Techniques*. BCS, Swindon.

Skidmore, S. and Eva, M. (2004) *Introducing Systems Development*. Palgrave Macmillan, Basingstoke.

Simsion, G. and Witt, G (2004) *Data Modeling Essentials*, 3rd edn. Morgan Kaufmann.

Yeates, D. and Wakefield, T. (2004) *Systems Analysis and Design*. FT Prentice Hall, Harlow.

12 DELIVERING THE REQUIREMENTS

Debra Paul and James Cadle

INTRODUCTION

Once the requirements have been defined, attention shifts to considering how they will be delivered. The business analysis work could provide the basis for a large-scale, broad-scope business change programme or could be much more focused on a particular area. As a result, delivering the requirements could include some or all of:

- **Business process change:** the business processes may be altered to be simpler, faster, more accurate or more effective.

- **People changes:** the jobs of the people involved may be redefined and new tasks and skills added. In turn, this would give rise to further requirements for training, coaching or mentoring, and to changes in the way people are recruited and appraised.

- **Changes to organisational structure:** often posts disappear, new ones are created and sections or departments are merged or split. Sometimes introducing a new structure (projects, for example) is seen as key to the business improvements sought.

- **Changes to IT systems:** that support the business processes and provide the information used by the organisation.

These elements must not be considered in isolation, and it is important that business analysts keeps their interdependence in mind. A holistic approach to the delivery of the requirements is essential for the successful delivery of the changes to the business.

DELIVERING THE SOLUTION

There are several lifecycles, methods and standards that may be used when developing solutions to meet the requirements. In deciding how to deliver the requirements it is important to consider a number of factors, which are summarised in Figure 12.1.

Figure 12.1 Factors in deciding the delivery approach

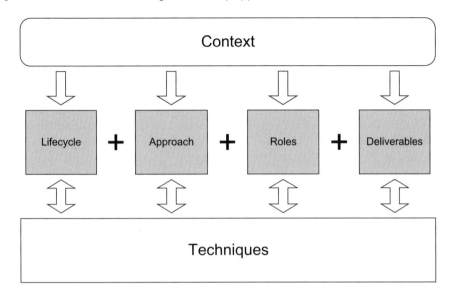

The factors are concerned with the following areas:

- **context:** the nature of the organisation and the project that will provide the basis for deciding how the solution will be delivered;
- **lifecycle:** the process adopted for developing and implementing the solution;
- **approach:** the methods and standards that are used during the lifecycle;
- **roles:** the key roles to be carried out during the project;
- **deliverables:** the products to be delivered by the project team;
- **techniques:** the management and development techniques used to plan, analyse and document the project work.

These areas are described in further detail in the following sections.

CONTEXT

The context for the organisation and the project will provide the basis for deciding how any business changes are to be delivered. Organisations are subject to external pressures from customers and competitors and to other business demands, and these usually determine the need for change and the constraints within which those changes need to be met. For example, if an organisation works in a safety-critical or highly regulated environment it may be essential for the entire set of change requirements to be defined in great detail and implemented in one group. Alternatively, if an organisation operates in a highly competitive business environment then it is likely that a rapid response to change will be required.

The issues to be considered are:

- **The culture and underlying philosophy of the organisation:** here we can consider questions such as what type of organisation this is, the nature of the business domain within which it operates, and the values and beliefs of the senior managers.

- **The business context for the proposed changes:** for example, what the organisation is hoping to achieve in terms of business benefit as a result of this project.

- **Constraints on the project:** for example, the timescale for delivering the solution, the budget, what resources are to be made available and the standards that the organisation uses.

- **The prioritised needs of the business:** for example, improved public image may be more important than cost savings or vice versa.

- **The drivers for the project:** for example, whether this project is based upon a need to comply with new legislation or whether it is concerned to offer additional or enhanced services to customers.

The context will vary from project to project and across change programmes. Whatever is the case, it is important that it is understood in order to ensure that we adopt the most appropriate approach to delivering the requirements.

DELIVERY LIFECYCLES

The business change lifecycle defined in Chapter 1 and reproduced in Figure 12.2 below shows in overview the sequence of stages to be carried out when analysing, developing and delivering business changes.

However, while this lifecycle shows in overview the areas of business change activity needed, it does not indicate how the solution is to be developed and delivered. There has been a great deal of effort devoted to defining lifecycles for IT systems development, and it is important to understand the nature of these lifecycles because they provide a clear basis for the project work. Although they focus on IT systems development it is important to align this work with the broader business changes, such as the definition of new processes and revised job roles. The lifecycles are described below.

The concept of a systems development lifecycle
The development approaches to IT systems are known as systems development lifecycles (SDLCs). These approaches have evolved over many years and are

Figure 12.2 Business change lifecycle

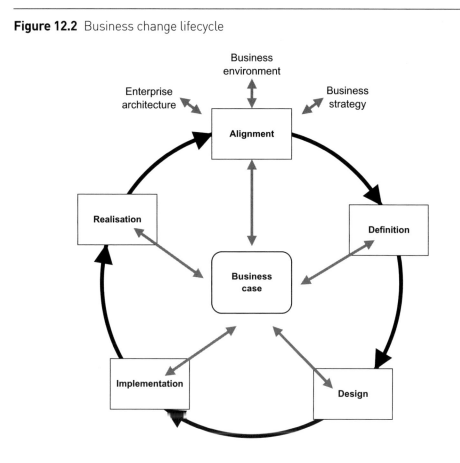

underpinned by philosophies that determine the route taken from analysis through to deployment of the system solutions.

A systems development lifecycle sets out the stages and their sequence that are undertaken in the process of developing and implementing an IT system. The lifecycle covers the entire life of a system from feasibility study to operation. The earliest established model of a SDLC is the waterfall lifecycle, but, over the years, variants and alternatives have been devised. Each has advantages and disadvantages.

The waterfall lifecycle

The waterfall lifecycle, illustrated in Figure 12.3, shows the development proceeding through a series of sequential stages. In theory, each is reviewed and signed off before the next starts. Thus we should only begin analysis once a feasibility study has been approved, and design should be based on an agreed set of requirements from the analysis. The backwards-facing arrows in the lifecycle indicate the need to check back at each stage to ensure that the project has

Figure 12.3 The waterfall lifecycle

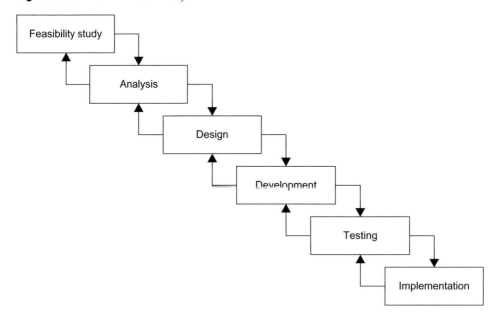

not expanded its defined scope, that the present stage builds logically on its predecessor and that modifications to the deliverables from the previous stage may be made where required.

Business analysts would typically be involved in the feasibility study and analysis stages of the project. They would also probably assist in the user acceptance that forms part of the testing stage and help the business users during implementation. During design and development, business analysts would be available to provide support to, and answer business-based queries from, the development team.

The principal benefit of the waterfall approach is that it provides good control from a project management perspective. In addition, the requirement to sign off each stage before the next starts should lead to a high-quality system. However, the highly structured nature of this lifecycle is also its weakness as it can lead to a long-drawn-out development that can leave the business in limbo. In addition, it does not handle change particularly well, since a whole sequence of deliverables requires adjustments in order to adapt to the change; for example, a change that occurs during development would require adjustments to the analysis and design documentation and possibly to the feasibility study as well.

The 'V' model lifecycle
The 'V' model, shown in Figure 12.4, is a variant of the waterfall model and consists of similar stages and a similar sequence of work. While the 'V' model is based upon the same principles as the waterfall model, in effect the waterfall has been bent back on itself following the development activity. This adds another

Figure 12.4 The 'V' model

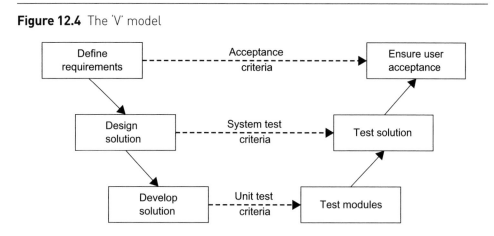

dimension to the lifecycle as it shows explicitly the connection between the earlier – developmental – stages of the project and the later – testing – stages. In particular, the derivation of the test criteria used at the different stages is explicit and it shows how the acceptance criteria should be derived from the requirements captured during the analysis stage.

An extended 'V' model, as shown in Figure 12.5, is sometimes used to reflect the link to the business needs. In this model the initial work concerns an analysis of the business needs and the development of the business case that justifies the recommended solution. This solution sets out the scope of the business change work to be explored further during the requirements definition stage. Again the

Figure 12.5 Extended 'V' model

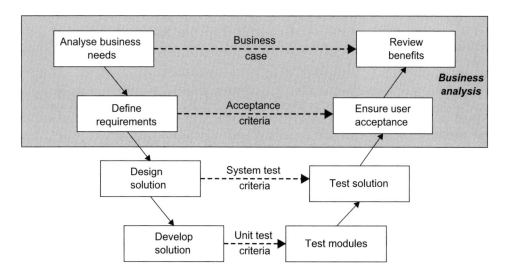

corresponding leg of the 'V' shows how the deliverables from the initial stages are used in testing the solution. The business case is used during the post-implementation review to test the success of the recommended solution by reviewing the predicted business benefits against the new business system. The aim is to confirm that the benefits have been achieved, or 'realised', and to identify further actions if this has not yet happened.

This model is also used to show the range of business analysis work in the light of an IT solution lifecycle. As can be seen in Figure 12.5, the business analyst is involved at the outset in assessing the business needs and defining the solution. The later activities of ensuring user acceptance and reviewing the benefits also form part of the business analyst role. Business analysis is not shown within these stages of the lifecycle because this model focuses on the design, development and testing of the IT element of the solution. These stages are primarily the remit of technical architects, developers and software testers. However, the business analyst should still be involved during design, development and testing, in order to:

- ensure that the business needs continue to be met;
- develop the process and job role definitions that will be implemented alongside the IT solution;
- assess the impact of proposed changes.

Incremental delivery

When analysing the requirements for the business change solution, it will be found that some of them will be more important or more urgent than others. For example, a regulatory deadline or an expected move by a competitor may make it imperative to implement some requirements quickly, whereas others may be less urgent and can be delivered at a later point. One way of achieving this is to develop and deliver the solution in a series of increments. The incremental delivery lifecycle is illustrated in Figure 12.6. This shows the analysis and design for the solution being completed initially. It is then followed by two incremental delivery phases, each consisting of development, testing and implementation. The most pressing requirements are in increment 1 and the rest follow in increment 2.

Something to be remembered if using the incremental lifecycle is that the total cost of delivering the solution is likely to be higher than that of delivering the complete solution in one release. This is because of the need to ensure that no increment will compromise the system when it is implemented. Also, in the second and subsequent increments it will be necessary to carry out 'regression testing' to make sure that the additional features do not cause something already implemented to stop working. What is more, the high-level analysis and design for the solution needs to be defined in order to future-proof the design for the later increments. If this is not done, aspects of the solution may be discovered during later increments that will necessitate changes to parts of the system already implemented.

Figure 12.6 Incremental lifecycle

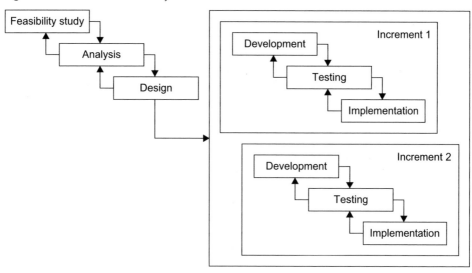

Figure 12.7 Boehm's spiral model

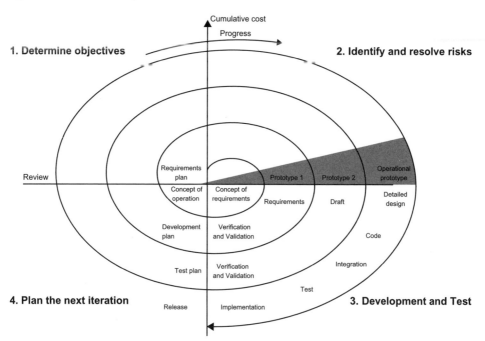

This lifecycle shows incremental development and delivery while using the structure of sequential stages defined in the waterfall lifecycle and the 'V' model. The need for a complete set of requirements and an overall design is one of the fundamental differences between the incremental approach described here and the iterative lifecycle, which is described next.

Iterative or evolutionary systems development lifecycle

A feature common to the waterfall, 'V' and incremental models is that a complete set of requirements is gathered at the start of the project and these form the basis for all subsequent work. An alternative approach is represented by a spiral model such as that shown in Figure 12.7.

The spiral model was devised by Barry Boehm (1986). The spiral model shows a different lifecycle for IT systems development, using iteration and prototyping to explore the requirements and develop the solution. Each turn around the spiral represents an iteration where a selected set of the requirements are analysed and developed using prototyping. During the final spiral, the operational prototype is used as the basis for detailed design, code production, testing and implementation. The quadrants of the spiral are as follows:

- In the first part of the iteration, the developers and business actors agree which requirements are to be included in the package of work. An important input to their decision is the agreed prioritisation of the requirements.

- Next the developers explore the technical possibilities, and the risks associated with them, for meeting the requirements. Much use is made of prototyping and it is essential that the business actors play an active role in assessing the prototypes and commenting upon them.

- Initially the prototype is reviewed to assess its strengths and weaknesses in delivering the requirements and to agree the requirements to be prototyped in the next iteration. Once the scope, design and appearance of the system (or the current part of it) have been agreed and an operational prototype developed, the project team completes the development and testing of the system.

- Finally this release of the software is implemented in the organisation and put into live operation. This release may be the entire system, as with the waterfall lifecycle, or it may be an increment that will be followed by further increments until the entire solution has been implemented.

As described above, the waterfall, 'V' model and incremental lifecycles incorporate a high level of control, which will offer some advantages. However, in practice there are some real difficulties in the way:

- There may not be time to define all the requirements at the outset, and only the most important or urgent ones can be defined in the time available.

- It is unlikely that the business actors will know exactly what they want, particularly if they are moving into new and uncharted areas of business.

- It is important to establish some of the business changes quickly in order to demonstrate capability and achievement, and to keep the support of the key stakeholders.

- The pace of business change is so rapid these days that a completely defined set of requirements can be out of date very quickly.

The most flexible delivery approach is achieved by utilising both iterative development and incremental delivery together in a coordinated and controlled way.

Developing the business solution
While the lifecycles described above are concerned with software development, the basic principles also apply to other business changes. For example, where the project is concerned with business process improvement the requirements for the new processes may be defined in detail prior to the development of the processes or an explorative, iterative lifecycle may be adopted. In reality most requirements are delivered through a mix of IT and process changes, causing the lifecycle chosen for the software elements to impose a lifecycle on the other aspects of the business solution. Where an incremental software release is to be delivered, we will need to define the process and job changes that will make that increment workable in practice, and these may need to change with the release of the next increment. Where a complete solution is to be implemented, the entire set of process and job definitions will be required.

APPROACH

Whichever lifecycle is adopted it will also be necessary to select an approach to carrying out the project work. The approach will determine the methods and standards to be adopted on the project. There are several published approaches to business process improvement and software development, such as the UML and DSDM Atern, each of which provides techniques and standards. Organisations will need to take account of the context and the lifecycles described above when deciding which approach to adopt. In deciding this, there are two key issues that should be considered: the approaches to the development and the delivery of the solution.

- **Delivery:** do we require one delivery of the entire solution or a phased delivery using incremental releases? The context described above will provide the basis for deciding whether the organisation requires the delivery of all of the requirements in one release, or whether a phased approach that delivers incremental change is necessary.

- **Development:** there are two key questions to answer. One is whether or not we are able to work closely with the business users during the development of the solution, and the other is whether or not the requirements are clear and well understood. When deciding on the development approach we need to consider whether the detailed requirements will need to be defined by working collaboratively with the business users during the solution development.

Where this is the case, it is vital that the business users are available to work closely with the project team so that the detail of the requirements may be uncovered as the solution evolves. Techniques such as scenario analysis and prototyping will be invaluable in this situation. However, if the requirements are sufficiently well understood to be defined prior to the solution development and testing and there is likely to be limited contact with the business users, formal documentation techniques such as detailed process and data models will be needed.

Software development approaches

There are several published, defined approaches to developing software solutions, each of which provides a framework and standards. Two key approaches are described here.

The **Unified Process** (UP) from the Object Management Group is a generic software development process that can be configured to meet the requirements of an organisation. Its structure acknowledges that no single development process fits all organisations, development environments and cultures. It is designed to fit small releases such as enhancements to existing systems as well as large systems development projects. The UP provides a guide on how to use the UML effectively (techniques from the UML are discussed in Chapter 11). It is both an iterative and an incremental approach, based upon the principle of using UML modelling techniques to explore and elaborate requirements through a series of iterations. Increments are developed that may be combined for one release of the entire solution or may be implemented as phased releases.

The software development approaches from the **Agile Alliance**, including methods such as DSDM Atern and Scrum, have become increasingly popular in organisations in recent years, for a number of reasons, including:

- the need for organisations to respond quickly to fast-changing business situations;

- the difficulty – indeed, sometimes the impossibility – of knowing what is wanted at an early stage of a project;

- the importance of flexibility when deciding how a requirement will be delivered. For example, a requirement to protect certain areas of the data may be defined, but there might be several possibilities as to how this is achieved. The solution to deliver this requirement may be decided through an exploration of various mechanisms.

The agile approach provides a framework for developing IT systems in an iterative and incremental way while still ensuring the quality of the software solution. This approach assumes that it is impractical to expect that systems can be built perfectly in one iteration, and is based upon the principle that 80 per cent of a total solution can be delivered using 20 per cent of the development effort that would be needed to produce the total solution. The focus is on meeting business needs when developing the solution, and key techniques such as evolutionary prototyping, timeboxing and prioritisation are engaged. One of the implicit assumptions underlying agile approaches is that revisiting previous steps in the development process is perfectly valid and that change, clarification of requirements and so on are inevitable. This is in contrast to waterfall systems development approaches where end-stage deliverables are 'signed off' and any proposed changes are subject to formal change control.

When using an agile approach, however, there is the danger that the emerging prototype systems are not documented properly or are not coherent, which leads to considerable difficulties later when they are in live operation. The methods mentioned above address this danger quite explicitly and stress the need for proper documentation and testing throughout the development.

The importance of prioritisation

We mentioned earlier that prioritisation is vital if we are using an incremental delivery lifecycle, possibly combined with iterative development. Clearly, if all the requirements are deemed to be of equal importance, there is no real way of determining what should go into each work package or iteration. It is here that a prioritisation scheme such as DSDM Atern's MoSCoW structure, which was introduced in Chapter 10, is particularly relevant. We need to relate the MoSCoW prioritisation allocations to the development and delivery of the solution as follows:

- 'Must have' requirements will make up the first deployed increment. If an iterative development approach is to be adopted, these requirements will form the first elements of the prototypes.

- 'Should have' requirements provide one of the mechanisms for introducing contingency and flexibility. The acceptance that they could be implemented as manual workarounds in the short term is extremely helpful when deadlines are tight. Any of these requirements that have not been delivered in the first release will be allocated a 'must have' priority in the second increment.

- 'Could have' requirements are often included in the set of requirements under development, particularly if they are relatively easy and inexpensive to incorporate with the higher-priority requirements. Where timeboxes are used, these requirements provide the contingency should the development team run out of time, since they can be left out if necessary.

- Finally, the 'want-to-have-but-not-now' requirements are recognised as those that will be set aside and considered during one of the later increments. This is an essential element for incremental delivery approaches as it provides a means of including requirements for later phases of the solution and specifically annotating them as such. These requirements will be allocated a different priority once the moment arrives for their delivery to be considered. For example, there may be a specific date when some of these requirements become mandatory; in the planning for that release the 'W' prioritisation may be changed to an 'M'.

The MoSCoW approach is also extremely useful for prioritising business changes. For example, when developing process documentation we can identify the elements that must be included at the outset, those that can wait for the next version and those that could be dropped if we run out of time.

Use case diagrams, described in Chapter 11, are also useful in prioritisation because they provide a highly visual way for business actors and developers to understand the entire range of areas covered by the requirements. They show the potential scope of the entire solution and provide a diagrammatic view that may be used to partition the solution into practical implementation packages for the short or the longer term. They also enable business analysts to see the extent of the business requirements so that they can then consider where IT functionality should be developed or whether process changes would suffice.

Software package approach

So far in this chapter we have considered the lifecycles and approaches that may be used to develop a software solution. The software may be built using an in-house development team or, more typically these days, using an outsourced software development supplier. However, in many situations organisations now have a preference for finding commercial off-the-shelf (COTS) solutions where at all possible, and using these to drive the business process changes. The reasons are not hard to find:

- Buying a COTS solution is almost certainly going to be cheaper for the organisation than having to fund the entire development process, since, by definition, the development costs are shared by all of the users of the package.

- Implementation should be faster, because the solution exists and only has to be set up in the way the customer wants.

- Support and maintenance packages are available from the software vendors.

- The vendors also keep their software up to date with, for example, changes in legislation.

As against these advantages, however, there are some drawbacks, including:

- No COTS package is likely to be a perfect fit with the requirements, so the organisation must either adapt its processes to what the package can do or pay for expensive tailoring and customisation, thereby partly negating one of the benefits of the COTS approach.

- If competitive advantage is required, it is unlikely to come from a package, since everyone else in the same business can buy the same software – although they still have to use it effectively.

If a COTS solution is desired, care must be taken that the requirements focus on what the system is required to do rather than how it is expected to work (unless the 'how' really is vital to the business, for example to improve competitiveness). And there must be a willingness to change processes where necessary to use what the chosen package is capable of providing.

Whichever approach is taken – bespoke development or COTS solution – and whichever lifecycle is chosen in the former case, the business actors must make a decision on how far they want to go with automating the processes and jobs.

Sometimes very complex decision-making, for instance, is better done by members of staff who can make judgements on a case-by-case basis rather than trying to anticipate and preprogram every eventuality.

ROLES IN DELIVERING REQUIREMENTS

The roles that are required in order to deliver the solution will depend upon these three factors:

- the context of the organisation and the project;
- the nature of the lifecycle selected;
- the approach adopted.

Typically there will be a project team that will include the following roles:

- project manager;
- business analyst;
- developer;
- tester.

However, the stage at which these roles are required will differ depending upon the nature of the solution, the lifecycle to be used and the approach chosen. If the solution is concerned with changes not to the IT systems but to the business processes that use them, the role of the business analyst will be to analyse and define the business process improvements, but there will be no need for the IT developers or software testers. Where there is a software solution and the 'V' model or the incremental lifecycle are selected, the business analyst may complete much of the early work without the need for involvement of the developer or tester roles. However, if a software solution is required and the spiral model lifecycle using agile development is adopted, the project will need development and testing skills at an early point.

There may also be a need for other roles. For example, a technical architect may be needed where the solution to be developed is complex and needs to be integrated with other software applications. A data analyst may also be needed where the software is underpinned by a complex data structure that will need to be designed carefully to ensure that all of the requirements will be met.

Within the business community there are also key roles such as that of the project sponsor and the business end user. These roles play an essential part in the development of the solutions. The project sponsor is the business representative who is the point of contact for the project manager and is responsible for providing the resources to the project team. The business users provide the details of the requirements. However, the nature of the work carried out by these roles, in particular that of the business user, will vary depending upon the approach adopted.

Where a waterfall, 'V' or incremental lifecycle is adopted, the business user role will be involved in the definition of the requirements and the acceptance of the solution. Where an agile approach is adopted, the business users have to work closely with the project team to collaborate in the prototyping work.

DELIVERABLES

The products that are to be delivered will also vary depending upon the nature of the solution, the standards of the organisation and the lifecycle and approach adopted. Sometimes we can deliver the requirements through a training exercise to improve the skills of the business users. In this case the deliverables may be course descriptions and training manuals. Sometimes the business rules applied by the business users need to be defined and documented and a follow-on training exercise conducted. In this case, the deliverables will also include the procedure descriptions.

Where business process changes are aligned with or supported by IT systems changes, the deliverables will be more extensive and will be linked to the software development lifecycle and approach. Early methods for systems analysis and design, such as the structured systems analysis and design method (SSADM), placed a strong emphasis on formal documentation through-out all stages of the systems development lifecycle. While this method is less used these days, some of the principles concerning documentation are still applied. For example, many organisations develop extensive requirements documentation prior to deciding upon the delivery approach, and maintain that documentation throughout the development lifecycle. Where an iterative development approach is to be adopted most organisations document the requirements in overview before exploring the selected requirements set in greater detail. During this exploration, the deliverables include the prototypes developed during each iteration. However, many organisations also enhance the requirements documentation as part of an iterative development and ultimately may produce similar deliverables to those resulting from a waterfall-type lifecycle.

One of the important aspects of the deliverables is that they should always be suitable for the purpose. Where documentation standards exist – whether they are organisational standards or part of a particular approach – there is little benefit to be gained (and potentially a lot of time to be wasted) in developing deliverables that do not contribute to the aims of the project.

TECHNIQUES

The techniques to be adopted during the development of the solution can vary considerably from project to project. They will depend upon the scope of the solution, the standards of the organisation and the lifecycle and approach adopted. Some typical situations are as follows:

- A waterfall-based lifecycle will require the use of formal documentation that has been reviewed and 'signed off'. This necessitates the use of formal and rigorous techniques for documenting and modelling requirements. For example, a technique such as entity-relationship modelling or class modelling is likely to be required.

- Where an agile approach has been adopted for a project, this will determine the techniques to be used. As stated earlier, prototyping is a vital element of the agile approaches. Essentially, when delivering the requirements, all of the factors described earlier will combine to determine many of the techniques used. It would not be sensible to consider using an iterative development approach without the use of prototyping.

- Organisations may have set templates for requirements documentation that may include standards for modelling business processes and IT requirements. They may also have templates for organisational documents such as job role definitions and job descriptions.

- Many organisations have adopted development tools that impose both a development process and the modelling standards to be used.

CONCLUSION

All of the aspects described above need to work together to ensure that a coherent approach to delivering the requirements is adopted. It is important to recognise that the context for the organisation and the project should determine this. An inappropriate lifecycle and approach will not reap the business benefits and is likely to result in wasted time and budget, possibly leading to the failure of the business initiative. The standard lifecycles and approaches are used in the main to develop or procure software, but we also need to consider them when delivering the other aspects of the requirements – the business processes and procedures, and the new jobs and people skills. In many situations we cannot deliver all of the requirements as we would ideally desire. The nature of the business constraints may mean that we have to explore alternative means of delivering some requirements in the short or even the longer term. The role for the business analyst is to identify where this is needed and seek out the options for delivery that will ensure that the business needs are met.

REFERENCES

Boehm, B. (1986) A Spiral Model of Software Development and Enhancement. *ACM SIGSOFT Software Engineering Notes*, August.

FURTHER READING

Arlow, J. and Neustadt, I. (2005) *UML 2 and the Unified Process: Practical Object-oriented Analysis and Design*. Addison-Wesley, Boston, MA.

Cadle, J., Paul, D. and Turner, P. (2010) *Business Analysis Techniques.* BCS, Swindon.

Cadle, J. and Yeates, D. (2007) *Project Management for Information Systems,* 5th edn. Pearson Education, Harlow.

DSDM Consortium (2008) *DSDM Atern: The Handbook.* DSDM Consortium, Ashford.

Schwaber, K. (2004) *Agile Project Management with Scrum.* Microsoft Press, Redmond, WA.

Skidmore, S. and Eva, M. (2004) *Introducing Systems Development.* Palgrave Macmillan, Basingstoke.

Yeates, D. and Wakefield, T. (2004) *Systems Analysis and Design.* FT Prentice Hall, Harlow.

13   MAKING A BUSINESS AND FINANCIAL CASE

James Cadle

INTRODUCTION

A business case is a key document in a business analysis project. It is where the analysts or consultants present their findings and propose a course of action for senior management to consider. This chapter considers the purpose, structure and content of a business case and provides some guidance on how to assemble the information and present the finished product. One thing worth remembering here is that, to some extent, a business case is a sales document, aimed at getting people to take a decision. Therefore, some of the key rules of successful selling apply: stress the benefits, not the features; sell the benefits before discussing the cost and get the 'buyers' to understand the size of the problem – or opportunity – before presenting the amount of time, effort and money that will be needed to implement a solution.

THE BUSINESS CASE IN THE PROJECT LIFECYCLE

A question often asked about the business case is 'When should it be produced?' This issue is addressed in Figure 13.1. As the illustration shows, a business case is a living document and should be revised as the project proceeds and as more is discovered about the proposed solution and the costs and benefits of introducing it. In addition, of course, organisations and the environments in which they operate are not static, and so the business case must be kept under review to ensure that changing circumstances have not invalidated it. The initial business case often results from a feasibility study, where the broad requirements and options have been considered and where preliminary estimates of costs and benefits are developed. The preliminary figures must, however, be revisited once more detailed analysis work has been completed and a fuller picture is available of the options available. They should also be examined again once the solution has been designed, when much more reliable figures should be available for the costs of development. The business case should next be reviewed before the solution is deployed, precisely because the business circumstances may have changed and it may now not be worth proceeding to implementation. Finally, once the proposed solution has been in operation for a while, there should be a post-project review to determine the degree to which the predicted business benefits have been realised and to identify actions to support the delivery of these benefits.

Figure 13.1 The business case in the project lifecycle

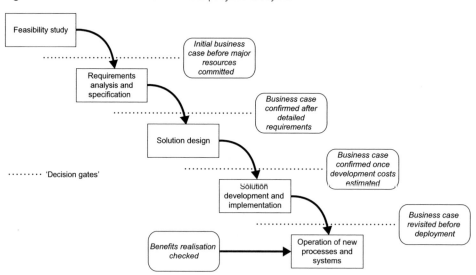

Figure 13.1 refers to each of these review points as a 'decision gate'. The concept here, now widely used in project management, is that projects should pass certain tests – not least those relating to their business viability – before they can be allowed to proceed to the next stage.

IDENTIFYING OPTIONS

The first step in putting together a business case is to identify and explore the various options that exist for solving the business issue. There are actually two kinds of options:

- business options, which explore **what** the proposed solution is intended to achieve in business terms – for example, 'Speed up invoice handling by 50 per cent' or 'Reduce the number of people we need to staff our supermarket';

- technical options, which consider **how** the solution is to be implemented, often through the use of IT.

At one time it was thought that these two elements should be considered separately and that the business elements should be dealt with first, the aim being to avoid the technical 'tail' wagging the business 'dog'. Nowadays, however, most changes to business practice involve the use of IT in some form and it is often the availability of technology that makes the business solutions possible. For example, one way of reducing the need for staff in a supermarket is to enable customers to scan their purchases themselves using the new 'smart' bar codes. For this reason it is a bit difficult nowadays to keep business and technical options separate, but it remains true that business needs, rather than the use of technology for its own sake, should drive the options process.

Figure 13.2 Process for developing options

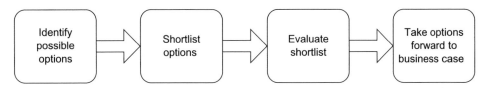

The basic process for developing options is shown in Figure 13.2. Identifying options is probably best achieved through some form of workshop, where brainstorming and other creative problem-solving approaches can be employed. Modelling techniques such as business activity modelling (see Chapter 7) and business process modelling (Chapter 8) are also useful to help generate options. The aim is simply to get all of the possible ideas out on the table before going on to consider which ones look most promising. Even if some of the ideas seem a bit unlikely, they may provide part of the actual solution or stimulate other people to come up with similar but more workable suggestions. Another way of identifying options is to study what other organisations – possibly competitors – have done to address the same issues.

Once all the possibilities have been identified, they can be evaluated to see which ones are worth examining further. Usually some ideas can be rejected quite quickly as being too expensive, taking too long to implement or being counter-cultural. The criteria for assessing feasibility are examined in more detail under the heading 'Assessing project feasibility' on page 228.

Ideally the shortlist of options should be reduced to three or four, one of which will usually be that of maintaining the status quo, the 'do nothing' option. The reason for restricting the list to three or four possibilities is that it is seldom practical, for reasons of time or cost, to examine more than this in enough detail to be taken forward to the business case. Each of the short-listed options should address the major business issues but offer some distinctive balance of the time they will take to implement, the budget required and the range of features offered. Sometimes, though, the options are variations on one solution, with one dealing only with the most pressing business issues and others offering various additional features. This situation is illustrated in Figure 13.3.

In Figure 13.3 the bottom option deals only with the most pressing issues as quickly as possible and at minimal cost. The next option adds some additional features to the solution but costs more and takes longer. The last option is a comprehensive solution but obviously takes the longest and costs the most.

One option that should always be considered – and that should usually find its way into the actual business case – is that of doing nothing. Sometimes it really is a viable option and might even be the best choice for the organisation. Often, though, there is no sensible 'do nothing' option because further problems may result from inaction. In this case the decision-makers may not be aware that action is imperative, and so spelling out the risks and consequences of doing nothing becomes an important part of making the business case.

Figure 13.3 Incremental options

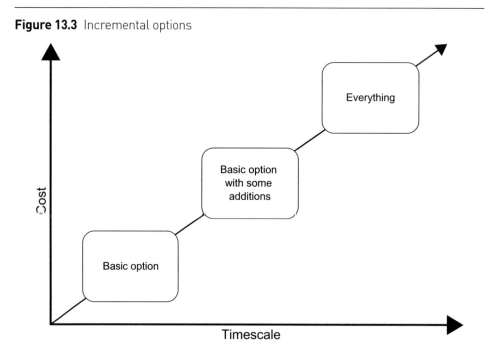

ASSESSING PROJECT FEASIBILITY

There are many issues to think about in assessing feasibility, but all fall under the three broad headings illustrated in Figure 13.4.

Business feasibility issues include whether the proposal matches the business objectives and strategy of the organisation and – in a commercial firm – whether it can be achieved in the current market conditions. There is also the question of whether the proposed solution will be delivered in sufficient time to secure the desired business benefits. The proposal must 'fit' with the management structure of the organisation and with its culture, as lack of cultural fit is often a cause of projects not meeting the expectations held for them. The solution must be capable of implementation within the physical infrastructure of the organisation, if that is a constraint. Although the proposal may be for major process change, it may still have to interface with other processes that are not changing, so compatibility with other areas must be considered. Whatever is proposed must be within the competencies of the organisation and its personnel, or there must be a plan for the development of these competences. Finally, many sectors are now heavily regulated and the proposed solution must be one that will be acceptable to the regulators and not infringe other law or treaty obligations.

In assessing **technical feasibility**, one is normally – though not necessarily – considering an IT solution. It must meet the organisation's demands in terms of system performance, availability, reliability, maintainability and security.

Figure 13.4 Aspects of feasibility

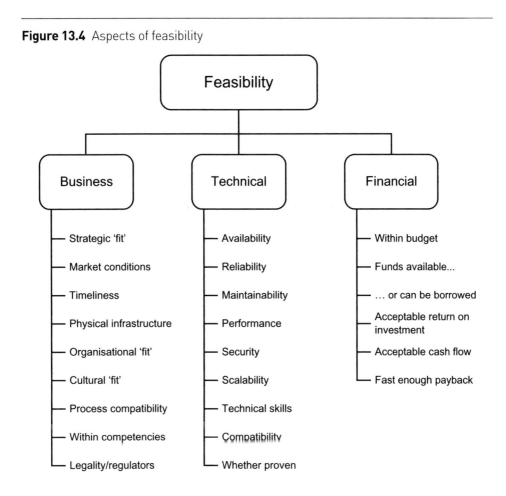

Its scalability – up or down – if the circumstances of the organisation change must be considered. The organisation must possess the technical skills to implement the solution, or supplement these with help from outside. Few IT systems are now completely standalone, and so the issue of compatibility with other systems must be considered. If the solution involves an off-the-shelf software package, thought should be given to the amount of customisation that would be required and whether this would cause technical difficulties. Finally, some thought should be given as to whether the proposed solution is a proven one or whether it places excessive reliance on leading-edge – that is to say, unproven – technologies. Many organisations would prefer a less ambitious but reliable solution to a more advanced one that comes with a lot of technological risk.

Financial feasibility is about whether the organisation can afford the proposed solution. There may already be a budget imposed. The organisation needs either to have the required funds available or to be in a position to borrow them.

Figure 13.5 Force-field analysis

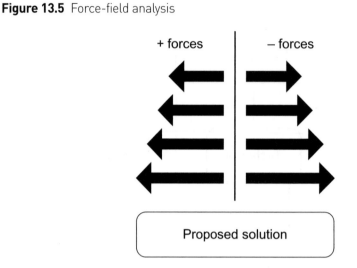

Every organisation will have some rules or guidelines about what constitutes an acceptable return on its investment, and methods of calculating this are considered under the heading of 'Investment appraisal' on page 239. Even if a project pays for itself in the end it may have unacceptably high costs on the way, and so cash flow must also be considered. Finally, all organisations specify some time period over which payback must occur, and in the case of IT projects the payback periods are often very short, sometimes within the same accounting year as the investment.

Another tool that can be used in assessing feasibility is a PESTLE analysis (see Chapter 3). PESTLE examines the environment outside an organisation, or perhaps within the organisation but outside the area being studied. It can be used to assess feasibility as follows:

- **Political:** is the proposed solution politically acceptable?
- **Economic:** can the organisation afford the solution?
- **Sociocultural:** does the solution fit with the organisation's culture?
- **Technological:** can the solution be achieved, technically?
- **Legal:** is it legal, and will the regulator allow it?
- **Environmental:** does it raise any 'green' environmental issues?

A final tool that can be employed to assess the feasibility of an option is a force-field analysis, illustrated in Figure 13.5.

With a force-field analysis, we consider those forces inside and outside the organisation that will support adoption of the proposal and those that will oppose it. We need to be sure that the positive forces outweigh the negative. The forces may include the PESTLE factors mentioned already, the elements identified in Figure 13.4 and also the key stakeholders in the organisation (see Chapter 6). If we conclude that the negative forces are just too strong, then the proposal is not feasible and must be abandoned or recast in a way that gets more positive forces behind it.

In considering the feasibility of options, we also need to think about their impacts and risks. Because these form part of the business case itself, we discuss them in the next section.

STRUCTURE OF A BUSINESS CASE

Organisations differ in how they like to have business cases presented. Some like large, weighty documents with full analyses of the proposals and all the supporting data. Others like a short, sharp presentation of the main points, and we have come across one organisation that mandates that business cases be distilled into a single A4 page. If this sounds cavalier, remember that the people who have to make the decisions on business cases are busy senior managers, with time at a premium. Whatever their size, however, most business cases are similar in their structure and content. They tend to include the following elements:

- introduction;
- management summary;
- description of the current situation;
- options considered;
- analysis of costs and benefits;
- impact assessment;
- risk assessment;
- recommendations;
- appendices, with supporting information.

We shall examine each of these elements in turn.

Introduction
This sets the scene, defines the scope and objectives of the change under consideration, and explains why the business case is being presented. Where relevant, it should also describe the methods used to examine the business issue and thank people who have contributed to the study.

Management summary
In many ways this is the most important part of the document, since it may be the only part that the senior decision-makers will study properly. It should be written after the rest of the document has been completed and should distil the whole of the business case into a few paragraphs. In an ideal situation, three paragraphs should suffice, covering:

- what the study was about and what was found out about the issues under consideration;
- a survey of the options considered, with their principal advantages and disadvantages;
- a clear statement of the recommendation being made and the decision required.

If you can't get away with only three paragraphs, try at least to restrict the management summary to one or two pages.

Description of the current situation

Here we explain the current situation and where the problems and opportunities lie. As long as this is consistent with explaining these issues properly, it is also important to keep this section as short as possible; senior managers often complain of having to read several pages to find out what they knew already! Sometimes, though, the real problems or opportunities uncovered are not what management thought they were when they instituted the study. In that case, more space will have to be devoted to explaining the issues and exploring the implications for the business.

Options considered

In this section we describe the options considered and explain – again as briefly as possible – why we are rejecting those that we do not recommend. More space should be devoted to describing the recommended solution and why we are recommending it. As we saw earlier – see Figure 13.3 – there may well be a series of incremental options, from the most basic to one that addresses all of the issues raised.

Analysis of costs and benefits

Cost/benefit analysis is one of the most interesting – and also the most difficult – aspects of business case development. Before we examine the subject in detail, though, it is worth mentioning that it is good psychology to present the benefits before the costs, since the decision-makers will then appreciate the benefits before they are faced with the costs of achieving them. In other words, what we are presenting is actually a benefit/cost analysis, even though by convention it is always referred to as a cost/benefit analysis.

Although cost/benefit analysis is interesting, it does pose a number of challenges:

- working out in the first place where costs will be incurred and where benefits can be expected;
- being realistic about whether the benefits will be realised in practice;
- placing a value on intangible elements such as 'improved customer satisfaction' and 'better staff morale'.

The last point brings us on to a discussion about the types of costs and benefits that we need to deal with. Costs and benefits are incurred or enjoyed either immediately or in the longer term. They are also either tangible, which means that a credible – usually monetary – value can be placed on them, or intangible, where this is not the case. Combining these elements, we find that costs and benefits fit into one of four categories, as illustrated in Figure 13.6.

Figure 13.6 Categories of costs and benefits

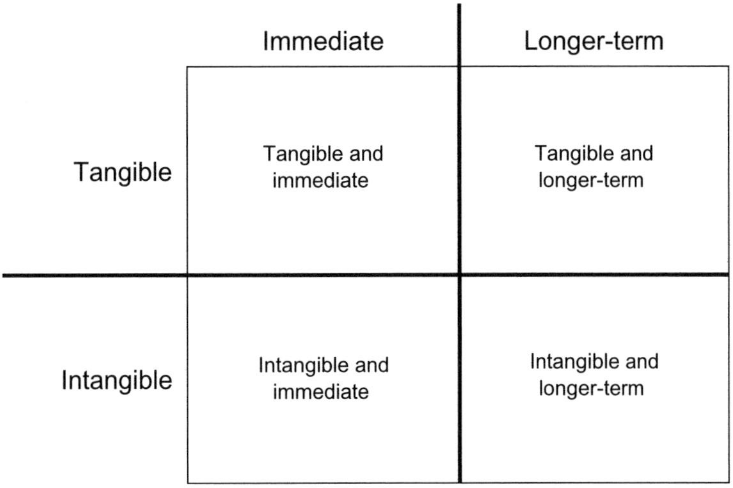

	Immediate	Longer-term
Tangible	Tangible and immediate	Tangible and longer-term
Intangible	Intangible and immediate	Intangible and longer-term

Costs tend to be mainly tangible, whereas benefits are often a mixture of the tangible and the intangible. In some organisations the managers will not consider intangible benefits at all, and this often makes it difficult – or even impossible – to make an effective business case. How, for instance, does one place a value on something like a more modern company image achieved through adopting a new logo? In theory, it should be possible to put a numeric value on any cost or benefit; the practical problem is that one seldom has the time or the specialist expertise to do so.

If intangible benefits are allowed, though, it is very important not to overstate them or, worse, to put some spurious value against them. The danger here is that the decision-makers simply disbelieve this value, and this then undermines their confidence in other, more soundly based values. With intangible benefits it is a much better policy to state what they are, and even to emphasise them, but to leave the decision-makers to put their own valuations on them.

Another pitfall in cost/benefit analysis is basing the values on assumptions. For example, we might say something like 'If we could achieve a 20 per cent reduction in the time taken to produce invoices, this would amount to 5000 hours per year or a cost saving of £25,000'. This will only prove acceptable to the decision-makers if the assumption is plausible. If you can, use assumptions that are common within the organisation and always err on the side of conservatism – that is, under-claim rather than over-claim.

Having stated some of the key issues, let us look at some of the places where costs and benefits might arise and how we might go about quantifying them. We shall use the four categories of costs and benefits already described.

Tangible costs

- **Development staff costs:** in many projects, particularly those that involve developing new processes or IT systems, these will be a major cost element. To work them out, we need a daily rate for the staff concerned – probably available from the HR or accounts department – and an outline project plan showing when and how the resources will be required. If external consultants are being used, then the costs here will be subject to negotiation and contract.

- **User staff costs:** these are often forgotten but can be significant. User staff will have to be available for the initial fact-finding, for the testing of any systems involved and to be trained in the new systems and methods of working. Again, daily rates can be used in combination with an outline plan of the amount of user involvement.

- **Hardware:** where IT is involved there will often be a need to purchase new hardware. For this, estimates or quotations can be obtained from potential suppliers.

- **Infrastructure:** this includes things like cabling and networks. Again, estimates will be required from suppliers.

- **Packaged software:** estimates of the cost of this can be obtained from package vendors, probably based on the proposed number of users. Where tailoring of a package is envisaged, estimates of the effort and cost involved can be requested also.

- **Relocation:** this can be quite difficult to cost. The costs could include those of the new premises (either rented or bought), refurbishment, new furniture and the actual moving costs. There may also be costs associated with surrendering existing leases and so on.

- **Staff training and retraining:** to work this out, we need to know how many people need to be trained and what they need to learn. Ideally this requires some form of training needs analysis. If there is insufficient time for that, then one can make a broad assessment of the training needed and multiply the delivery time for one course by a factor of 10 to get a rough estimate of the course development effort.

- **Ongoing costs:** once any new systems are in place they will require maintenance and support, and quotations for this can be obtained from the vendors. If this is not possible, a very rough rule of thumb is to allow support costs of 15 per cent of operational costs in the first year after installation and then 10 per cent thereafter. However, this is very crude, and actual quotations are much to be preferred if they can be obtained.

Intangible costs

- **Disruption and loss of productivity:** however good a new process or system is in the long run, there is bound to be some disruption as it is introduced. The level of disruption is very difficult to predict when implementing any business change. Also, if parallel running of old and new IT systems is undertaken in order to smooth the transition, then there will be a tangible cost involved as well.

- **Recruitment:** this ought to be tangible, but organisations often have little idea of the total cost of recruiting someone, although elements of this cost, such as agency fees, will be tangible. But if new staff members or skills are needed, there will be costs involved in obtaining the new people and inducting them into the organisation.

Tangible benefits

- **Staff savings:** this is the most obvious saving, though many organisations are now so lean that it is hard to see where further reductions will come from. In calculating the savings, we need the total cost of employing the people concerned – including things like national insurance, pensions and other benefits, and sometimes the space they occupy. The HR or accounts departments should be able to supply this information. Don't forget, though, that if people are to be made redundant, there will be one-off redundancy costs that must be set against the ongoing saved staff costs.

- **Reduced effort and improved speed of working:** if staff posts are not completely removed, it may be possible to carry out some tasks in a shorter timescale thus freeing up time for other work. This is a tangible benefit if the effort to carry out the task is measured and compared with the expected situation after the change.

- **Faster responses to customers:** again, it would be necessary to make a pre-change measurement of the time taken to respond to customers' needs in order to quantify any possible benefits.

- **Reduced accommodation costs:** these may have already been factored into the cost of employing staff (see 'Staff savings' above), but smaller computers may also save space and, perhaps, people may be able to work from home some or all of the time. The facilities or finance department should have some idea about the cost of accommodation.

- **Reduced inventory:** new systems – especially 'just in time' systems – usually result in the need to hold less stock. The finance and logistics experts should be able to help in quantifying this benefit.

- **Other cost reductions:** these reduced overtime working, the ability to avoid basing staffing levels on workload peaks, and reductions in time and costs spent on travel between sites and in the use of consumables.

Intangible benefits

- **Increased job satisfaction:** this may result in tangible benefits such as reduced staff turnover or absenteeism, but the problem is that we cannot prove in advance that these things will happen.

- **Improved customer satisfaction:** this, too, is intangible unless we have sound measures to show, for example, why customers complain about our products or services.

- **Better management information:** it is important to distinguish between better management information and simply more management information. Better information should lead to better decisions, but it is difficult to value.

- **Greater organisational flexibility:** this means that the organisation can respond more quickly to changes in the external environment, through having more flexible processes and systems, and staff members who can be switched to different work relatively quickly.

- **More creative problem-solving time:** managers freed from much day-to-day work should have more time to study strategic issues.

- **Improved presentation or better market image:** new systems often enable an organisation to present itself better to the outside world.

- **Better communications:** many people report poor communications within their organisation as a problem, so improving communications would clearly be beneficial. However, again, how would one place a value on this?

Avoided costs

One special form of benefit worth thinking about is what we might call 'avoided costs'. For example, in the run-up to the year 2000, many organisations were faced with the costs of making their computer systems 'millennium-compliant'. IT departments often instead suggested the wholesale replacement of systems, thereby avoiding the costs of adapting the old systems. In such a case, an investment of, say, £2 million in a new system might be contrasted with an avoided cost of £1 million simply to make the old legacy systems compliant. There are often situations where an organisation has to do something and has already budgeted for it, and that budget can be offset against a more radical solution that would offer additional business benefits.

Presenting the financial costs and benefits

Once the various tangible costs and benefits have been assessed, they need to be presented so that managers can see whether and when the project pays for itself. As this is a somewhat complex topic, it is examined separately under the heading of 'Investment appraisal' on page 239.

Impact assessment

In addition to the costs and benefits already mentioned, for each of the options we need to explore in the business case any impacts that there might be on the organisation. Some of these impacts may have costs attached to them but others may not – they may simply be the things that will happen as a result of adopting the proposed course of action. Examples of such impacts include:

- **Organisation structure:** it may be necessary to reorganise departments or functions to exploit the new circumstances properly, for example to create a single point of contact for customers or more generalist rather than specialist staff roles. This will naturally be unsettling for the staff and managers involved, and a plan must be made to handle it.

- **Interdepartmental relations:** similarly, the relationships between departments may change and there may be a need to introduce service level agreements or in other ways redefine these relationships.

- **Working practices:** new processes and systems invariably lead to changes in working practices, and these must be introduced carefully and sensitively.

- **Management style:** sometimes the style that managers adopt has to change. For example, if we de-layer the organisation and give front-line staff more authority to deal with customers, then their managers' roles will change as well.

- **Recruitment policy:** the organisation may have to recruit different types of people and look for different skills.

- **Appraisal and promotion criteria:** it may be necessary to change people's targets and incentives in order to encourage them to display different behaviours – for example, to be more customer focused.

- **Supplier relations:** these may have to be redefined. For example, outsourcing IT services would work much better with a cooperative customer/supplier relationship than with the adversarial situation that too often seems to exist.

Whatever the impacts are, the business case needs to spell them out. It must also make clear to the decision-makers what changes will have to be made in order to exploit the opportunities available to the full, and the costs these changes will incur.

Risk assessment

No change comes without risk, and it is unrealistic to think otherwise. A business case is immeasurably strengthened if it can be shown that the potential risks have been identified and that suitable countermeasures are available. A complete and comprehensive risk register (sometimes called a risk log) is probably not required at this stage – that should be created when the change or development project proper starts – but the principal risks should be identified. For each risk, the following should be recorded:

- **Description:** the cause of the risk should be described together with its impact, for example 'Uncertainty over the future leads to the resignation of key staff, leaving the organisation with a lack of experienced personnel'.

- **Impact assessment:** this should attempt to assess the scale of the damage that would be suffered if the adverse event occurred. If quantitative measures can be made, so much the better; otherwise a scale of 'small', 'moderate' or 'large' will suffice.

- **Probability:** how likely is it that this risk will materialise? Again, precise probabilities can be calculated but it is probably better to use a scale of 'low', 'medium' or 'high'.

- **Countermeasures:** this is the really important part, the question being what we can do either to reduce the likelihood of the event occurring or lessen its impact if it does. We may also try to transfer the risk's impact to someone else, for example through the use of insurance.

- **Ownership:** for each risk, we need to decide who would be best placed to take the necessary countermeasures. This may involve asking senior managers within the organisation to take the responsibility.

If there seem to be many risks associated with the proposal, then it is a good idea to document only the major ones – those that could stop the project or destroy the business rationale – in the body of the business case and to put the rest in an appendix.

Recommendations

Finally, we need to summarise the business case and make clear the decisions that the senior managers are being asked to take. If the business case is for carrying out a project of some sort, then an outline of the main tasks and timescales envisaged is useful to the decision-makers. This is best expressed graphically in the form of a Gantt/bar chart, as illustrated in Figure 13.7.

Figure 13.7 Gantt/bar chart for a proposed project

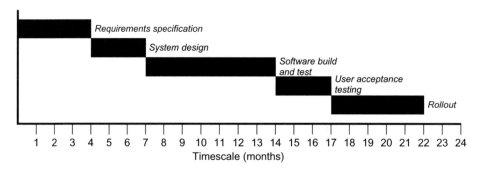

Appendices and supporting information

Where detailed information needs to be included in the business case, this is best put into appendices. This separates out the main points that are put in the body of the case from the supporting detail. If supporting statistics have to be provided, they too should go into appendices, perhaps with a summary graph or chart in the main body. The detailed cost/benefit calculations may also be put into appendices.

INVESTMENT APPRAISAL

In this part of the business case the financial aspects – in other words, the tangible costs and benefits – are contrasted in order to see whether and when the project will pay for itself. The simplest way of doing this is by using what is called a payback calculation, which is in effect a cash-flow forecast for the project. An example of a payback calculation is given in Table 13.1. It shows immediate costs of £200,000 for hardware and £150,000 for software for a new system, and ongoing costs of £30,000 per year for hardware maintenance and £30,000 for software support and upgrades. The tangible benefit will be the removal of some clerical posts, valued at £150,000 per year.

Table 13.1 Example of a payback calculation

Item	Year 1	Year 2	Year 3	Year 4	Year 5
Hardware purchase	200,000				
Hardware maintenance	30,000	30,000	30,000	30,000	30,000
Software purchase	150,000				
Software support	30,000	30,000	30,000	30,000	30,000
Staff savings	150,000	150,000	150,000	150,000	150,000
Cash flow for year (savings less costs)	−260,000	90,000	90,000	90,000	90,000
Cumulative cash flow	−260,000	−170,000	−80,000	+10,000	+100,000

In the first year the costs considerably outweigh the benefits because of the large capital expenditures, but thereafter benefits exceed costs by some £90,000 per year. By working out the cumulative positions we discover that the accumulated benefits finally exceed the accumulated costs after year 4 and thereafter build up at a rate of £90,000 per year.

Payback calculations have the virtue of being easy to understand and relatively easy to construct, although getting reliable figures can sometimes be a headache. Where interest rates and inflation are low they provide a reasonable forecast of what will happen. However, they do not take account of the 'time value of money'. This is the simple fact – which we all understand from our personal experience – that money spent or saved today is not worth what it will be worth next year or in five years' time. In part this is the effect of inflation, but, even with low or zero inflation, there are other things that we could do with the money besides investing in this project. We might, for instance, leave it in the bank to earn interest. Or, conversely, we might have to borrow money and pay interest to finance the project.

A method that takes account of the time value of money is known as discounted cash flow (DCF). This leads to a 'net present value' (NPV) for the project, which means that all of the cash flows in years after the current one are adjusted to today's value of money. Management accountants work out the discount rate to use in a discounted cash flow calculation by studying a number of factors including the likely movement of money-market interest rates in the next few years. The mechanism for doing that is outside the scope of this book, and interested readers are referred to the 'Further reading' section at the end of this chapter. Let us suppose, though, that the management accountants decide we should be using a discount rate of 10 per cent. We can then find the amounts by which we should discount the cash flows in years 2–5, either by using the appropriate formula in a spreadsheet or by looking up the factors in an accounting textbook. For a 10 per cent discount rate, the relevant factors are shown in Table 13.2.

Table 13.2 Example of a net present value calculation

Year	Net cash flow	Discount factor	Present value
1	−260,000	1.000	−260,000
2	90,000	0.909	81,810
3	90,000	0.826	74,340
4	90,000	0.751	67,590
5	90,000	0.683	61,470
Net present value of project:			25,210

Table 13.2 represents the same project that was analysed in Table 13.1. With the cash flows from years 2–5 adjusted to today's values, we can see that the project is not such an attractive investment as the payback calculation suggested. It does pay for itself, but now only in year 5 and not by as great a margin as before.

We can perform a **sensitivity analysis** on these results to see how much they would be affected by changes in interest rates. If we had used a discount rate of 5 per cent, for example, we would have got a NPV of £59,140, and a 15 per cent rate would have produced a NPV of −£2960.

One final measure that some organisations like to use is the internal rate of return (IRR). This is a calculation that assesses what sort of return on investment is represented by the project in terms of a single percentage figure. It can then be used to compare projects one with another in order to identify the better investment opportunities, and to compare them all with what the same money could earn if just left in the bank. So, for example, if the IRR of a project is calculated at 3 per cent and current bank interest rates are 5 per cent, then on financial grounds alone it would be better not to spend the money.

The IRR is worked out by standing the DCF/NPV calculations on their head. The question we are asking is: what discount rate would we have to use to get a net present value of zero after five years (or whatever period the organisation mandates should be used for the calculation)? In other words, at what point would financial costs and benefits precisely balance each other? The problem is that this cannot be worked out by a formula. One has to set up a spreadsheet and try different discount rates until an NPV of zero is produced – Microsoft Excel has an automated function to do this. In the case of our example project, the result is around 14.42 per cent. If this were being compared with another project offering only, say, 5 per cent, then our project would be the more attractive one. However, IRR does not take account of the overall size of the project, so the project with the smaller IRR may produce more actual pounds, Euros or dollars in the end. For this reason, most accounting textbooks agree that DCF/NPV is the best method of assessing the value of an investment, whilst acknowledging that many managers like the simplicity of the single-number IRR.

PRESENTATION OF A BUSINESS CASE

There are two basic ways in which a business case can be presented, and often there is a need for both. It can appear as a written document and as a face-to-face presentation. In both cases the way the business case is presented can often have a major impact on whether it is accepted. There are some simple rules that apply to both approaches:

- **Think about the audience:** readers of reports and attendees at presentations have a variety of interests and attitudes. Some like to have all of the details and others prefer an overview. As far as possible, try to address the concerns of each of the decision-makers in the report or presentation. (See the information in Chapter 6 on stakeholder management for more on this.)

- **Keep it short:** you may have to use a preset format or template for your report, in which case the actual sections may force you into creating a long document. However, try as far as possible to keep the business case concise.

- **Consider the structure:** we have provided here a good basic structure for a written business case. For a presentation, the old rule still holds good:

  o Tell 'em what you're going to tell 'em.

  o Tell 'em.

  o Tell 'em what you've told 'em.

You need to build to a logical conclusion that starts with the current situation and leads to the decision you need made.

- **Think about appearances:** again, you may be constrained by a template here, but, if not, remember you have to induce the decision-makers to read your business case! Use lots of white space, pictures and diagrams instead of tables, and use colour as well. For a presentation, avoid dozens of bullet-point slides, which tend simply to repeat what's in the report anyway; instead use pictures, diagrams and colour to show the decision-makers what you're talking about.

BENEFITS MANAGEMENT AND REALISATION

In recent years organisations have become increasingly interested in benefits management and realisation, which can be summarised as managing projects such that they are able to deliver the predicted benefits and, after the project has been implemented, checking progress on the achievement of these benefits and taking any actions required to support their delivery. The basic approach is shown in Figure 13.8.

Figure 13.8 Benefits realisation approach

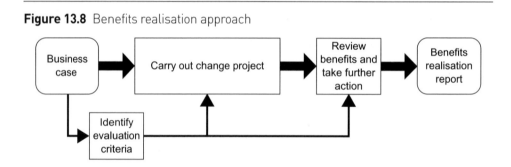

When a business case is being constructed, some thought should be given to how the claimed benefits will be measured. For some tangible benefits this may not be too difficult: for example, either we make the expected cost savings or we do not. However, even then there are some problems, such as the question of how we disaggregate the effects of this project from those of other projects that may be happening at the same time. Or how do we adjust for changes in the external environment, for instance a general upturn or downturn in sales? For intangible benefits, the obstacles are even greater: how can we measure a change in staff morale, for instance? It may be possible to measure reduced staff attrition, but what if there is no other work locally and attrition drops anyway? Whatever the difficulties, however, some thought needs to be given to measurement. This may involve surveying the situation before the change takes place, so that the situation afterwards can be compared with it.

Benefits will not appear by themselves, simply as a result of carrying out the change project. Where a project has a large technical component – as do most that involve the use of IT – there is a natural tendency for the planning to focus mainly or even exclusively on technical issues, but this is wrong; the business changes that are needed to secure the benefits must also be planned for. It should be appreciated, too, that such planning is not generally the responsibility of the project manager, whose focus is on the technical aspects; rather, it is the responsibility of the project sponsor, who may appoint a business change manager to oversee the detailed planning work.

Planning the steps needed to secure the business benefits can take the form of the construction of a benefits map, as shown in Figure 13.9.

Figure 13.9 Example of a benefits map

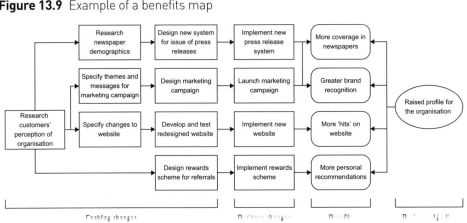

A benefits map is created from right to left, starting with the overall business objectives that the change project is designed to achieve. We then work backwards to the set of benefits that will contribute to those objectives. Next we consider what business changes will be required to secure those benefits, and finally we identify the enabling changes that will lead to the business changes. As the example in Figure 13.9 shows, at least one stream of enabling and business changes represents the technical aspects of the project, but the other streams highlight the non-IT changes that will be required if the overall benefits and objectives are to be achieved. It will be noticed that the arrows from the objective face back towards the benefits (right to left), indicating dependency, whereas other arrows are go from left to right, indicating the sequence of the enabling and business changes and the business benefits.

The advantage of constructing a benefits map like that in Figure 13.9 is that it forces us to consider all of the work, not just that related to IT systems development, that is required to achieve the project's business benefits. It also helps us to identify who should take responsibility for each stream. The technical stream, relating to the website redevelopment, for instance, is obviously the responsibility of the IT project manager, whereas the stream relating to improved press coverage should probably be managed by the PR function or, if the organisation does not have one, by the marketing department.

Returning now to Figure 13.8, we notice an arrow from the evaluation criteria leading back into the change project itself. This highlights the need to try and manage the project in such a way as to maximise the hoped-for benefits. For example, allowing a lot of changes may drive up the costs of the project and therefore extend the period of time it will take to pay for itself, or even wipe out any gains altogether.

Management processes are needed in order to ensure that the benefits are reviewed in two circumstances:

- **Scheduled reviews:** at each of the 'decision gates' shown in Figure 13.1 at the beginning of the chapter, the expected benefits should form a major part of the review. At each stage careful consideration should be made of whether the expected benefits are still available and whether they are still sufficient to compensate, for example, for an increase in the expected costs of the project. In the light of such a review, it may be necessary to re-scope the project in order to improve the prospects of securing the maximum business benefit.

- **Unscheduled reviews:** these should be triggered whenever a significant event occurs that could potentially affect the expected benefits. Proposed changes are an obvious example of this, since they could cause the project to cost more, to take longer or to deliver something different, and all of these changes might affect the benefits. Other significant events could include a change in the key stakeholders (especially the project sponsor) or developments in the external business environment or the organisation's business strategy.

The business case should be reviewed frequently during the project in order to check whether the predicted benefits can still be achieved and to identify any changes required to the project in order to enable those benefits to be delivered. The main evaluation, however, takes place after the project has finished. Consideration should be given to the timescale required for the expected benefits to appear. Depending on the type and scale of the project, this could happen months or even years after the project ends. The evaluation will also focus on the progress towards achieving the benefits and consider whether any further action needs to be taken to enable the benefits to be achieved.

Ultimately a benefits realisation report, which assesses frankly whether or not the hoped-for benefits have been gained, should be produced. This report has four important uses:

- Where the hoped-for benefits have not yet been achieved, it can identify any additional actions that could be taken in order to retrieve them. For instance, if users are not taking full advantage of a new system, additional training may be required.

- It can reassure the decision-makers and the wider organisation that the time, effort and cost of the project has been justified.

- It can provide input to future business cases and future projects to help make them more successful.

- It can enable the organisation, over time, to get better at choosing which projects to undertake.

SUMMARY

A coherent and well-researched business case should be an important guiding document for any change project. Developing a business case involves the identification of the possible options and the assessment of their feasibility. The business case itself follows a fairly clearly defined format, leading to clear recommendations to the decision-makers. There are several approaches to investment appraisal, which assesses the financial costs and benefits of a proposed change project. After the project has been completed there should be a review to determine whether the expected benefits have been realised in practice and to identify any actions required to support the delivery of those benefits.

FURTHER READING

Blackstaff, M. (1999) *Finance for IT Decision Makers*. Springer-Verlag, London.

Boardman, A.E., Greenberg, D.H., Vining, A.R. and Weimer, D.L. (2001) *Cost–Benefit Analysis: Concepts and Practice*, 2nd edn. Prentice Hall, Upper Saddle River, NJ.

Remenyi, D. (1999) *How to Prepare a Business Case for IT Investment*. Butterworth-Heinemann.

Remenyi, D., Money, A., Sherwood-Smith, M. and Irani, Z. (2000) *The Effective Measurement and Management of IT Costs and Benefits*, 2nd edn. Butterworth Heinemann, Oxford.

Schmidt, M.J. (2002) *The Business Case Guide*, 2nd edn. Solution Matrix, Boston, MA.

Schmidt, M.J. (2009) *Business Case Essentials: A Guide to Structure and Content*. Solution Matrix, Boston, MA.

Ward, J. and Daniel, E. (2005) *Benefits Management: Delivering Value from IS & IT Investments*. John Wiley & Sons, Chichester.

14 IMPLEMENTING BUSINESS CHANGE

Keith Hindle

INTRODUCTION

It is important to appreciate that the business analyst role is vital if organisations are to benefit fully from business changes. Earlier chapters have explored many aspects of business analysis work and have covered a range of techniques that will help analysts to identify and specify the changes required to improve the operation of their organisations. In this chapter we look at the factors that need to be considered when implementing change. We examine the general characteristics of change, the stages of change and the different levels within an individual that can be affected by change. We also discuss a four-part change process that includes:

- understanding the impact of the change;
- planning what needs to take place for the change to be successful;
- carrying out the planned change;
- making sure that the change becomes embedded in the organisation.

INTRODUCING A NEW BUSINESS SYSTEM

Introducing new business processes and a new IT system can have many consequent effects, some obvious and easy to handle but others not so straight-forward. End users may require new skills or they may find that their existing jobs disappear and they have to take on new roles, possibly at a different location. The change of role may also result in changes to the social group or the department to which they currently belong. Some staff may be made redundant whilst new staff with different skills and aptitudes may be hired. The new or changed roles that they are required to undertake may call for a different approach compared with their old ones. They may for instance have more responsibilities or a wider range of tasks to complete, or they may be asked to make decisions that were previously left to others. Any change can be unsettling if it is not well managed. It is usual for those in changing circumstances to feel anxious about the change, their ability to adapt to it and its long-term effects on their career prospects. Such anxiety will affect the performance of their jobs as their morale drops. In more extreme cases it can lead to overt resistance to the change. Those who have the opportunity, usually the more able and adaptable staff, may leave for jobs elsewhere that they regard as safer or more predictable.

Change initiatives can differ in scope and components. Many change projects include the implementation of new processes and procedures and the IT systems that support this work. The smooth introduction of these elements will help the change process, but it will not guarantee success – and yet so often this is the main area on which many projects concentrate. The other, often neglected, area deals with the people issues: what are sometimes described as the 'hearts and minds' aspects. This involves understanding how people respond to change, the ways in which their initial negative reactions can be reduced, and how their acceptance of the new processes, procedures and IT system can be achieved quickly and smoothly.

THE NATURE OF CHANGE

Change is becoming more common and far reaching. Organisations, their structures and product sets are changing more frequently. These internal changes are forced on the organisation by shifts in the external world. Organisations think that if they do not change, their rivals will whittle away their competitive advantage. In the past, businesses could remain the same for considerable periods of time. Now customers are looking for products with improved functionality and higher quality, backed up by more individualised customer service. Consequently the organisation's processes must be refined, if not completely reengineered. This affects not only the way employees are required to behave but more importantly how they need to think; their attitude to the customer can be critical for success.

At the same time, change is difficult. Although the need for them has increased, change programmes are often less successful than management would have liked. Introducing change is not a mechanistic process like programming a computer. Senior management cannot simply decide what change is required and tell the rest of the organisation to get on with it. For a start, senior management do not know the detail of the required changes. Neither can they predict exactly how their staff are going to react to them. Instead of a linear set of steps that can be rolled out sequentially, change requires much more monitoring and adaptation in light of the feedback we receive from those involved in it.

Change is an organic process. When you are growing a new seedling, you have to be aware of and cater for the plant's needs for water, nutrients and the right temperature. Even if the seedling's needs are met, it will not always grow successfully – there may be limiting factors such as slugs or other insects that eat the young plant as soon as it pokes its leaves above the surface. It's the same with change. It requires the positive support – the nutrients and the water – and the reduction or elimination of the negative factors – the slugs and pests – if it is to be successful. Change cannot be imposed from above but requires time and nurturing.

THE ENVIRONMENT FOR CHANGE

Change does not take place in a vacuum but in a particular context that influences how the change occurs and how successful it will be. This context consists of three sets of factors, related to:

- the individual who is undergoing or being affected by the change;
- the organisation in which the individual works;
- the external environment in which that organisation operates.

These factors may be represented as three concentric circles, as shown in Figure 14.1. The closer we are to the centre of the diagram, the more influence we can exert. Individuals, for example, can be encouraged to take a more positive attitude to change through training, support and involvement with the change project. Whilst some aspects of the organisation may be within the scope of the project, many other aspects will have to remain as they are. These could include processes and functions outside the scope of the project and the culture of the organisation. The external environment is even less under the control of the project.

Figure 14.1 The environment for change

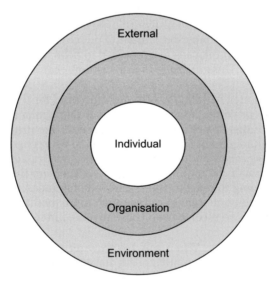

The external environment
The external environment includes everything outside the organisation. Sometimes this is subdivided into the general environment that applies to all organisations and the business domain within which the particular organisation operates. The broader external environment is often summarised by the PESTLE framework, which was described in Chapter 3.

The business domain consists of those individuals, groups and organisations with which our organisation has contact. In Chapter 3 we also introduced Porter's five-forces model, which helps us to understand how our organisation relates to others within the business domain.

The external environment is important from a change perspective because it often provides the initial impetus for change. Thus the development or introduction of new technology may be attractive because it can help an organisation to be more efficient than its competitors. If the competitors get there first, it may have to react in order to defend its present position. The behaviour of the organisation's competitors is often a major driver for change.

Inside the organisation

The major aspects of the organisation as a whole that influence or are affected by change include:

- strategy;
- structure;
- resources;
- experience of change.

Strategy can be described as matching external demands with internal capabilities. As the external environment changes, the strategy helps to differentiate between those changes that we need to do something about and the others that we can ignore. A well-thought-out strategy is stable; it does not change frequently. Over time, however, it will need to adapt to the changing situation

The **structure** of an organisation may be affected by change as well as affecting the feasibility of that change. Organisations with different types of structure have differing abilities to handle change. Consultancies, media companies and some engineering organisations are geared up to work on projects; the project approach is designed to accommodate change. As one project ends and another begins, the staff are regrouped and possibly reskilled to meet the needs of the next assignment. In contrast, a hierarchical organisation is made up of functional units that may be less receptive to change. Many organisations have introduced matrix structures in order to benefit from the best of both of these approaches.

The **resources** of the organisation and how well they are managed can differentiate the flexible from the rigid. If we manage our resources well, this implies that we know:

- what resources we have;
- what those resources can do;
- how they can be developed to support particular change initiatives.

Central to an organisation's resources are its employees. If we know what skills and competencies they have, we can make sure that they are appropriately equipped to deal with the change. Other significant resources from a change perspective include business processes, systems and the data and technology that support those systems. In order to assess the full impact of a proposed change, it is useful to have high-level descriptions of the different resources. These models or pictures are referred to as the relevant architectures.

The final element contributing to the organisation's ability to handle change is its **experience of change**. Success breeds success; previous successful change projects give us the confidence to do it again. Furthermore, we can learn from our initial attempts at change to improve our skills and techniques. There is a danger, however. Significant change requires a big commitment from all involved. This may be a particular problem when people have previously been asked to put in a lot of effort but have seen little success or reward. Too often change projects seem to fizzle out as senior personnel change and enthusiasm for the new approach fades. Those who suffer as a result of these initiatives finish up taking a jaundiced view, summarised as 'We have seen these change initiatives before – they didn't work then and they won't work now'. That sounds like a self-fulfilling prophecy, so be on the watch for change fatigue.

The individual

Change is implemented through people carrying out the new or different processes and working with the new IT systems. This is often considered the most difficult aspect of introducing change, because the reaction of the people involved will have a major impact on the success of the change. From the start of the change process, we need to understand:

- who the stakeholders are;
- the nature of their interest;
- their likely reaction to the change.

Identifying stakeholders was covered in Chapter 6. Here we need to ensure that the important stakeholders understand their role within the project and hence contribute to the success of the change.

People have different attitudes to change. Some are very positive, seeing the change as an opportunity from which they could benefit. The benefits they identify may vary from the promise of a more interesting job to better career development prospects. Others adopt a negative attitude, emphasising the difficulties and risks facing them in making the change. The attitude of the staff members whose work will change will be affected by what happens during the project. It has been said that most people are not resistant to change itself; what they do not like is having change forced on them by somebody else. Explaining why the change is necessary and involving the staff in defining the details of it will often minimise resistance. Unfortunately, underlying management assumptions can undermine this consultative approach. At one extreme it might be assumed that people dislike work, need controlling and are motivated by threats of punishment. This can become a self-fulfilling prophecy – if the management treats its employees in this way, the staff will react accordingly. This controlling approach commonly leads to poor results. Alternatively, at the other extreme it might be assumed that people are naturally innovative and will respond to encouragement and recognition. This is more conducive to successful change. These two different approaches and the circumstances of their use were proposed by Douglas McGregor (2006) as theory X and theory Y styles of management in *The Human Side of Enterprise*, originally published in the 1960s.

Figure 14.2 Maslow's hierarchy of needs

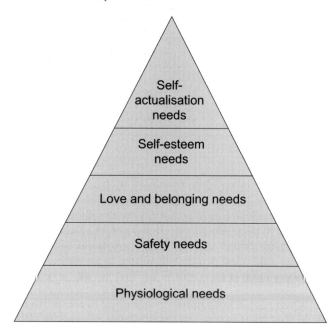

These ideas build on work on individual motivation by Abraham Maslow, described in his theory of the hierarchy of needs (Maslow 1943). This hierarchy is shown in Figure 14.2. Maslow realised that people have an innate desire to develop by satisfying a set of needs. The most basic needs, including food and shelter, form the base of the hierarchy. Once these are met, people will then try to satisfy the second level, the physical and psychological safety needs, so that they feel secure. The third level covers social needs, for friendship, love and the rewards of belonging to a group. All three levels described so far motivate people because they fear their absence. They are the basis of theory X – you are motivated by the threat that one of these needs will not be met. The higher levels of need, or theory Y needs, concern:

- self-esteem arising from doing something well and being recognised for it;

- self-actualisation from one's ability to achieve one's full potential.

Research has shown that people respond to change in a similar way, whether that change is good or bad. The diagram in Figure 14.3 illustrates the kind of emotions that an individual goes through.

Figure 14.3 Emotions and the change process

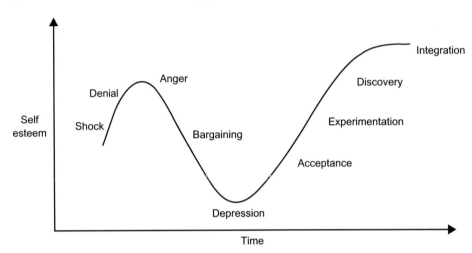

This change curve is based on work by Elizabeth Kubler-Ross (1970) with terminally ill patients and their reactions to life-threatening change. It is, however, typical of change that involves loss of something with which you are familiar and which you do not want to lose. Whilst the stages are represented sequentially in this description, in practice there may be many variations. Not everybody goes through all the stages, and often people will return to an earlier point on the curve or get stuck at a particular point.

Denial can occur when people are unable or unwilling to recognise that a change will affect them. At this point people may shut down, refusing to talk about the possibility of change. When they do start to acknowledge that the change will take place, they react emotionally, with anger and anxiety. This is natural because they are facing an unsure future with little control over it, which has the effect of reducing confidence in one's ability to handle the unknown impact of change. Morale as well as competence suffers. As a result people may resist the change either actively or passively. Going through the dip is a very uncomfortable experience, involving grief at the loss of the old ways and, possibly, of the social groups that are often disturbed by change.

Once people start to accept that the change will take place and that it will have some benefits, they begin to look forward (maybe with excitement) rather than backward. From this point things are starting to get better, even though the situation is very fluid at the start of the climb. There is a lot of experimentation as people work out how they can best operate in the new process and the new work group. Many new ideas are generated as the change beds down. These ideas need to be captured and evaluated, and thanks given to their originators. The final stage is commitment, when people sincerely believe that the change was worthwhile and it is fully bedded into the way the business works. With the benefit of hindsight it may be difficult to see what all the worries were about at the beginning of the change.

The purpose of describing this change cycle is to help prepare for the change. There may be an unrealistic expectation that the change will not cause any disruption amongst the staff. This is unlikely, and management will be better able to support their staff if they know what problems are going to crop up. Such knowledge can also help in avoiding inappropriate interventions. By planning ahead, we can minimise the impact of the change and keep the staff feeling positive as they find that their concerns are being addressed and they are getting the help they need.

The business change lifecycle

In the following sections we shall look at implementing business change in the light of the business change lifecycle that was introduced in Chapter 1. This lifecycle is shown in Figure 14.4. We shall consider the five stages: alignment, definition, design, implementation and realisation.

Figure 14.4 Business change lifecycle

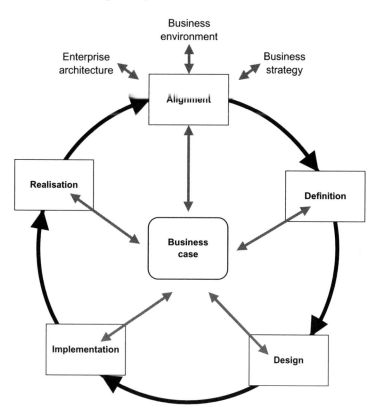

ALIGNMENT

There is a continuous need to check the strategic direction of the organisation as we react to the changing circumstances and challenges. This is referred to as strategic management and is the main activity of the alignment stage within the business change lifecycle. As explained above, the strategy helps to link the organisation with the external environment. This is shown in Figure 14.5. The strategy outlines how we intend to achieve our long-term objectives and highlights what we have to be good at if we are to succeed. It helps us to focus on those changes in the outside world that are particularly significant for our organisation. Thus some new but costly technology that could be the basis of a new product may be very important for an organisation that concentrates primarily on innovation. On the other hand, leading-edge technology may be less important for a value-for-money, low-price business unless it can lead to lower costs.

Figure 14.5 Strategy links the internal and external factors

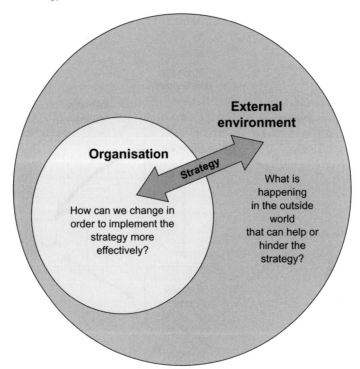

As the environment changes, the organisation has to adapt. There are many examples of organisations that have died because they failed to see that their customers had changed and were no longer interested in the products on offer. Consequently, the organisation's direction and strategy will have to be updated in light of external changes. In fact, an important part of the strategy statement explains how the organisation intends to change over the medium to long term in order to meet the challenges it faces.

The strategy is a high-level, medium- to long-term plan. More detailed analysis and planning is required to identify how the organisation is going to change internally. One way to do this is through the use of the balanced business scorecard (BBS). This effectively develops a cause-and-effect chain showing how overall financial objectives are achieved by giving the customers what they want. Customers, in turn, are happy if they are satisfied with the products and services they receive. Good products and services rely on effective and efficient processes, which, in their turn, require high-quality staff and innovation. This allows us to see how the key elements of the organisation support the business as a whole. Furthermore, it allows us to spot the significance of change. If we know that particular aspects of customer service are vital for sales, any improvement by a competitor could be a threat. Similarly, a new way of improving our levels of service might provide us with a competitive edge.

The BBS can also help us in another way by identifying businesses' critical success factors and how they relate to each other. The BBS defines measures and targets that can be used to monitor performance. For example, improved customer service performance by a competitor might indicate that we should improve our own customer service key performance indicators (KPIs) if we want to retain our existing customers.

It would be nice to think that the majority of change initiatives come out of the strategic analysis and are closely aligned with the strategy. In practice, change may be initiated in a bottom-up fashion. Problems at the operational level may be tackled piecemeal and, whilst this may result in short term benefits, we can find that the independent solutions implemented in different areas fit poorly together. Sub-optimisation may occur, where an improvement in one part of the business actually causes extra work elsewhere. As a result, the overall effectiveness of the organisation is reduced.

One way of avoiding the dangers of a piecemeal approach is to check any proposed changes against the overall business strategies. Alignment with a strategy depends on how well the change is likely to support the objectives or KPIs associated with that strategy. This link between the change and the achievement of objectives can be an important part of the business case. There is, for example, some evidence that projects are now finding it more difficult to base their business cases on quantifiable cost savings. This is to be expected if most of the cost savings have already been squeezed out by earlier projects. As an example, consider a project that is improving the provision of management information. Typically there are few cost savings to be made beyond reducing the manual effort in producing existing reports. Management knows that it needs more and better information, which will lead to improved business performance, but it is very difficult to quantify those benefits with sufficient certainty to support the cost/benefit analysis. Demonstrating how the information can support the achievement of particular objectives through better decision-making can overcome this difficulty.

Change can be wide ranging, affecting many different aspects of an organisation. The IT function has long used high-level pictures that show how the constituent elements of the systems, data and technology interrelate. These models are referred to as the application/system architecture, the data architecture and the technology architecture. They are very useful when examining the impact of a proposed development project. Some organisations are now using the same approach on the business to show, for example, how the business processes interact. The models are called process or business architectures. Checking a business change against the set of architectures can reveal the full extent of the impact of that change.

Aligning with the culture

As well as aligning with the strategy and the architecture, any proposed change must also align with the culture of the organisation. Unfortunately, culture is much less well defined and understood than are the more formal aspects that we considered above. It is sometimes described as 'the way we do things round here', which gives an indication of what we are dealing with but is not very useful for understanding the elements that make up the culture. Asking people about the culture may not get us very far because many employees are only dimly aware of its presence and could not describe it in any detail. In some situations, published information even conflicts with the actual culture.

Why is it so important, then, to understand the culture? When we propose a change we may have ensured that it aligns with strategy and other formal aspects, but nevertheless we might find that the change does not 'take'; for some unforeseen reason the users do not use the new system as intended and we never achieve all the anticipated benefits. In some sense the new methods do not fit in – they are not 'the way we work round here' – and they are rejected. In some extreme cases the culture may be the problem that is holding the organisation back. As the market changes, customers may expect much higher levels of service and understanding of their needs. An organisation that has always emphasised high-pressure selling may find it difficult to change employee mindset and attitudes and its processes, performance-monitoring and reward mechanisms. Needless to say, culture is not easy to change.

If culture is so loosely defined, how can we go about analysing and understanding it? We cannot simply ask people, since they may not know or they may have difficulty explaining what the culture is like. Somehow we have to use more indirect approaches, looking for evidence, for example, in the stories that are told about the organisation, how it operates and what makes it tick. Johnson, Scholes and Whittington (2008) have suggested that identifying an organisation's 'cultural web' will clear the picture. They suggest paying attention to the following areas:

- **Stories:** what the staff, customers and other stakeholders say about the organisation. Many organisations relate stories about their founders to highlight the values and beliefs that underpinned the original company and are still important. Hotels and other businesses that emphasise customer care publicise stories about particular employees who have gone to extraordinary lengths to help guests who have had problems that threatened to ruin a trip or vacation.

- **Rituals and routines:** the behaviour that defines what is acceptable and valued by management. How are customers treated when they visit the business – are they made to feel at home, given a cup of coffee and helped or do they have to fend for themselves? How well are new employees introduced to the organisation and their role when they start? Do employees gather round the coffee machine to chat and to discuss problems and progress on their projects or are they expected to get back to their desks as quickly as possible?

- **Symbols:** the status symbols, images and jargon commonly used. Some organisations have:

  - a standard uniform that everyone in their manufacturing plants wears, from apprentices starting on day one to the most senior plant managers;

  - open-plan offices for the entire staff;

  - awards displayed around the buildings;

  - catchphrases such as 'The ultimate driving machine' or 'Every little helps'.

- **Organisational structures:** both formal and informal. Do the different parts of the organisation adopt a silo mentality? Is the structure hierarchical or flat? Do the parts of the organisation cooperate or compete? What are the informal relationships that help the organisation get round the practical problems imposed by the hierarchy?

- **Control systems:** how finance, quality and performance are measured and rewarded. Employees may expect their expense claims to be checked very closely. Where are the tightest controls – money, quality or customer service? Is there use of display boards to show the performance of the team, for example the number and average length of calls taken in a call centre? Is the emphasis on rewarding good performance or on punishing bad?

- **Power structures:** where the real power lies. Which parts of the business are most successful or tipped for success and hence have the ear of the CEO? Who are the behind-the-scenes influencers whom the decision-makers trust? What are the main blockages to change, and who is behind them?

Exploring these issues will give you a feel for the state of the existing culture when thinking through the implications of any necessary changes. The existing culture may be incompatible with the way we would like to operate in the future. It is difficult to see how all the different functions within a business could work closely together to provide top-class customer service if there is an entrenched silo mentality across those functions. Such a mentality would highlight conflicts between end-to-end process performance, for example on cycle times from order placement to completion, and individual functional objectives – to meet sales targets, maximise production throughput or minimise stockholding costs. A silo mentality means that the functional objectives are considered more important, especially if they are tied in with incentives. The gap between the existing and the ideal future culture indicates what needs to change.

DEFINITION

Planning the human dimension of change is necessary if we are to succeed. It is worthwhile remembering, however, that the transition from the old to the new way of working is not a mechanical activity, the pace of which can be accurately predicted in advance. Different people will make the transition at different rates. There will be unanticipated problems that seem to threaten the progress of the whole project. Unless the change is relatively straightforward, you might think of the transition as an experiment in which people find their own ways of adapting to the new circumstances. As a result, the plan cannot be set in concrete – it must be flexible enough to handle the problems that occur.

Change requires trust between its instigators and those affected by it. Whether or not that trust already exists, we need to develop it and ensure that it remains. At the beginning of the project, it will help to develop and communicate a set of ground rules that outline how the project is to be conducted. These are high-level statements that need the active support of senior management. They may be described as principles and they should cover aspects such as business values, customer focus, the project itself, the impact of the project on staff, and management behaviour.

By reiterating our main business values, we are assuring the staff that the organisation is fundamentally the same even if the detailed activities are changing. This provides continuity and guards against any accusations about loss of integrity. The project principles will assure staff of the professionalism and fairness of the proposed changes. Examples of these might be statements that staff members will be involved in the decisions that affect their jobs and that existing processes will be analysed to decide which elements can continue unchanged. The staff impact principles will address the fears that individuals often have when changes are announced concerning redundancy, relocation or change of organisational structure. Examples of these might include statements that staff will be trained and coached when they take on new jobs and that there will be no compulsory redundancy.

The management principles address people's concerns over management's intentions. They will help to undermine the rumours and suspicions that inevitably go around. They could include statements to the effect that management will be available for formal and informal discussions about the change and will be open in those discussions, and that two-way dialogues will be encouraged.

The purpose of publishing these principles is to build up greater trust, and consequently everyone must act according to them. Trust will make the change process much easier. Because the principles are so far reaching, they must be agreed with senior management. Ideally, those managers should present them to the staff. The project members can then develop the trust created by the principles as they work with the individuals in the business. If the principles are later abandoned, all that trust can disappear and this will damage the change process significantly.

A popular change process plan has been developed by John Kotter (1996) of Harvard Business School. Kotter's eight steps may make the change process appear formulaic – which it is not. Treat the steps as necessary but not sufficient components for a change programme. Each programme will have its own specific additional needs. In the list that follows only the first four steps fit into our definition stage, but for the sake of completeness all eight are described.

Establish a sense of urgency

Organisations and the people in them need to be convinced that change is absolutely necessary. Successful change is based on widespread buy-in, so the sense of urgency also needs to be felt by a significant part of the management team. The urgency comes from the realisation that staying as we are is not an option. The push factor, moving us away from the status quo, can be developed by revealing how poor the present performance is against our main competitors and examining the future under a range of options. This step develops a 'felt need' for change that goes beyond simply knowing, at an intellectual level, that change is required; it becomes an emotional realisation as well.

Form a powerful guiding coalition

Using the outputs from stakeholder analysis and the investigation into the cultural web, identify a group of people from the different functions and levels who have influence derived from position, experience and political vision. These are not necessarily the formal leaders – the power structures contain those trusted individuals who have been around for a long time and who know how the business really works. If you can get them involved as early as possible, they can be very useful in bringing on board their particular constituency. Once this coalition has been developed into a proper team, it can drive the other stages through.

Create a vision

The vision is a clear, brief outline of a destination with a strategy for achieving it. The sense of urgency is a negative factor pushing us away from the existing situation. The vision, on the other hand, is a pull factor and is more positive. It describes how much better we will be when we have implemented the vision. Together, the push and the pull factors will win both the hearts and the minds of those affected by the change. Together they help to overcome the inertia or resistance to change. People describe this as 'unfreezing' or unlocking the status quo.

Communicate that vision

You are not going to be able to communicate the vision in a few short presentations. It requires constant repetition and hence the need for a communications plan. At this point we are involved in enrolling those involved with the change and explaining why we need to change, as well as the wider implications of the change for attitudes, beliefs and values.

Empower others to act on the vision

Here we are moving out of the definition stage of the change lifecycle and into the more detailed work that is part of the design stage. As we said at the start of the chapter, change will only occur successfully if we ensure that all the supporting factors are in place and that the negative or blocking factors have been minimised.

Plan for and create short-term wins

A gradual development approach is more supportive of the organic idea of a change programme. If you can achieve early successes within the first month or two, this will carry more weight than all the presentations and estimates of what might happen sometime in the future. Publicise the successes as widely as possible and use them as a stepping stone to further change and further success, but also learn the lessons by not repeating the initial mistakes and by refining what worked well.

Consolidate improvements and produce still more change

Momentum should be maintained. Keep in mind that the vision is to transform a specific aspect of the business, not to make minor changes here and there. Be agile, adapting the work to changing circumstances.

Institutionalise new approaches

Make the change stick by building it into the 'way we do things round here'. Without attention to this step, it is possible to slip back into the old ways and lose all the benefits we have been striving to achieve.

DESIGN

This stage covers the design and development of:

- the new or refined business processes;
- the IT applications that support the changed processes;
- the job definitions of the staff carrying out the processes;
- the updated organisation structures along with changes to management responsibilities;
- testing for all of these elements so as to ensure that they work correctly and in an integrated manner.

In this stage we aim for better-quality design geared to the detailed needs of the actual users rather than the needs as perceived by others, greater acceptance of the change, recognition by users that this is their design and a willingness to iron out any problems that may subsequently occur. Useful techniques to be employed here include design workshops, prototyping and demonstrations.

During workshops the business users are actually participating in the design of the new processes, system interfaces and so on. In a workshop to design a new process, for example, the business analyst may facilitate the work of the workshop delegates in developing swimlane diagrams, testing the various paths through the flowchart to ensure that all the different business scenarios are covered. Demonstrations of the proposed interface of the IT system will help the business users appreciate what the new system will be like. As with business process modelling, the users can test out how the design will handle a variety of scenarios. This will allow them to identify errors, omissions and refinements before development work begins.

We should do everything possible during this stage to ensure that the implementation will go as smoothly as possible. Thorough testing during the development is essential to avoid problems and delays in implementation later. For example, by testing the interface under realistic operational conditions with real users, we can identify and correct deficiencies. This is much more cost-effective than waiting for the problems to occur during implementation.

It also helps if the requirements have been defined with some consideration of how they will be tested. Some aspects of testing are, however, very difficult and it may, for example, be impossible to predict the performance of a new system, and hence of the business process that it supports, accurately. After development, performance testing is not easy because of the difficulty of simulating the operational environment in which the new system will run. For significant change, it may be worthwhile building models of the system and the process to estimate how well they will work under different combinations of loads and resources. This will allow performance problems to be identified and resolved before implementation.

IMPLEMENTATION

Throughout this stage the change team have a major influence on how well implementation proceeds. In this phase we need to consider the need for professionalism in the delivery of the business changes. The involvement of key staff members can help to cascade the message and the sequence of activities as they are rolled out. Learning and adapting the plan as the roll-out takes place will be important, as will training, coaching and dealing with practical issues as they arise.

Professional delivery of the message is essential on two counts. First, we are trying to build up people's confidence and trust. Sloppy presentations, inconsistent content and an inability to handle objections will undermine that confidence. Second, communication is a two-way process that requires quick thinking and the ability to adapt to varying needs and circumstances. On the first count we could call upon skilled staff to prepare brochures, newsletters and websites. Accomplished speakers will be able to deliver the messages and can also generate enthusiasm for the changes. The goal for the change team is to show that they are well organised, know what they are doing and are capable of leading the change project. On the second count, as well as the typical presentation and writing skills, more developed communication skills such as facilitation, negotiation, conflict resolution and problem solving will be important. Successful communication requires the development of rapport with the audience. This will help to create an open discussion, engage the audience and enable them to contribute comments and ideas.

In any organisation there are key staff members – often called change agents or change champions – who influence what happens. They are not necessarily part of the management structure, but, because of their experience, knowledge, personality and contacts, others go to them for help and advice. If we can identify these key individuals, we may be able to speed up the acceptance of the changes. People trust them already, so if the key players endorse the change, the others will accept it more easily. Getting the buy-in of the key staff members is not necessarily easy.

They may have concerns themselves about the change, but in order to develop these people as 'early adopters' it is important that we identify their current attitude to the change and any concerns they have. We need to identify, with them, how those concerns could be addressed as well as assessing their potential to influence others. If their influence is significant, we can then work with them closely so that they can act as change agents. In this role they will take others through the same steps and will help to cascade the change through the organisation.

Awareness of the change stages by management and staff provides a framework for everyone to discuss their problems and feelings about the change. It tells people that it is acceptable to experience emotions and that they can talk about these emotions. If people are forewarned and understand why they might feel the way they do, then they are more likely to be able to get through the negative period with minimum disruption. The roles of business managers and business analysts are important here. They themselves are impacted by the change and feel a similar set of emotions to those of the business system users. They need to deal with this before they can support users through the implementation cycle.

Training is important in order to improve people's skills and competences, and it often takes place away from the workplace. Training units are standard modules, designed to meet the needs of the average member of staff. The timing of the training sessions may not coincide directly with the scheduled roll-out of the new system. Consequently, much of the training effort may be wasted. Coaching can overcome these problems. It is tailored to suit the individual's needs, takes place as required and relates directly to the job in hand. Change leaders, business analysts and managers can develop their coaching skills so that they can support their staff.

When designing the training material, it is worthwhile considering the learning styles of the course delegates. Different people learn in different ways. One analysis by Richard Felder and Linda Silverman (1988) identifies four dimensions of learning styles:

- **Sensory versus intuitive:** sensory learners prefer practical information and look for facts, unlike intuitive learners who prefer conceptual information and look for meaning.

- **Visual versus verbal:** visual learners like diagrams, pictures and graphs whereas verbal learners prefer the written or spoken word.

- **Active versus reflective:** active learners want to do something such as a physical experiment or problem-solving in a group. Reflective learners, on the other hand, like analysis and thinking things through on their own.

- **Sequential versus global:** sequential learners work bottom-up, putting all the details together in order to understand the resulting big picture. Global learners start with the high level and then go into the detail.

There are no right or wrong learning styles. Most of us adopt a position that is a mixture. Some person may prefer the detailed view but not exclusively; they can learn globally as well. The difficulty is in getting the right balance, and in preparing material that offers opportunities to each of the different styles. Consider, for example, a very detailed, verbal learner on a training course run by a global and visual trainer. The material is likely to be delivered in a way that makes a lot of sense to the trainer but is very difficult for the delegate to handle. This example helps us to identify two lessons. First, identify your own preferred learning style and try to make it more balanced. If you are a detailed learner, drag yourself out of the detail and try to work out how the detail fits into the overall picture, how it supports the high-level objectives. Second, as a trainer understand where your delegates are coming from: what are their learning styles? Develop your material so that it is balanced, and is not geared to your own style or that of any one delegate but appeals to them all. In this way you will have the best chance of getting your message across.

A useful approach to achieving this helpful result is to use the action learning approach (Revans 1982), which applies these ideas by mixing 'doing' with thinking about what has to be learned. It is based on the learning cycle shown in Figure 14.6. After some initial instruction, the learners get some concrete experience. Then they are asked to think about what they have done, what was good about it and how it could be improved. In other words, they are required to explain the lessons learnt from the experience. The learners are then presented with some theory or concepts about the experience. This could be presented by a trainer or read in a book or manual. The learners can see how the experience illustrates what the theory is saying. If there are further aspects of the theory that the learners want to investigate, then they can plan how to do that before putting it into practice once more. They can go round the cycle as many times as they require in order to develop an appropriate level of understanding.

Figure 14.6 Action learning approach

Experience
Put ideas into
practice

Plan
What to do next

Action
Learning

Reflection
Learn the lessons

Conceptualisation
Extend the lessons
learnt

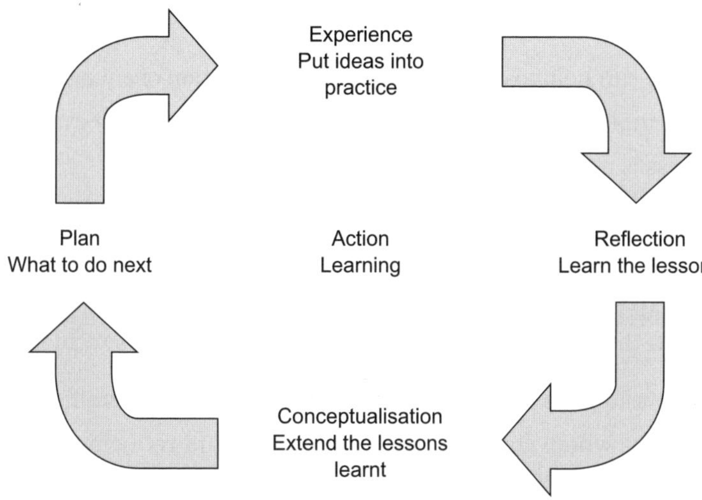

Figure 14.7 First cycle of an iterative change programme (based on action learning)

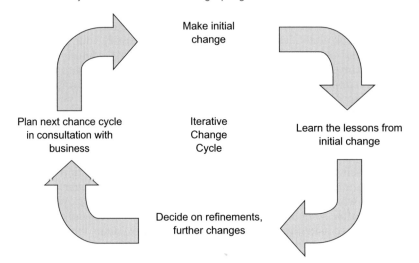

Make initial
change

Plan next chance cycle
in consultation with
business

Iterative
Change
Cycle

Learn the lessons from
initial change

Decide on refinements,
further changes

Action learning does not apply only to training. It can become the basis of an iterative change programme as shown in Figure 14.7, which is an adaptation of the previous diagram. It is far more successful if it is implemented in a series of cycles. This has a number of advantages:

- Those affected by the change find each cycle more manageable.
- The organisation starts to benefit from the initial changes quickly rather than having to wait until everything has to change at one time.
- The initial changes provide feedback from real use of the changed process or system.
- The feedback can help to determine the future direction of changes.
- External factors can also be considered when planning further cycles.
- The business is involved throughout the change cycles.

As well as skills training, other aspects of behaviour may need support. Process and system changes may also affect social groups and teams within the workplace. Team-building events can help the individuals to bond as a group as well as understand the personal changes that they will need to make to operate effectively in the new business. Other support mechanisms include:

- super-users who have the task of helping less experienced staff;
- support groups where staff can discuss problems and refinements with others from across the organisation;
- help desks to deal with technical and other problems;

- help facilities built into the IT system; this could be a complete training version of the software that users can switch to when they do not know how to carry out a particular action.

The Concerns-Based Adoption Model (CBAM) extract shown in Figure 14.8 (Hord, Rutherford, Hurling-Austin and Hall, 1987) is very useful when planning the training and support that people need as they adapt to change. It highlights the concerns that people have and the questions they ask as they progress through the change. People have to be aware of the change before they are likely to ask for information. Once they have been given background information about the change, their questions then become personal: 'How will this change affect me?' 'How can I make use of and manage the new technology?' The later stages then start to move away from the personal concerns by considering what kind of

Figure 14.8 Stages of concern (from the concerns-based adoption model)

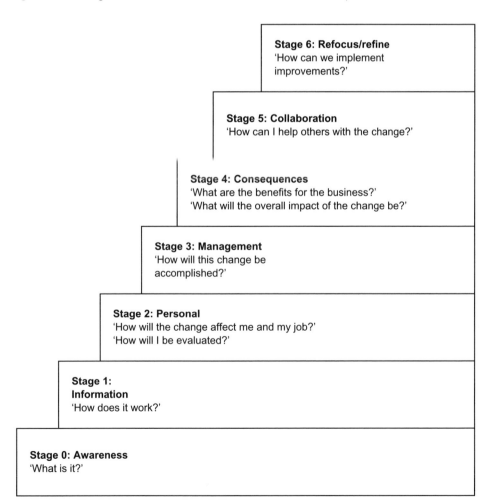

results or benefits we will be able to get from the change. This is referred to as the Consequence stage. Collaboration brings out questions about fitting the change into a larger picture: 'How does this change link in with and support other initiatives?' 'How can I relate what I am doing to the work of other colleagues?' The final stage focuses on how the change could be made even better.

When we are implementing change, we can use the model in many ways. By understanding the concerns displayed by a particular person, we can identify the type of training, coaching or other development they need. The diagram emphasises that people must go through the stages sequentially. There is no point, for example, in telling people how the change will affect them personally unless they already know what the change is. The training will not address their current concerns and it will be ignored. Similarly, concentrating on the results of the change before people know what impact the change will have on them will also be ineffective. Use of the model by professional development staff has revealed that people take a considerable time to get through all the stages. Whilst the needs associated with the initial stages are usually met by training courses, the later stages are often ignored. Experience indicates that without support, those undergoing change get stuck at the most recent stage reached. Often this may be at stage 2, with the consequent outcome that they do not see the benefits of the change to the business.

Reward systems can have a powerful influence on how we behave. That, after all, is what they are meant to do. As we change processes, we also may want changes in behaviour. But if we forget to change the rewards we give to our staff, we may find that the behaviour does not change and the benefits we were looking for do not materialise. The examples in Table 14.1 illustrate the point.

Table 14.1 Reward system problems

What we say we want	What we actually do
Teamwork and collaboration	Reward the best employee and not the team
Innovation and risk-taking	Punish mistakes
Better people skills	Reward only technical achievements
Empowerment	Enforce strict controls

REALISATION

Realisation is about ensuring that the planned change has taken place. As change is carried out in order to improve business performance, realisation is also about benefits realisation: checking that the predicted benefits have actually been achieved. In total, realisation asks the following questions:

- Has the change has been implemented appropriately?
- Have the anticipated benefits have been achieved?
- Will the change be sustained? Is it embedded in the organisation?
- Can the change become the basis of further refinements and improvement?
- Can the change be adopted elsewhere within the organisation and hence result in further benefits?

The problems encountered during realisation can be technical; perhaps the process does not perform as planned because the IT system that supports it does not respond quickly enough. In the majority of cases, however, realisation centres on people issues. If the users have not been properly prepared for the change, they may accept it initially during the excitement of implementation but then drift away when attention is transferred elsewhere.

Business change is made because business benefits are expected. This means that the business case is the benchmark against which benefits are measured. A formal benefits realisation exercise brings many advantages:

- We know how well we have done and can determine the reasons for any underperformance or over-performance.
- Everyone involved with the project takes the achievements of benefits seriously when they are aware that the project will be reviewed after implementation.
- Feedback on estimated costs and benefits compared with actual costs and benefits will help improve the estimating and project management processes in the future.
- It may be discovered that some predicted benefits have not been realised, but actions to achieve them can be determined.
- Often the changes result in unexpected benefits that were missed in the original business case; their inclusion can make the case look more attractive.

Although benefits realisation may be considered a technical exercise, adding another stage on to the end of a project, there is a deeper question of values. The increased emphasis on benefits changes the overall perspective of the project from one of introducing a new IT system into a business improvement project aimed at achieving benefits. Another important aspect of benefits realisation is to highlight what predicted benefits have been missed and then to identify what is blocking them. Once we have reduced or eliminated those blocks, some or all of the missing benefits may be realised.

Once the change has settled down, it is time to normalise the new situation and embed it as the new business as usual. Solidifying the change means that the organisation really changes. All references, forms and manuals about previous processes, procedures and systems should be removed. We can replace them with posters, handy reference cards and other publicity material describing the new processes and systems. Indirect documentation such as job descriptions should be updated. Adoption of the new approach should be part of each employee's appraisal in order to emphasise the importance of the change and show the rewards for supporting it. Another positive way of encouraging take-up is to publicise and celebrate the improvements in business performance resulting from the change. The benefits realisation effort helps this when it discovers unanticipated benefits.

As well as ensuring that the change has taken root where it was targeted, it may be beneficial for the whole organisation if the change is adopted elsewhere within the business. Changes are more likely to spread if the following factors apply:

- There are clear advantages over the current situation.
- The change is compatible with existing values and systems.
- The change is simple to implement.
- It is easy to test out the change before full commitment.
- It is easy to see the change and its impacts.

The more closely a particular change initiative matches these characteristics, the higher the chance of its further take-up. We also need to understand the steps in the adoption process. For a change to take place, those responsible must:

- be aware of the need for change;
- know how they might change in order to meet that need;
- evaluate the possible ways of changing to see which is most appropriate;
- take actions to make the change.

This indicates that we need to tell people about our change if we want it to spread. But simply telling them may be insufficient on its own; they may not realise that they need to change. Once someone has expressed an interest in our change, we can help them by demonstrating the new way of working, outlining its benefits and explaining how we organised the change project. If they decide they wish to adopt the change themselves, we may be able to support them in the light of our experience.

At this point it is worth standing back and asking what exactly we want to sustain and spread to other parts of the organisation. The obvious answer is the change initiative that we have just been working on. The problem with transferring a new process, however, is that often it does not fit into the new environment. Consequently, the adopters must adapt the solution we have implemented to suit their needs, culture and operating environment. A more general approach is to publicise the performance improvements that we have achieved and encourage others to determine how they could achieve similar improvements, either by adapting our ideas or by coming up with their own. This can be backed up by explaining the underlying change principles that we applied. These might include eliminating non-value-adding tasks, minimising hand-offs between tasks within the process and automating tasks wherever possible. Thus we are providing people with a set of general techniques that they can apply as they see fit.

CONCLUSION

'Human change isn't something we do, it's everything we do.' (Burlton 2001) All process and IT system improvement projects aim to change the way in which people do their jobs. Change management is not something that can be tacked on to the end of a project. Instead, it should affect all aspects of the project, from the start to the end.

Just as we cannot relegate change management to a particular phase of a project, neither can we think of it as a particular person's responsibility. Change projects require several job roles in order to ensure their success. Alongside programme and project managers, we have change managers whose job it is to plan and coordinate the change effort. But the role that involves working directly with the stakeholders to accommodate their needs is that of the business analyst. We act as a bridge between the business and the IT function or the outsourced provider, and play a crucial role in ensuring that all aspects of the business change are successful. The business analyst role has expanded significantly in the last few years so that we now need to have a wider understanding of the change process, why change needs to be managed and what has to happen for change to be successful. The successful business analyst will be seen as an agent for beneficial change and our successes will ensure that the role will be invaluable to our organisations as they strive to compete in the global economy.

REFERENCES

Felder, R.M. and Silverman, L.K. (1988) Learning and Teaching Style in Engineering Education. *Engr. Education*, 78(7), 674–681 (1988).

Hord, S.M., Rutherford, W.L., Huling-Austin, L. and Hall, G.E. (1987) *Taking Charge of Change*. Alexandria, VA: ASCD.

Johnson, G., Scholes, K. and Whittington, R. (2008) *Exploring Corporate Strategy*, 8th edn. FT Prentice Hall, Harlow.

Kotter, J. (1996) *Leading Change*. Harvard Business School Press, Cambridge, MA.

Maslow, A. (1943) A theory of human motivation. *Psychological Review*, **50**, 370–396.

FURTHER READING

Burlton, R. (2001) *Business Process Management: Profiting From Process.*
Sams Publishing, Indianapolis, IN.

Cameron, E. and Green, M. (2004) *Making Sense of Change Management.* Kogan
Page, London.

Kübler-Ross, E. (1970) *On Death and Dying.* Tavistock Publications, London.

McGregor, D. (2006) *The Human side of Enterprise (Annotated edition).*
McGraw-Hill Professional, New York, NY.

Revans, R. (1982) *The Origins and Growth of Action Learning.* Krieger Pub Co.

Senge, P.M. (1999) *The Dance of Change: The Challenges to Sustaining
Momentum in a Learning Organization.* Nicholas Brealey, London.

INDEX